The Stranger in Shakespeare

BY LESLIE A. FIEDLER

Nonfiction

An End to Innocence
No! in Thunder
Love and Death in the American Novel
Waiting for the End
The Return of the Vanishing American
Being Busted
Collected Essays

Fiction

The Second Stone
Back to China
The Last Jew in America
Nude Croquet

THE
Stranger
IN
Shakespeare

LESLIE A. FIEDLER

STEIN AND DAY/*Publishers*/New York

First published in 1972

Library of Congress Catalog No. 70-186219

Published simultaneously in Canada by Saunders of Toronto Ltd
Designed by David Miller
Printed in the United States of America
Stein and Day/*Publishers*/7 East 48 Street, New York, N.Y. 10017
ISBN 8128-1454-1

To Margaret: ACT V

Hang there like fruit, my soul,
Till the tree die!

CONTENTS

PREFACE

TO HAVE WRITTEN this book at last means to have kept at last a promise made to myself some twenty-five years ago, a promise long deferred and nearly despaired of. In one of the first lectures I ever gave before an audience of my academic peers, "Shakespeare and the Paradox of Illusion," I listed what seemed to me in 1948 his "four essential myths," then went on to say that "I hope some day to treat all four . . . in some detail. . . ." When this talk was reprinted in 1960, however, I felt obliged to confess in a footnote, "I no longer believe I shall really come to terms at great length with Shakespeare, but I leave the hope of 1948 in the text to remind myself of what seemed possible twelve years ago." Yet, twelve *more* years having passed, here is that impossible book. And though not exactly the one I dreamed earlier, it ends with the same paragraph as my original lecture—only a little changed to suit its new context.

It is primarily for myself, then, that I have written this book: to bind my past to my present and to refresh my soul by immersing myself for a little while in a stream of living words and images. I have grown desiccated on the long march through the arid flatlands of ordinary language: the language of law courts and committee meetings, of newspapers and demonstrations. And toward what Sinai I thought I was advancing I find it difficult to remember. Perhaps it was always Shakespeare, though I did not know it.

Nonetheless, I consider this study not an act of self-indulgence but rather one of *ascesis,* since anyone confronting Shakespeare begins with chutzpah and joy but ends in humility and terror. Moreover, he must also come to terms with the body of Shakespearean criticism, at least walk penitentially past library shelves full of unreadable books on the most readable of poets. And taking down the handful that survive for him, he finds little confirmation of the Shakespeare he thinks he perceives, the Shakespeare he sometimes fears he has invented—only a few hints here and there.

Such hints are enough, however, to persuade him that it is pride rather than humility which suggests that his Shakespeare is a mere invention. Indeed, the case seems more often the exact opposite, as if instead our world were the invention of Shakespeare, in whom we find selves more interesting than we had suspected our skins might contain. I have tried to write, then, not another book about "Our Shakespeare," but one about "Shakespeare's Us." Still, my sense of the dialectical relationship between poet and living audience comes not just out of my own head and the text before me. Certain critics have mediated between me and it, critics it would be churlish not to mention here, though I have acknowledged particular insights I owe them elsewhere in the pages which follow.

I feel especially indebted to Wyndham Lewis's *The Lion and the Fox,* G. Wilson Knight's *The Crown of Life,* Kenneth Muir and Sean O'Loughlin's *Voyage to Illyria,* and Jan Kott's *Shakespeare Our Contemporary,* as well as to various comments by Frank Kermode, Northrop Frye, and I. A. M. Stewart. A couple of detective stories by the last, written under the pseudonym of Michael Innes, have also provided me clues for my quest. In fact, as my readers will soon discover, works of fiction have sometimes proved as helpful to me as self-declared critical works: notably, Eugène Sue's *The Mysteries of the People,* James Fenimore Cooper's *The Last of the Mohicans,* John Peale Bishop's *Act of Darkness,* and James Joyce's *Ulysses.*

The last especially has influenced my strategies of explication, since Stephen Dedalus's discourse on *Hamlet* revealed to me first that literary analysis can also be literature: a fiction about another fiction attributed to a fictional character destined to outlive his actual author.

If I do not draw directly on Joyce-Dedalus's insights in the present book, it is because my chosen theme has meant concentrating on some plays at the expense of others, among them Joyce's favorite tragedy. My book represents in fact an attempt to present the Prince without *Hamlet.* That deliberate exclusion is due in part to my conviction that we must leave off talking about that balefully fascinating play for a little while if we are to avoid forever repeating ourselves, which is to say, our fathers and grandfathers.

Still, if my central concern had been the relation of fathers and sons, or mothers and sons, or even brother and brother, there would have been no way not to deal with *Hamlet* at considerable length. But I have been concerned rather with the relations between America and Europe, white men and black, Gentiles and Jews, masters of arts and savages, males and females, and within the family, as it has turned out, between fathers and daughters.

This has meant concentrating on *Henry VI, Part I, The Merchant of Venice, Othello,* and *The Tempest,* though it has also compelled my returning again and again—a little unexpectedly, I must confess—to *Macbeth, Cymbeline,* and *Twelfth Night.* And it has given me an excuse for full-scale analyses of works especially difficult or customarily scanted, including the *Sonnets, Love's Labor's Lost, Titus Andronicus,* and *Pericles.* Even the first four alone constitute a representative sample of Shakespeare's work, beginning with the very earliest and ending with the very latest, and including a chronicle play, a comedy, a tragedy, and a romance. Moreover, though my selection may lack something in breadth, it necessarily leads deep into the archetypal underworld of Shakespeare's drama, a world inhabited by witches and ogres, devils and sorcerers, elementals and vices and fools.

But if I have been much obsessed, on the one hand, with the past, the "dark backward and abysm of time" from which Shakespeare's images and characters emerge, I have, on the other, been as much intrigued by the future toward which they tend, a future symbolized for me by the medium of film. The reader will discover, therefore, that my discussions of the plays are framed between evocations of fairy-tale material old before Shakespeare was born and projects for movies still unproduced: the kind of narrative which preceded print and that which threatens to survive it.

My own study, in fact, was spoken words before it was a manuscript or a book, having been delivered as a series of four lectures first at University College in London, then to a colloquium of the Department of English at the State University of New York in Buffalo. I am grateful, once more, to Frank Kermode, who made possible the first occasion, and to my colleagues and students at Buffalo, who sponsored the second. The listeners in both countries to a text which I am writing down in a third proved more active collaborators than passive audience, and if I name no particular names at this point, it is because I feel indebted to too many.

I must give special thanks, however, to John and Miranda Villiers for having left on the bookshelves of their house in Brighton, in which I lived for a year, a Fourth Folio edition of the plays, which I took for a sign that it was finally time to keep my promise to myself and Shakespeare. I feel gratitude as well to Gordon Ray and the Guggenheim Foundation for having had faith in this book before it was born. And finally my thanks are due to Susan Groenheck for having decoded and transcribed the palimpsest of notes and emendations, visions and revisions with which I ended my long quest.

LESLIE A. FIEDLER
Paris, May 1, 1971

SONNET 27

Weary with toil, I haste me to my bed,
The dear repose of limbs with travel tired.
But then begins a journey in my head,
To work my mind, when body's work's expired.
For then my thoughts, from far where I abide,
Intend a zealous pilgrimage to thee,
And keep my drooping eyelids open wide,
Looking on darkness which the blind do see.
Save that my soul's imaginary sight
Presents thy shadow to my sightless view,
Which, like a jewel hung in ghastly night,
Makes black night beauteous and her old face new.
    Lo, thus, by day my limbs, by night my mind,
    For thee, and for myself, no quiet find.

INTRODUCTION:

The Passionate Pilgrim

At the heart of any continuous body of work—the total production of an age, a school, a single author—there is always present a set of assumptions about the nature of man and, more particularly, about the limits of the human. Sometimes these assumptions are stated explicitly as ideas or themes, but more often they are projected in obsessive fables and characters, perceptible everywhere beneath the nominal plots and dramatis personae which may seem at first glance to vary completely from one work to another. Traditional criticism began by calling the kind of character who, for an age, a school, an author, embodies an ideal of the human, the "hero," and the kind who embodies its opposite the "villain"; but these terms have long since fallen into disrepute. And, in any case, there exists in all literature an archetypal figure who escapes both poles of the classic definition—appearing sometimes as hero, sometimes as villain, sometimes as clown.

That borderline figure, who defines the limits of the human —customarily from the farther side, though never without some ambiguity—has been named variously the "shadow," the "other," the "alien," the "outsider," the "stranger." And it is with the stranger in Shakespeare that this study is concerned: primarily with the stranger as woman in *Henry VI, Part I,* the stranger as Jew in *The Merchant of Venice,* the stranger as Moor in *Othello,* the stranger as New World savage in *The*

Tempest, but also with the Jew, the black, the "savage man of Ind" and, most especially, the witch as they appear in the complex web of the whole Shakespearean corpus.

Though related in some ways to what earlier critics have identified as the "odd man out"—to such characters as Mercutio, Falstaff, and the two Antonios of *The Merchant of Venice* and *Twelfth Night,* those equivocal lovers excluded from the happy endings Shakespeare felt it incumbent on him to provide—such strangers differ in one essential aspect. Whatever marginal ambivalence Shakespeare may have felt at their final discomfiture or defeat, in the main he subscribed consciously to the values of the popular audience, which demanded their symbolic casting out. Othello represents, perhaps, if not an exception to, a severe qualification of this general rule; but by and large, the affective resonance of women, Jews, blacks, and Indians is the same in the private mythology of Shakespeare and the public mythology of the world for which he wrote. And this is notably *not* so when he portrays men whose deepest affection is bestowed on those of their own sex, so that they will not or cannot make a satisfactory last act–last scene marriage.

Nor is the stranger quite the same as the "spoilsport" (also identified by earlier critics): the kind of bad boy who, irked by the rules of the game, wants to take his ball and go home—or failing that, will sit on the sidelines and sulk. The spoilsport appears frequently in Shakespeare—initially as a courtly mocker like Berowne in *Love's Labor's Lost* and "the melancholy Jacques" in *As You Like It,* perhaps also, vestigially, as Hamlet himself; and he reappears in surly and unregenerate form as Malvolio in *Twelfth Night* and Thersites in *Troilus and Cressida.* But, after a while, he is cast chiefly in the privileged role of the jester or fool, as Feste on scene and Yorick off; as that faithful companion of Lear, so oddly identified toward the play's close with the doomed Cordelia; and as the cosmic jester, Puck, to whom all mortals seem finally the fools he pretends to be for his master's sake and the plot's.

In the fool, the spoilsport is, as it were, institutionalized, taken into the game he begins by refusing to play; but outside that role, he blends disconcertingly into the odd man out, as in Falstaff, or even into the stranger, as in Malvolio and Shylock or, most ambiguously of all, Iago. Such role confusions must not, however, be allowed to blur the difference at the poles between the stranger and the spoilsport. And the figure of the mocker, in any event, seems not to belong to the deepest and earliest level of Shakespeare's fantasy, the private mythology which preceded any poem or play.

It is, however, precisely with that private mythology that any examination of the stranger in Shakespeare must begin, though obviously the communal mythology which he inherited from his sources, along with plot structures and casts of characters, must also be taken into account. Especially important is the body of myth implicit in those fairy tales, fabliaux, and *novelle* to which he turned constantly in search of story material and most especially, the *Metamorphoses,* which possessed his imagination from the time of his school days, making him in the profoundest sense, as his contemporaries already surmised, another Ovid, Ovid reborn an Englishman.

Even less obviously archetypal sources, like travelers' journals and historical chronicles, helped sustain the tension between private and public, personal and communal, that characterizes his work at the mythic level. Certainly, a study of such documents can illuminate such vexing, though apparently peripheral, problems as why a poet committed to propagating the Tudor myth (on which Henry VIII so largely based his claim to legitimate succession) and, afterward, the Jacobean (by which James I hoped to sustain his theories about the divine right of kings) almost entirely ignored the myth of the

Virgin Queen (sponsored by Elizabeth I to help maintain her delicate balance of power). It was, however, that final myth which fired the imaginations of his most distinguished fellow poets, including Spenser and Raleigh, since they found the celebration of woman congenial on a personal as well as a public level. Shakespeare, on the other hand, began with an antifeminist bias; and it is the private mythology bred by that bias which most directly influences his view of the stranger, as well as his over-all theories about the nature of love.

The very scriptures, the holy text, of that personal mythology is the *Sonnets,* and, in particular, Sonnet 144. In it is distilled Shakespeare's vision of Eros as good and evil, a vision so camouflaged in the sequence as a whole that for generations scholars took it for the most conventional of poems. This mistake his first publisher, that pirate-entrepreneur William Jaggard, did not make, selecting texts which illuminate what is at once most unique and universal in the *Sonnets*—the heart of their archetypal appeal. Jaggard's collection, with which we must begin, since it is, in fact, the beginning, appeared in 1599, a year after Francis Meres had first mentioned in print Shakespeare's "sugared Sonnets among his private friends."

Jaggard's volume, which he chose to call *The Passionate Pilgrim,* contained not only the sonnet presently numbered 144 but also 138. And it included as well three poems extracted from *Love's Labor's Lost,* along with four sonnets on the theme of Venus and Adonis and eleven other pieces of verse, among them "Live with me, and be my love." The last is by all odds the favorite poem of the age—written and rewritten by Christopher Marlowe, Sir Walter Raleigh, and John Donne, among others, and surviving into an alien age in the cadences behind the opening lines of Milton's *L'Allegro* and *Il Penseroso;* but it is not one ordinarily associated with Shakespeare. Yet Jaggard's collection carries Shakespeare's name on its title page, so that scholars ever since have felt obliged to wrestle with the problem of the authenticity of its contents. No one can finally doubt, however, that Jaggard's selection, whatever the sources of the individual poems, reflects Shakespeare's own view of what he was after, or, at least, that of someone from the circle of "private friends" in which the Sonnets had first circulated.

The title itself carries assurance that the compiler was aware of one key image in the sequence: the image of the poet whose unquiet mind, even from afar, travels toward the beloved, as in Sonnet 27, "For then my thoughts, from far where I abide, / Intend a zealous pilgrimage to thee. . . ." And finding in second place among the twenty poems which constitute Jaggard's collection Sonnet 144 is doubly encouraging, for this is one sonnet which explicitly joins the praise of the fair friend to the outpouring of self-torturing lust for the dark lady. As printed in *The Passionate Pilgrim,* its octave runs as follows:

> Two loves I have of comfort and despair,
> Which like two spirits do suggest me still,
> The better spirit is a man right fair,
> The worser spirit a woman colored ill.
> To win me soon to Hell, my female evil
> Tempteth my better angel from my side,
> And would corrupt my saint to be a devil,
> Wooing his purity with her foul pride.

If all the sonnets except for this were to disappear tomorrow, we would be left in possession not only of the story Shakespeare tries to tell but also of the moral it is intended to convey. Beginning as an account of one who would divide his love in two, directing all that is noble in it toward one object, all that is vile toward another, it ends with his discovery of the two in each other's arms—the noble contaminated by the vile. The significance is clear enough, since such a story becomes inevitably a parable concerning the ambiguity of passion. Moreover, Sonnet 144 contains also the unconventional symbols through which Shakespeare chose to project both plot and theme: friend and mistress, boy and whore.

Finally, fable, moral, and symbol are rendered in a special tone, sustained also in Sonnet 138, whose opening betrays under the show of easy cynicism a sense of deep disgust: "When my love swears that she is made of truth, / I do believe her, though I know she lies. . . ." And the pun barely suggested by the last word is picked up in the concluding couplet, more clearly in its revised form than in the earlier text used by Jaggard: "Therefore I lie with her and she with me, / And in our faults by lies we flattered be." In both sonnets, the doubleness of tone finds expression in the *double-entendre;* and reading them at the head of *The Passionate Pilgrim,* the reader will recall how many poems in the entire sequence are precisely of this kind.

Indeed, the brand of humor they exploit must have been a staple amusement for young noblemen, contrived on demand by such privileged entertainers as Shakespeare, who made the mistake in fact (or fancy) of falling (or imagining he fell) in love with one of his elegant benefactors and who thereafter made love rather than mockery his essential theme. There must have seemed at first no contradiction, for the love his heart compelled was directed toward a male, while the cynicism demanded of him by fashion was directed toward the female.

It is *woman's* sexuality that Shakespeare's puns excoriate with special fervor, the play on "lie" and "lie" in Sonnet 138 equating their facility at falsification with the ease with which they are bedded down, the two meanings of "hell" in the sestet of Sonnet 144 equating the vagina with the place of eternal punishment, and the quibble on "fire" attributing to the dark lady the power both to damn and venereally infect the youth.

> And whether that my angel be turned fiend
> Suspect I may, yet not directly tell,

But being both from me, both to each friend,
I guess one angel in another's Hell.
  Yet this shall I ne'er know, but live in doubt
  Till my bad angel fire my good one out.

In the dark lady segment of the *Sonnets,* similar puns abound, reaching one climax in Sonnets 134 and 135, which ring changes on the several meanings of "Will": not only the name of the poet and perhaps also the friend but also a word signifying "testament" and "volition" and "carnal desire": "So thou, being rich in *Will,* add to thy *Will* / One will of mine, to make thy large *Will* more." A second such climax comes toward the very end of the sequence, in a series of puns on the male's erection, the unwilled response to woman's "Will." The couplet which concludes Sonnet 150 first suggests the double meaning ("If thy unworthiness raised love in me, / More worthy I to be beloved of thee"), which is then made explicit in Sonnet 151 ("flesh stays no farther reason, / But rising at thy name doth point out thee / As his triumphant prize") and confirmed wryly in the final couplet ("No want of conscience hold it that I call / Her 'love' for whose dear love I rise and fall").

This kind of wit, trembling always on the edge of disgust, is, however, found also as early as Sonnet 20 (whose punning close has occasioned much soul searching among the critics), which, despite its position among the sonnets of praise, is quite as antifeminist as any specifically directed against the dark lady. Its sestet begins, "And for a woman wert thou first created, / Till Nature, as she wrought thee, fell a-doting. . . ," and it ends, "But since she pricked thee out for women's pleasure, / Mine be thy love, and thy love's use their treasure." Involved here is a play not only on the word "pricked," but also on "use," which in Shakespeare's lexicon means, besides "employment," "usury" or "interest" and also "the sex act."

On these meanings Shakespeare loves to quibble, speaking in *Measure for Measure* of the "two usuries," by which he means moneylending and copulation, and making throughout *The Merchant of Venice* an implicit contrast between the consummation of love and the extortion of interest. It is clear which usury Shakespeare would prefer, but it is also clear that ideally he would choose neither; for his peculiar wordplay tends to identify the carnal love of women with a commercial practice that his age still regarded as an "unnatural" sin. In Dante (more orthodoxly), it is homosexuality which is associated with usury, the sins of Sodom and Cahors being punished in the same circle; but in the *Sonnets,* there is a tendency to make heterosexual love seem guilty by association.

Indeed, if a third sonnet out of the sequence had been included in *The Passionate Pilgrim,* it might well have been Sonnet 20—and not on the grounds of tone alone; for in comparing the friend to women whose hearts are given to "shifting change" and whose eyes are practiced in "false . . . rolling," Shakespeare implicitly comments on the theme of the two loves. What the poet insists on in Sonnet 20 is the epicene character of "the Master-Mistress of my passion" ("passion" here meaning "song" *and* "suffering" *and* "libidinal love"), what he shares with women as well as what distinguishes him from them. What differentiates him from the despised sex, the poem explains, is double: the male organ (alas!) and purity of heart (thank God!); what makes him like them is his physical beauty, as "womanly," in this sense, as theirs.

Many contemporary readers find it a little difficult, perhaps, to empathize with the taste for a kind of beauty in males identical with that sought in females; and they are likely to be brought up short when in Sonnet 53 the youth is compared in a span of three lines to both Helen and Adonis. But the latter allusion provides a clue, suggesting that the roots of the epicene ideal must be sought in Hellenistic culture, which for Shakespeare means especially Ovid, a clue whose importance is underlined by the inclusion in *The Passionate Pilgrim* of four sonnets by a single hand retelling the story of Venus and Adonis.

Whether that hand was Shakespeare's remains still unclear, even though one of them had been claimed in 1596 by a certain Bartholemew Griffin; Shakespeare had treated the theme in a long erotic poem, which, we are tempted to think, should have been sufficient. On the other hand, the four doubtful sonnets combine, quite as does *Venus and Adonis,* certain elements out of Ovid's account of Venus's passion for Adonis with his version of the love of Salmacis for Hermaphroditus. And that combination constitutes a compulsively repeated Shakespearean theme, a private myth of great power: the encounter between a passive male and an aggressive female, between modest reason and shameless lust, symbolized respectively by a boy and a woman.

In *Venus and Adonis,* the poet who makes a triangle of this encounter in the *Sonnets* is lacking. And there are, therefore, strange equivocations, as Shakespeare, lacking another mask, is compelled to embody in Venus—whom he basically fears—his own desire for epicene beauty. He actually puts into her mouth the argument that great beauties have a special obligation to marry and reproduce ("Seeds spring from seeds, and beauty breedeth beauty"), which in the *Sonnets* he speaks through his mouthpiece. We may, indeed, agree with one editor of the poems that "there is more of Shakespeare himself" in Venus than in Adonis, as there is more of him in Cleopatra than in Antony, in Falstaff than in Prince Hal.

But we remember, too, that Venus remains for him as late as the time of *The Tempest,* "Mars's hot minion," supreme representation of all he most distrusts in naked passion. No wonder then, that the end of *Venus and Adonis* is a catastrophe more unmitigated than the conclusion of the *Sonnets,* involving not the mere corruption of a boy by a woman, but the death of that boy, a death which Adonis seems all along to have felt as preferable to seduction; and that it is followed by

Venus's curse on the kind of love she embodies: "It shall be fickle, false and full of fraud; / Bud, and be blasted, in a breathing-while. . . ."

In the four Venus-Adonis sonnets of *The Passionate Pilgrim,* the rich, almost cloying texture of Shakespeare's long poem and its tragic tone are replaced by a show of easy irony quite like that which characterizes the two sonnets with which Jaggard opened his collection. Their meanings are simple, the puns obvious and undisturbingly obscene—one is tempted to say childishly obscene. The last three lines will do by way of illustration, foreshadowing as they do the goring and death of Adonis, but all in the guise of a joke.

> "See, in my thigh," quoth she, "here was the sore."
> She showèd hers. He saw more wounds than one,
> And blushing fled, and left her all alone.

What terror or sexual queasiness is implicit in all this is not permitted to show, as it is not in Jaggard's poem VI, which tells of Venus's passion for the youth as he stands naked on the edge of a pool—a scene derived from Ovid's tale of the lust of Salmacis for Hermaphroditus. But this reminds us once more that if in order to understand the fair youth of the *Sonnets,* we must see what in him is derived from the myth of Adonis, we must also understand how much of Shakespeare's Adonis is Hermaphroditus, that son of Hermes and Aphrodite whose body was blended with that of the water nymph Salmacis when she perceived that only thus could she attain the union she desired.

In Ovid, it is *not* Adonis but Hermaphroditus who struggles against love, adamantly preferring his own beardless beauty to that of woman; and it is Hermaphroditus who becomes, in his final transformation, the prototype of the "Master-Mistress" in Sonnet 20.

And the two bodies seemed to merge together,
One face, one form . . .
So these two joined in close embrace, no longer
Two beings, and no longer man and woman,
But neither, and yet both. . . .

In the museums of half the world, there are yet to be found Alexandrian images in marble and alabaster of the boy-woman Hermaphroditus, images worked in love by the craftsmen of a culture which considered pederasty a grace of civilized living. The beholder who first comes on the mythical figure, sees him from the rear, half curled up as if in sleep; and noting the lovely sweep of back and flank, takes him for a woman, a mistake apparently confirmed when the beholder peers round the hyacinthine head into the beautiful face. But looking lower he discovers, surprised, that the body is "pricked . . . out for women's pleasure," and knows he has found the Hermaphroditus.

Just such an image seems to have possessed the imagination of the Renaissance, in Italy first, in England afterward; and it is this image which, projected in the theater by boy actors of women's parts, gave sensual substance to the cult of friendship and the literary tradition of the praise of lovely boys. That the Elizabethans had no suspicion of the homosexual basis of that cult seems unlikely, particularly since any grammar school boy of the time was likely to have parsed the legend of Hermaphroditus in class. He knew, therefore, that, like Shakespeare's version of *Venus and Adonis,* the story ended with a curse, a curse no less terrible, though somewhat different in form. It is Hermaphroditus who speaks, according to Ovid, after his transformation in the pool, crying out in "a voice whose tone was almost treble":

. . . O father and mother, grant me this!
May every one hereafter, who comes diving

Into this pool, emerge half man, made weaker
By the touch of this evil water!

It is hard to believe that the group of Shakespeare's poems which included *Venus and Adonis* and the *Sonnets* is not centrally concerned with this problem of unmanning, with the price paid for attempting to flee woman. And one's suspicions are further strengthened in turning from Book Four of the *Metamorphoses,* which contains the myth of Hermaphroditus, to Book Ten, in which the story of Adonis is told. Book Ten opens with the legend of Orpheus and Eurydice, which, as Ovid recreates it, serves chiefly as a preface to a group of songs sung by the bereaved Orpheus. Overwhelmed by grief for his lost wife, we are told, the poet disowned women and turned for love to boys.

His love was given
To young boys only, and he told the Thracians
That was the better way: *enjoy that springtime,*
Take those first flowers.

Orpheus is not content, moreover, merely to celebrate pederasty; he dedicates himself, too, to the vilification of women, invoking Jupiter, lover of Ganymede, to inspire him:

. . . for I would sing of boys
Loved by the gods, and girls inflamed by love
To things forbidden, and earned punishment.

Shakespeare's hermaphroditic revision of Adonis assimilates him to those "boys loved by the Gods," Ganymede and Hyacinthus and Cyparissus. And his version of Venus makes her just another of those "girls inflamed by love to things forbidden," like the "foul Propoetides," whom Ovid portrays as the first whores, and Myrrha, who, seducing her own father, begot the very Adonis doomed to die beneath the boar's tusk.

In his own time and among the "private friends" for whom

his nondramatic poems were written, Shakespeare surely assumed he could evoke by simple allusion any section of the *Metamorphoses.* So Marlowe seems to have assumed when, in the concluding speech of *Doctor Faustus,* he quotes a tag from the Ovidian account of Jupiter's night of love with Alcmene, *"O lente lente currite noctis equi!"* All the more so, then, might one in whom, according to his contemporaries, "the sweet witty soul of Ovid lives" feel free to evoke in passing an aspect of Ovid's retelling of the Orpheus myth which is commonly expurgated in a day which requires scholarly studies to make us aware of Shakespeare's indebtedness to a text we know only casually if at all.

The context in which *The Passionate Pilgrim* sets the *Sonnets* is not, however, defined entirely by Ovid and Shakespeare's most Ovidian long poem; it includes as well *Love's Labor's Lost,* from which *The Passionate Pilgrim* extracts three lyrics, two of them also in sonnet form. These two, in fact, alternate with the first two Venus and Adonis sonnets near the beginning of the collection, thus serving to remind us early on that further clues to Shakespeare's private mythology can be found in this eccentric early play, the freest, least source-bound and mass-audience-oriented of all his dramatic works.

The first poem from *Love's Labor's Lost* is attributed in the play itself to a minor character called Longaville; the second, to Berowne, its spoilsport *raisonneur;* and both represent shamefaced attempts at erotic verse by young aristocrats who earlier had abjured love and retired to a kind of Neoplatonic academy in the woods. In that ascetic, all-male community, they had planned to pursue fame through single-minded "study," thus triumphing not only over their own feeble flesh but also over "cormorant devouring Time." The actual poems (perhaps verses of his own which Shakespeare had come to find intolerable) are miserable enough, philosophically as well as formally, to deserve the scorn of Berowne, who says of Longaville's rhymes what he surely knows applies also to his own:

> This is the liver vein, which makes flesh a deity,
> A green goose a goddess—pure, pure idolatry.

Indeed, the tone of the play throughout is close to that of the more troubled sonnets; yet, though presumably written for a select rather than general audience, it is more circumspect and oblique than the poems composed to be read in private by an even-smaller group.

In certain scenes, however, particularly those in which Berowne pays begrudging and witty court to an equally reluctant Rosaline, a relationship is developed clearly analogous to that of the poet and the dark lady of the *Sonnets.* Quite like the deceived lover of the *Sonnets,* Berowne in *Love's Labor's Lost* insists on the blackness of his beloved, describing her as:

> A whitely wanton with a velvet brow,
> With two pitch balls stuck in her face for eyes—
> Aye, and, by Heaven, one that will do the deed,
> Though Argus were her eunuch and her guard.

And reading these lines, we remember "Therefore my mistress' eyes are raven-black" in Sonnet 127. But "pitch" is the operative word here, and it is picked up again when Berowne speaks of falling in love as "toiling in a pitch—pitch that defiles."

Finally, however, he decides to brazen out his capitulation to the dark Rosaline though the play has already reminded us (once more like Sonnet 127) that if one opposite of "fair" is "black," another is "foul." "No face is fair that is not full so black," he boasts; and the King is moved to answer, reflecting surely Shakespeare's own sense of the metaphorical resonance of the adjective which happened to suit the complexion of the woman whom he happened to desire:

> Oh, paradox! Black is the badge of Hell,
> The hue of dungeons and the school of night, . . .

But this re-echoes the key words of the closing couplet in Sonnet 147:

> For I have sworn thee fair, and thought thee bright,
> Who art as black as Hell, as dark as night.

And it recalls the reworking of the same pair of lines in Sonnet 152:

> For I have sworn thee fair, more perjur'd I,
> To swear against the truth so foul a lie!

"For I have sworn" becomes by a kind of ellipsis "forsworn," a leitmotif of both the dark lady sonnets and *Love's Labor's Lost.* But though Jaggard fairly represents in his sampling Shakespeare's concern with the fate of love in a world forsworn, and though, further, he does justice to the theme of youth and age, which also obsesses the poet, he scants the equally important contrast of fair and black. Yet this contrast, along with that of boy and woman, true and false, age and youth, serves centrally to define the two loves, good and bad, between which he sees man eternally torn. The darkness of the dark lady is of her essence; and fair and black turn out to mean, moreover (though this level of significance is not made manifest until the later plays), what we have come to call white and black, Caucasian and Negro. Indeed, *Love's Labor's Lost* contains allusions in jokes, asides, and casual metaphors to all three of the alien races, those ethnic strangers we shall be discussing later: the "Ethiope," the Jew, and the "savage man of Ind."

In Jaggard, however, the theme is represented only by the passing contrast of "a man right fair" and "a woman colored ill," which opens Sonnet 144, and is overwhelmed immediately by an insistence on the theme of self-betrayal and self-deceit: "Therefore I'll lie with love and love with me. . . ."; "If love make me forsworn. . . ."; "Though to myself forsworn. . . ." Yet this is, in one sense, just; since at the close (not end, there being no end, happy or otherwise) of *Love's Labor's Lost,* there rings still in the ear of the audience the melancholy couplet in which Berowne accepts on behalf of us all man's comic-tragic fate:

> We cannot cross the cause why we were born;
> Therefore, of all hands must we be forsworn.

What is added by that play to the myth of the two loves is, then, a new version of the Fall of man, in which woman and the serpent are identified with each other and Adam is condemned to leave the garden arm in arm with his temptress—if she will have him.

It is a variant form of a theme found throughout Shakespeare's work: men bound together by friendship are sundered by the love of woman (as in *Two Gentlemen of Verona*) and must somehow make another, more fragile compact or sadly learn to part. Sometimes there are political considerations which persuade a younger man to reject his older friend (as in *Julius Caesar* or *Henry IV);* but more customarily, what causes the rift is the intervention of the female. Certainly this is the case in *Love's Labor's Lost,* as in the *Sonnets* themselves, though in the former, the conventions of comic theater require that the conflict between friendship and passion be played out in lighthearted wit combats. Only in the darkest sonnets and tragedies (most notably *Othello* and *Lear*) do the hatred and fear of female sexuality pass over into hysteria, as in Lear's mad rant:

> Down from the waist they are Centaurs,
> Though women all above.

But to the girdle do the gods inherit,
Beneath is all the fiends'.
There's Hell, there's darkness, there's
 the sulphurous pit,
Burning, scalding, stench, consumption, fie, fie, fie!
Pah, pah!

In *Love's Labor's Lost* such shrillness is avoided, even though, as the play moves toward its anticlimax, it is the women who seem to have triumphed, the men who appear to have been made fools in a tangle of disguises and counter-disguises, quite Mozartean both in complexity and in lightness of tone. What is being mocked, it becomes clear, are male pretensions to immunity from passion, perhaps even a specific all-male academy, around whose members charges of atheism and homosexuality floated at the time, that circle of "soul-loved friends" which included Derby, Northumberland, and Sir Walter Raleigh, and which boasted as its poet laureate George Chapman, favored candidate for the role of rival poet in Shakespeare's sonnet sequence. Speculation about this circle consists largely of scholarly attempts to reconstitute history out of ancient gossip, and skeptics have argued that the whole thing is a fabrication of bored twentieth-century academics. It seems likely, however, that Shakespeare knew of some such group, finding it a suitable butt for satire, since it competed with the Southampton circle, in which he seems to have played the role presumably accorded Chapman in the other.

But caricaturing Chapman and the intellectual-dandies whom he served, inevitably Shakespeare also caricatured himself and the lords he admired—even the one lord he truly loved. That is to say, the ironies of *Love's Labor's Lost* are not all directed outward at detested others. Self-hatred is everywhere an undercurrent, reflected especially in the self-tormenting wit of Berowne, who seems often another version of the poet of the *Sonnets*. In neither the *Sonnets* nor this most high-brow and personal of all Shakespeare's plays, however, is the last word a cynical acceptance of the pre-eminence of passion, the inevitable triumph of woman over men's vows of dedication to study and chastity and each other. As the title of the play declares, *no* kind of love triumphs in the end; for even as the irrational desire for the female has driven out reason, so the shadow of death cools irrational desire.

The play climaxes not, as it seems to have promised, in a mass wedding, but in the departure of the ladies and the imposition on their lovers of certain unforeseenly grim tasks. Berowne, for instance, is commanded by his beloved to remit his suit for a year and visit hospitals, where he is bidden "With all the fierce endeavor of your wit / To enforce the painèd impotent to smile." Not only is the evocation of pain and impotence an odd antiending for what opened as a comedy, but the suggested necessity of seeking an antidote to both more effective than wit undercuts, as well as the character to whom it is directed, the witty play in which he appears and its jesting author. The net effect is that of a palinode, just such a denial of love and joy as Shakespeare makes in Sonnets 129 and 146 and which appears four or five times over in *The Passionate Pilgrim,* most notably in the single stanza it reprints from the answer to Marlowe's "Live with me, and be my love," a poem originally signed "Ignotus" and more usually attributed to Raleigh.

> If that the world and love were young,
> And truth in every shepherd's tongue,
> These pretty pleasures might me move
> To live with thee and be thy love.

If these lines are, indeed, not Shakespeare's but those of a member of the rival group he presumably satirized in *Love's Labor's Lost,* the fact should serve to remind us of how many assumptions (imported from Italy, perhaps, and become the mode) were shared by the antifeminist academies. Shakespeare or Raleigh, it makes little difference; either might have spoken those hermetic words. "The words of Mercury are harsh after the songs of Apollo" reads the tag which closes *Love's Labor's Lost.* And this line, too, the scholars hesitate to give to Shakespeare, taking it instead for the comment of a reader distressed by the final turn of the play, in which its comic characters return after the failed happy ending to represent the debate of the cuckoo and the owl, a debate without a difference, in which spring is presented as the season which brings fear to married men and winter as a time presided over by red-nosed and "greasy" kitchen wenches.

There is one other major concern of Shakespeare's private mythology unrepresented in *The Passionate Pilgrim* though present in the sonnet sequence as a whole: the myth of the two immortalities. But the perplexity in response to which it is generated is, in fact, suggested by the "Ignotus" stanza and all the other selections which deal with the problem of youth and age. If love is based on beauty and beauty depends on youth, how can love survive in a world which, like ourselves, from moment to moment grows older? Beauty, the *Sonnets* begin by stipulating, since it exists in the flesh, must seek its perpetuity in the flesh, by begetting, or "breed," as Shakespeare prefers to say. But before he has gotten very far into the poem, he is also insisting that beauty can survive eternally if it is turned into art, recreated as a poetic image. In either case, love is the spur: either the love which attracts man to woman, body to body, thus ending in marriage and the family, or the love which draws man to man, soul to soul, thus ending in—literature.

Obviously, this is the doctrine of Diotima, as reported by Socrates in the *Symposium* of Plato. "What object do lovers have in view?" the prophetess asks, and answers herself, "The object . . . is birth in beauty, whether of body or soul. . . . Wherefore love is of immortality." The final phrase could stand as the motto of the *Sonnets,* and their meaning is further illuminated as Diotima continues, "Those who are pregnant in the body only, betake themselves to women and beget children . . . but souls which are pregnant . . . conceive that which is proper for the soul. . . . And such creators are poets. . . ." Here, then, is the second classic context for Shakespeare's personal mythology of love: the homosexual apologetics of the *Symposium,* derived via various Italian middlemen (Michelangelo, Bembo, Bruno, Florio) and already given, before reaching Shakespeare, an anti-Petrarchan or anti–courtly love cast.

Shakespeare is clearly not alone in his attempts at undermining the idealization of woman and the pseudosanctification of adultery which lie at the roots of courtly love. In his own country, both Donne and Raleigh had recorded cynical reservations about women and love not very different from his; and even Wyatt, who imported into England the courtly love mythos in its Petrarchan form, undercut from time to time the image of the adored lady as angel and savior. The convention and anticonvention grow up together, and neither necessarily arises from a deeper or more honest perception of the world. When Shakespeare writes the well-known bitter sonnet beginning, "My mistress' eyes are nothing like the sun," he is inventing nothing new, only providing an already expected titillation. Yet his *Sonnets* are unique, though not in this aspect of their antifeminism.

What is peculiar to Shakespeare's sequence is its attempt to preserve the mystique of courtly love and much of its traditional imagery by transferring them to a male beloved. Like the poets of ancient Provence, as well as their ironical codifier Andreas Capellanus, Shakespeare seems to have believed that love is "a certain inborn suffering," but a suffering which redeems. And like his predecessors, he seems also to have been convinced that *only* love redeems—makes a gentleman, perfects a poet, improves manners, and refreshes the soul—so that, like them, he pretends to find in the joy of loving a sufficient counterbalance even to the pain inflicted by the indifference of the beloved.

Like earlier theorists, too, he apparently discriminated between two kinds of love, *amor purus* and *amor mixtus;* though, once more like them, he believed even "pure" love to be necessarily physical, implying, besides the communion of souls, a sensual delight in the cheek, lip, all the lovely flesh of the loved one—so long as there was no actual penetration of flesh by flesh, no expenditure of seed. Finally, like his Provençal forerunners, Shakespeare thought of both the lower and higher kinds of love as existing outside of marriage, as being, in some sense, adulterous. No more than any love poet of the Middle Ages would he have considered addressing an erotic poem to his wife.

In language, too, Shakespeare emulated his great predecessors, referring to his beloved as a rose, a muse, an angel, a Helen of Troy; but, unlike them, he found his rose-muse-angel-Helen in a boy rather than a woman. There is no use pretending that such a procedure is, either in the history of literature or of society, merely "conventional." It is extraordinary, even a little disturbing; and there is something more honest in earlier attempts to bowdlerize the text by changing "he" to "she" than in the modern pretense of having proved by an analysis of Sonnet 20 that Shakespeare did not actually have physical relations with boys. The point is that the poet confesses to sleeping with women and considering it filthy, while chastely (but passionately) embracing an idealized male.

How was he driven, fictionally at least, to advocate so extraordinary a splitting of love, to endure so profound a division between sentimentality and desire? What ended as a division began as a dream of synthesis, the desire to reconcile the lesson of the Scriptures and the burden of vernacular poetry as written in Europe for some six hundred years; and to understand Shakespeare, we must first understand the way in which courtly love, which began as a pastime for idle courtiers, became a counterreligion irreconciliable with the reigning orthodoxy. Between the deification—half in sport, half in earnest—of woman and the Christian teaching that such adulation of any creature is idolatry, there can be no compromise; and even less tolerable is the view that human love, like the love of God itself, is a sufficient source of grace. *Amor purus* required the worship of a mistress remote and unattainable; the flesh demanded sexual consummation; the love of God required the renunciation of both. And in any case, the love of another man's wife remained adulterous, consummated or unconsummated; adding a pseudoreligious note merely aggravated the sin.

Yet beyond this nest of paradoxes the Provençal poets could not go, leaving the next step to Dante, who completed in the *Divine Comedy* what he had begun in the *Vita Nuova.* For every man, he suggests in the earlier work, there is somewhere a woman who is his personal mediator, a "miraculous" avenue to salvation. Dante cannot resist reminding us the name "Beatrice" means "she who beatifies," and he extends the pun until he seems to be hinting that Beatrice is, in some sense, the Christ! At this point, the Inquisition moved in to expurgate his little book, and Dante moved on to the allegory of the *Divine Comedy,* which turns the actual Beatrice into Divine Theology. It is a solution which, operating in the empyrean, leaves unresolved on earth the contradiction from which it began, thus bequeathing to the soul of the West an institutionalized schizophrenia.

Shakespeare's theory of the two loves, one angelic, the other diabolic, is at least a new way of stating the old problem, especially when he directs the first impulse toward a fair youth (loved as purely as any Italian poet of the sweet new style ever loved his lady) and the second toward the black woman (lusted after in self-hatred and disgust). Love as grace is attached to the homoerotic Beatrice, love as sin to the dark lady. This means that sentimental salvation is attributed to the male, passionate damnation to the female, thus resolving one age-old contradiction at least: that between the popular-orthodox conception of woman as temptress and the courtly view of her as savior. By loving a boy rather than a daughter of Eve, Shakespeare insists, one can find salvation.

But the taint of homosexuality clings to such a suggestion, and Shakespeare is painfully aware of the proverbial fickleness of boys, declaring through the Fool in *Lear,* for instance, that "He's mad that trusts . . . a boy's love, or a whore's oath." After all, he lived with boys in the theater, watched them off-stage as well as on; and though he can praise his fair youth with a tenderness so genuine that generations of men have read his words to their mistresses, the fable of the *Sonnets* does not end on a note of tenderness.

The poet, troubled from the first, finally sees in dismay his two loves in each other's arms, the untainted boy betrayed into the embrace of a gonorrheal whore. "Boy" and "whore"—no wonder these two words have a special affinity in Shakespeare, for in his world, boy actors daily put on and doffed the allure of women, *played* women. And who can doubt that on occasion their blatant homosexuality travestied behind the scenes the pure and rational love of males he dreamed, as mincing little queens caricatured those ambiguous boy-girl heroines so essential in their transvestite loveliness to such plays as *As You Like It* and *Twelfth Night.* In the end, for him, too, there remains, therefore, the terrible cry, as old as Christianity itself: "The expense of spirit in a waste of shame / Is lust in action. . . ."

It seems to have become clear to him finally that the seed of corruption was in the friend from the start, already present in the "chaste" relationship between him and the poet; since there is no pure masculine principle, no male is immune to the evil impulse represented by the female. Only the legendary "he that was not born of woman," the motherless man, can break out of the trap of sin. The youth, however, is very much his mother's child; and the poet desiring him has no way of being sure that he has not desired in him what Posthumus Leonatus in *Cymbeline* calls the "woman's part," the "motion that tends to vice." The poet cannot even be sure that he has not himself played that "woman's part," has not been the Venus who, in fantasy at least, has assailed the virtue he loves. When the youth falls, the poet cannot help suspecting that he has willed that fall, somehow collaborated in it; for the dark lady is a projection of something in his deepest imagination, too, and he has been the link between her and the fair friend.

Certainly, in the plays which deal with analogous love affairs—in *Henry IV, Julius Caesar,* and *The Merchant of Venice*—there is not only a pervading sense of melancholy, a presentiment that the relationship which joins youth and age, boy and man is doomed, but also a hint of guilt, the feeling that the relationship should never have existed. As Shakespeare imagines it, the older lover does not escape unscathed, but is condemned, as in *Julius Caesar,* to be stabbed to death; or destined, as in *Henry IV,* to be cast off to die of a broken heart; or permitted, as in *The Merchant of Venice,* to make the gesture which hands over his friend to woman forever. Shakespeare, at the moment of writing the *Sonnets,* could not condone in himself the highest love he could conceive, but foresaw its dissolution in betrayal and lust, felt it deserved to be thus dissolved. And so he falls back, as generations of poets had before him, into the Christian palinode.

In the myth of the *Sonnets,* the Uranian strategy will not finally work; and the poet in the end abandons the solution of the *Symposium,* the dream of Diotima, in favor of the Christian doctrine that there is no rebirth of beauty except in God, that here on earth all beauty must be yielded up in order to ransom it from time.

Buy terms divine in selling hours of dross,
Within be fed, without be rich no more.
    So shalt thou feed on Death, that feeds on men,
    And Death once dead, there's no more dying then.

In the plays, however, Shakespeare does not come to this point until, with *The Tempest,* he is approaching the close of his career; and it is the long foreground to Prospero's Christian Epilogue that must be examined first, beginning at the beginning.

SONNET 144

Two loves I have of comfort and despair,
Which like two spirits do suggest me still.
The better angel is a man right fair,
The worser spirit a woman colored ill.
To win me soon to Hell, my female evil
Tempteth my better angel from my side,
And would corrupt my saint to be a devil,
Wooing his purity with her foul pride.
And whether that my angel be turned fiend
Suspect I may, yet not directly tell,
But being both from me, both to each friend,
I guess one angel in another's Hell.
    Yet this shall I ne'er know, but live in doubt
    Till my bad angel fire my good one out.

I

The Woman as Stranger: or "None but women left. . . ."

Obviously, the beginning for Shakespeare is the problem of woman, or, more exactly perhaps, his problem with women. Certainly, in his first plays, members of that sex are likely to be portrayed as utter strangers: creatures so totally alien to men as threaten destruction rather than offer the hope of salvation, much less the possibility of a union in which male and female might become, as the Christian Scriptures seem to promise, one flesh and one soul. Hard enough, Shakespeare apparently felt, for two unique individuals of the same kind, two males, to achieve unity in love; impossible for male and female (i.e., alien beings), each the other's other, to attain such communion.

One does not need to search, as the naïver biographical critics of the late nineteenth century were tempted to do, for episodes in the poet's early life—such as a forced marriage to an older, pregnant woman—to explain his stance. It may not be shared by *all* male and most female authors in our culture, as the naïver feminist critics of the late twentieth century have been suggesting. But it surely appears in many key works of the Western world—from Plato's *Symposium* through Melville's *Moby Dick* to Henry Miller's *Tropic of Capricorn*—especially, it is worth noting, in works of prime mythological importance.

Indeed, men of a particular culture seem impelled to invent

myths whenever they encounter strangers on the borders of their world,* that is to say, whenever they are forced to confront creatures disturbingly like themselves in certain respects, who yet do not quite fit (or worse, seem to have rejected) their definition of what it means to be human. Such creatures are defined—depending on whether the defining group conquers or is conquered by them—as superhuman or subhuman, divine or diabolic; and the confrontation with them is rendered in appropriate terms, honorific or pejorative. In either case, however, there is a considerable margin of ambivalence, since the process which underlies the creation of stranger myths is, psychologically speaking, projection: more specifically, the projection onto the venerated or despised other of human possibilities not yet developed or rejected for the sake of something else by the defining group.

In the long course of its history, many sets of strangers have been thus encountered and mythicized by our culture, some to the point where we can scarcely recognize any longer the historical event behind its archetypal transformations. But we dimly surmise that the legends of the Greek gods, for instance, arose out of the confrontation of an indigenous Mediterranean people and certain Aryan invaders from the great outside; while the myths of faërie arose out of the meeting of Celt and Saxon, just as earlier, more primitive stories of kobolds and gnomes had emerged from the encounter of Homo sapiens and the preceding humanoid species.

More recently, white Europeans have come face to face with the black man in Africa and the red man in America; and the archetypal stories generated by those events continue to confuse us, since we are likely to take what is *our* myth of Negro or Indian for *their* actual history. The more ancient

* I have dealt theoretically with this problem in *The Return of the Vanishing American,* a book which begins precisely where this one will end—with the Indians. But I risk repeating myself in order to be clear on what seems to me a vital point.

encounters, however, have long since been resolved either by annihilating or coming to terms with the disturbing stranger; but "coming to terms" means, on a psychological level, introjecting what has been projected outward onto that other, modifying or extending the definition of our own humanity to accommodate their challenging divergences. And we are aware, all of us except the few pledged still to the archaic alternative of extermination, that a similar kind of accommodation with red and black is the order of the day.

But there remains among us—the "us" of Europe, all the way to its remote American and Russian poles—an unassimilated, perhaps forever unassimilable, stranger, the first other of which the makers of our myths, male as far back as reliable memory runs, ever became aware. And that stranger is, of course, woman, as scarcely anyone has to be told in a time when—after a couple of generations of celebrating their minor triumphs—the spokesmen of women are crying out in rage and hysteria that their sisters are still aliens in a culture and society dominated by men. But this the arts have, of course, always taken into account; and, indeed, one function of drama arises precisely from this awareness, shared on different levels by writer and audience, that such unredeemed strangers move always in our midst.

To begin at the simplest and most vulgar level, we know, for instance, that large numbers of men will even now pay for the privilege of watching female impersonators do their acts, those tawdry turns which simultaneously embarrass and amuse, depress and yet profoundly satisfy, the beholder. However secularized and vulgarized such impersonations may have become, they represent the survival on the level of popular entertainment of a ritual, an archetypal magic. And they will continue to be performed, presumably, as long as the female continues to be felt and to be made to feel herself a stranger in a culture whose notion of the human is defined by males afraid of, though desperately drawn to express, everything in their psyches which they have denominated "womanly" or "girlish."

Generally speaking, play acting, the theater itself, represents always and everywhere an attempt to mitigate, if not bridge, the mythological gap which men feel between themselves and the other, whoever that other may be, by permitting representatives of the reigning group in a culture (at first the sons of the best families, then their paid surrogates or servants) to *play,* that is, mythically to become, the feared and desired other. "Disguising" is another word for the process, a term still used in fact to describe a favorite form of dramatic entertainment at the courts of Henry VII and Henry VIII, and one which reminds us of the link between acting and the child's "dressing up" like his parents, on the one hand, or the gods' mythological changing of shape, on the other. Acting is, in any case, no mere matter of imitating another individual, at least when drama is most alive, but of metamorphosing into another kind.

So, for instance, in the heyday of Greek drama, men played gods or the half-divine children of gods, thus creating possibilities for the kind of dramatic punning practiced by Euripides in *The Bacchae,* in which the god who, inside of the play's fiction, plays he is a man, becomes, once we fall back into our own realm of truth, a man playing he is a god playing he is a man. This can be read, on the final level of myth, as the god in us all (whom we have been ordinarily too obtuse to know) playing he is a man playing he is a god playing he is a man. And so at the climax of his career, Shakespeare, in a final involution of drama's essential device, turned it back onto the nature of acting itself, creating in *The Tempest* that play within a play, which (as Tillyard long ago remarked) "is executed by players pretending to be spirits, pretending to be real actors, pretending to be supposed goddesses and rustics."

Long before this, however, he has brought that same device

to bear on the problem of the original stranger, the woman, most spectacularly in *As You Like It,* in which the full meaning of the play is only established by the last turn of the mythological screw, when the boy who has been playing Rosalind playing she is Ganymede playing Rosalind, steps out of his role and stage-sex to speak the Epilogue. And though in his-her wedding dress still, he-she informs the audience that, "If I were a woman I would kiss as many of you as had beards that pleased me, complexions that liked me, and breaths that I defied not." Then he-she curtsies with that strange perfection of grace possible only to a male playing the idea of femininity and sets throbbing—we are free to imagine—more than one male heart in that largely homosexual circle of gallants, which, sitting on stage rather than standing in the pit, must have felt itself sometimes more actor or chorus than audience.

But the Shakespeare who manipulated the four contrasted boy-girls in *As You Like It*—voice against voice, style against style, and complexion against complexion—was immensely more sophisticated and artful than the beginning playwright of *Henry VI, Part I.* He had not yet, of course, discovered how the device of disguising could be used to make his heroines seem as much boys as girls, and therefore less disturbingly alien. Nor could he even manage to differentiate the female parts demanded by his fable, creating over and over the same abstract dark lady. In the first part of *Henry VI,* there are actually three female characters: Joan of Arc, the Countess of Auvergne, and Margaret, who becomes Queen of England; but they never appear on the stage together and could easily have been played by a single actor. Indeed, mythologically speaking, they *are* one, being all "black," all French, and all bent on betraying the male champion of the English.

The Countess of Auvergne, to be sure, though she begins, like Joan, as the enemy of the play's archetypal English male, Talbot, ends with a quick, unconvincing capitulation before his power. "Alas," she cries on first confronting him, "this is a child, a silly dwarf! / It cannot be this weak and writhled shrimp / Should strike such terror to his enemies." But once he has, like some latter-day Roland, wound "his horn" to call up reinforcements and reveal that he is more than his single self, being all England, all masculine chivalry, the lady concedes, "I find thou art no less than fame hath bruited / And more than may be gathered by thy shape." She attempts vainly, that is, to play Delilah to a "weak and writhled" English Samson, destined by the irrelevant exigencies of history to die at other hands. And she is dismissed in a single scene, having illustrated in baldest allegory that the enemy=France=traitor =woman=the blackness of darkness, which is to say, Hell, but also that in the end, that enemy is powerless against England and Saint George.

Margaret, on the other hand, who also demonstrates the same equation, is permitted to appear on stage in all three of the *Henry VI* plays and in *Richard III,* as well. But she does not enter until the Countess of Auvergne has disappeared into the wings and Joan herself has exited, discomfited and in chains. She seems in fact to be, in some real sense, Joan's successor, a relationship made manifest in the speech with which she introduces herself to the other players and us: "Margaret my name, and daughter to a King, / The King of Naples. . . ." But Joan, who reappears once more after Margaret's entrance, is led off to her death asserting (in what may be her last lie or her first truth) that precisely the father of Margaret has also fathered the unborn bastard she claims to be carrying in her belly. " 'Twas neither Charles nor yet the Duke I named," she explains, "but Reignier, King of Naples, that prevailed."

Reflecting afterward on the line—for the play's quick pace at this point scarcely leaves time for reflection—we realize that given a few more months, another act, Joan might have borne a half sister to Margaret, who succeeds her on stage as "the English scourge." Or, let us rather say that in the nighttime illogic of dream and myth, she *did* bear a "banning hag" quite like herself in Margaret, an archetypal daughter–alter ego.

That daughter–alter ego, at any rate, continues to dominate the scene throughout the rest of Shakespeare's first historical tetralogy, the sole character who survives the bloody events from almost start to almost finish, though transformed step by step from a fatal Aphrodite to a cursing Hecate. She constitutes, in fact, the sole principle of unity in a series of events otherwise rendered in all the formless confusion of the Lancastrian wars themselves. How sad, in light of all this, to see modern productions of *Richard III* which, heedlessly or ignorantly, cut her out, thus cheating us of that final confrontation of male and female as "hog" and "hag"—for so Shakespeare calls the humpbacked King and the aged Queen at last.

In the final play of the tetralogy, the character who begins as the Duke of Gloucester and ends as Richard III remains, quite as Talbot was, an enemy to women, crying for drums and trumpets to drown them out when they rail at him ("Let not the Heavens hear these telltale women / Rail on the Lord's anointed"), and despising them when they capitulate to his evil charm ("Relenting fool, and shallow, changing woman"). But he is the enemy of chivalry and male honor as well, so that there seems finally little to choose when he and the ancient Queen—a bereaved mother now, though she had begun as a bereaver of fathers—scream insults at each other. "Devil," she calls him, "murderous villain" and "cacodemon," to which he responds, "Foul wrinkled witch" and "hateful withered hag." The final word, however, is hers, as she mounts to a pitch of invective worthy of Joan herself:

> Thou elvish-marked, abortive, rooting hog.
> Thou that wast sealed in thy nativity
> The slave of nature and the son of Hell!
> Thou slander of thy mother's heavy womb!
> Thou loathèd issue of thy father's loins!
> Thou rag of honor!

The omission of Margaret deprives us as well of that chilling scene in Act IV, scene iv, of *Richard III,* after which she exits to France (whose alien significances she has embodied throughout), but not until—squatting on the ground with Queen Elizabeth and the Duchess of York—she has helped project the image of the Triple Goddess in darkest form. A triad of Norns or Furies, those three black mothers fall to cursing, which, according to the early Shakespeare, is woman's role when she is not foolish enough to love or weak enough to weep. There is something about the ritualistic scene which reminds us of *Macbeth,* as the three ladies echo and re-echo each other like an early version of the weird sisters, picking up rhyme and cadence.

"When didst Thou sleep when such a deed was done?" asks the Duchess of York; and Queen Margaret answers, "When holy Harry died, and my sweet son." But here the antiphonal exchange reaches its climax in the recital of the names of the dead, the shared names fewer than the victims. Margaret leads off:

> I had an Edward—till a Richard killed him.
> I had a Harry—till a Richard killed him.
> Thou hadst an Edward—till a Richard killed him.
> Thou hadst a Richard—till a Richard killed him.

And the Duchess responds:

> I had a Richard too, and thou didst kill him.
> I had a Rutland too, thou holp'st to kill him.

Then the Queen ends the series, capping the list with a curse:

> Thou hadst a Clarence too, and Richard killed him.
> From forth the kennel of thy womb hath crept
> A hellhound that doth hunt us all to death.
> That dog, that had his teeth before his eyes. . . .
> dear God, I pray,
> That I may live to say, "The dog is dead!"

But when Richard III does in fact die, there are no women present to rejoice (indeed, in the whole fifth act, the only female on stage is a ghost); and the words that echo Margaret's curse are spoken by Richmond, who is to be Henry VII, "the bloody dog is dead." It is as if Shakespeare, at this point in his career, can imagine no final reconciliation, no hope of peace except in an all-male world. At the end of his second tetralogy —which includes *Richard II,* the two parts of *Henry IV,* and *Henry V*—he will try to imagine a more conventional ending, a marriage rather than a truce of exhaustion on the field of battle.

But to do this he must imagine a Frenchwoman, a daughter of the enemy, fit to marry his English hero-king, who is Prince Hal before he becomes Henry V—which is to say, a character is some ways much like the fair youth of the *Sonnets.* Only so could their union be made to symbolize not merely the reconciliation of two hostile kingdoms, but of two polar sets of human possibilities as well—all that is represented by the contrast of male and female, fair and black. Try as he would, however, Shakespeare could not, even at that later moment, keep his fear of women and his disgust with sex from breaking through.

The key to it all is to be found in the fourth scene of Act III, a comic scene written almost entirely in French and dealing with the effort of Katherine, Princess of France, to learn English—out of a sense, perhaps, that until the two countries and two sexes had a language in common (and how could English Hal learn French?) no real *détente* would be possible. At first all goes well with the Princess and her teacher, "Alice, an old Gentlewoman," for it is solely in nouns that the French girl seems interested, chiefly the parts of her own body, and she has little trouble learning to say "de hand" for "la main" or "de fingres" for "les doigts." With "col" and "menton," however, the situation begins to change, though the audience realizes it before Katherine herself does, since in Katherine's mouth these become "de nick" and "de sin."

"En vérité," says Alice, underlining the ironies lest we have missed them, "vous prononcez les mots aussi droit que les natifs d'Angleterre" ("Truly, you pronounce the words as accurately as the natives of England"). And though we laugh, we feel the scene grow dark at the evocation of the Devil under his fashionable name of Nick, along with that of sin, whose wages, we recall, are death.

Almost immediately, however, Katherine is wanting to go on, asking the English for "le pied" and "la robe," which she is told is "de foot" and "de coun" (the latter, apparently, Alice's approximation of "gown"); but to her ears these sound like *foutre* and *con,* which is to say, "fuck" and "cunt"—what were for Shakespeare the act of darkness and the organ he identified with hell itself. If the cadences of Sonnet 144 recur in our heads at this point ("Mine be thy love, and thy loves use their treasure"), they are surely not irrelevant. The Princess herself is aware of the bilingual puns, and commenting on them, makes us doubly so: "Oh, Seigneur Dieu! Ce sont mots de son mauvais, corruptible, gros, et impudique. . . ." And further, whenever such dirty *double-entendres* rise unbidden to the surface of Shakespeare's work, we are close to his queasiness before the sexuality of women, whether he is, as in this case, doing his best to escape it for the sake of a happy ending or, as in the case of *Henry VI, Part I,* giving it free rein.

Indeed, at the heart of the latter play, too, there is such a bilingual pun, on the French *pucelle* and the English "puzzel," meaning, respectively, "virgin" and "whore," or more precisely perhaps "stinking whore," since behind the English cant word must lie the Italian *puzzare,* with its evocation of the "burning, scalding, stench" of Lear's diatribe against women. "Pucelle or puzzel, dolphin or dogfish," Talbot cries on first hearing Joan's name, "Your hearts I'll stamp out with my horse's heels. . . ." "Dolphin" represents, of course, a pun on "Dauphin," who strikes the simple-minded Englishman as representing a kind of effeminacy as monstrous in its way as

Joan's unwomanly aggressiveness in its. Both of them, that is to say, seem to Talbot to challenge that clear-cut distinction of roles according to sex on which his view of man is based. His bitter dream of stamping them out, trampling them into the muck with his horse's heels, is, consequently, the product not of simple sadism, but rather of a desire to find some outward and visible sign for the destruction of the rebellious female principle that he believes necessary if peace is to be restored to the polity and men's hearts.

His rhetoric is extreme almost to the point of hysteria, as he continues, "And make a quagmire of your mingled brains." But it is no more extreme finally than the terrible soliloquy of Posthumus Leonatus in *Cymbeline,* so chillingly genocidal in respect to women that the genteel and chivalrous editors of the nineteenth century tried hard to prove that Shakespeare had never written it.

> Is there no way for men to be, but women
> Must be half-workers? . . .
>   Could I find out
> The woman's part in me! For there's no motion
> That tends to vice in man but I affirm
> It is the woman's part. Be it lying, note it
> The woman's; flattering, hers; deceiving, hers;
> Lust and rank thoughts, hers, hers. . . .

Fortunately for him, it turns out that in his case woman was not quite a "half-worker," since he was untimely snatched from his mother's womb—just such a man not born of woman as was Macduff in *Macbeth* or Julius Caesar first of all. It is Shakespeare's favorite quibble, though not such a quibble at last as it may first seem, since the boy whose mother dies bearing him grows up solely his father's son. And this, for Shakespeare, precisely qualifies him to be a hero, that is, one capable of confronting and defeating the female principle.

In the *Henry VI* tetralogy, however, there is no Caesarean

hero. Indeed, the series of plays begins with a lament for that most phallic of English kings, Henry V, of whom the Duke of Gloucester says, "His brandished sword did blind men with his beams. / His arms spread wider than a dragon's wings," and who, the Duke of Bedford boasts, was superior to Caesar: "A far more glorious star thy soul will make / Than Julius Caesar. . . ." But even he, being born of woman, did not possess the mana of Posthumus or Macduff, the sole effective antidote against the female "arts." And consequently, the Duke of Exeter suggests, "the subtle-witted French / Conjurers and sorcerers . . . / By magic verses have contrived his end."

With his death, at any rate, his country seems on the verge of losing its last claim to the male principle, which is to say, its own identity, since in Shakespeare's mythological geography, England represents masculinity as France does femininity. In the very first scene of *Part I,* the keening wail has gone up: "Our isle be made a nourish of salt tears, / And none but women left to wail the dead." *"None but women left":* it is the threat which hangs over a realm ruled by a boy king obviously destined never to become a real man. In all England, so far as the play will permit us to see, there is only a single claimant to the role of male champion, one warrior capable of resisting the incursion of the female from without and creeping feminization from within. And this is Talbot, "English John Talbot," contrasted from the start with the "coward" John Fastolfe, who, his accusers assert, "doth but usurp the sacred name of knight. . . ." Yet he is by an irony no less real for being unintended, destined to be transmogrified into the antihero of *Henry IV,* the craven tub of guts loved by Shakespeare's readers more than any hero, not excepting his own beloved Prince Hal.

Though Talbot speaks sometimes of his wife, it is impossible to imagine him at home; for the battlefield is where alone he becomes himself, joined in mutual loyalty with his fighting men and with that son for whom he feels the deepest affection he can sustain. To be faithful father to son and son to father: this is for Shakespeare, at the moment of writing *Henry VI,* the greatest of all virtues. And the two Talbots enact that faith almost allegorically in the emblematic scenes which portray the death of both. They begin with a sticomythic exchange, flat and stiff as an engraving on a sepulcher.

> TAL: Shall all thy mother's hopes lie in one tomb?
> JOHN: Aye, rather than I'll shame my mother's womb.
> TAL: Upon my blessing, I command thee go.
> JOHN: To fight I will, but not to fly the foe.
> TAL: Part of thy father may be saved in thee.
> JOHN: No part of him but will be the shame in me.

Then in the very midst of battle, both become less cryptic and more allusive.

> JOHN: Surely, by all the glory you have won,
> And if I fly, I am not Talbot's son.
> Then talk no more of flight, it is no boot;
> If son to Talbot, die at Talbot's foot.
> TAL: Then follow thou thy desperate sire of Crete,
> Thou Icarus. Thy life to me is sweet.
> If thou wilt fight, fight by thy father's side,
> And, commendable proved, let's die in pride.

It is the beginning of their mutual transformation into their mythological prototypes, Daedalus and Icarus, another father and son lost in the maze of female lechery and dreaming the flight that is to kill them. Toward the end of the play, the Minotaur is mentioned by Suffolk, who, contemplating adultery and treachery, admonishes himself, "But, Suffolk, stay. / Thou mayst not wander in that labyrinth. / There Minotaurs and ugly treasons lurk." In the Talbot scenes, however, the dark female chamber at the center of the maze is not evoked, only the open masculine heavens, where what seems to have been lost in time ("and there died, / My Icarus, my blossom, in his pride") is preserved in eternity:

> Two Talbots, wingèd through the lither sky,
> In thy despite shall 'scape mortality.

But this is not Talbot's final word, for even more than immortality, he seems to have desired the filial-paternal *Liebestod* he celebrates with his last breath.

> Poor boy! He smiles, methinks, as who should say,
> "Had Death been French, then Death had died today."
> Come, come and lay him in his father's arms.
> My spirit can no longer bear these harms.
> Soldiers, adieu! I have what I would have;
> Now my old arms are young John Talbot's grave.
> [*Dies.*]

Actually—as Shakespeare knew very well from his sources—John Talbot did not die with his son, but survived both him and Joan, outliving her in fact by twenty years. As Eugène Sue retells the legend two and a half centuries later in *The Mysteries of the People,* Talbot does not exit from the scene until he has tried to rape Joan in prison. It is a particularly ignominious encounter, in which the English captain, who has been made Joan's official guard after her recantation before the ecclesiastical court, only dares to assault her with the aid of an accomplice as drunk as himself—and fails. They beat her mercilessly, however, before retreating in confusion, to leave her virginity intact. "THEY STRIKE JOAN WITH THEIR FISTS. . . . HER FACE IS SMASHED IN . . . BLOODY. . . . She still resists. . . ."

But for Shakespeare, Talbot's dignity must be preserved to the last, though his personal mythology demanded that, however inconclusive their meetings in battle, the female principle triumph over the male by sheer longevity. To be sure,

Shakespeare had also departed from the historical record in order to grant Talbot a minor triumph over that minor French temptress the Countess of Auvergne. Joan, however, is given the last word, allowed to undercut—with a kind of ironic realism not unlike Falstaff's in his famous reflections on honor—the code by which Talbot lived and died.

The exemplar of that code, as well as of the heroic style which sustains it, is Sir William Lucy, who just after Talbot's death, enters the French camp, crying:

But where's the great Alcides of the field,
Valiant Lord Talbot, Earl of Shrewsbury,
Created for his rare success in arms,
Great Earl of Washford, Waterford, and Valence;
Lord Talbot of Goodrig and Urchinfield,
Lord Strange of Blackmere, Lord Verdun of Alton,
Lord Cromwell of Wingfield, Lord Furnival of Sheffield,
The thrice-victorious Lord of Falconbridge;
Knight of the noble order of Saint George,
Worthy Saint Michael and the Golden Fleece;
Great Marshal to Henry the Sixth
Of all his wars within the realm of France?

After this grandiloquence, the Pucelle answers so quietly and with such good sense that for one instant the balance of Shakespeare's sympathy (along with ours) tilts in her direction. For the first time in his career, perhaps, he betrays his ambivalence about the reigning values of his time, his suspicion, later expressed in certain speeches of Shylock and Caliban, that by virtue of his strangeness the stranger in our midst can sometimes see the silliness of the games we play in deadly earnest. And though such perceptions are not all the truth they are, like Joan's rejoinder, *also* true.

Here's a silly stately style indeed!
The Turk, that two and fifty kingdoms hath,

Writes not so tedious a style as this.
Him that thou magnifiest with all these titles,
Stinking and fly-blown lies here at our feet.

To make matters worse, Shakespeare's ironic strangers often possess a mythic dimension lacking in the official spokesmen they challenge. Certainly, this is the case in *Henry VI, Part I;* for Talbot is a provincial hero and Joan a universal myth, a figure of inexhaustible archetypal resonance. Even inside the play, he cannot ever touch her; they exist, as it were, in different dimensions, and she fades from his solidity like a dream. True, he is permitted to abuse her roundly, calling her "Devil or Devil's dam," "witch," "high-minded strumpet," "foul fiend of France," "hag of all despite," and "railing Hecaté." But it is she who pronounces his epitaph, not he, hers.

Moreover, as the play lives on in the mind, it has undergone the kind of posthumous transformation against which textual critics protest in vain, but of which mythopoeic artists dream. We consider it no longer, as Shakespeare's contemporaries did, an occasion for extorting patriotic tears by making the wounds of Talbot bleed again after two hundred years. In fact, Talbot has predeceased Joan in our imagination, even as Shakespeare compelled him to do in his prophetic revision of history. And this was inevitable, since all truly mythic characters and events escape the works which give them birth and survive in the public domain. There they belong to no one and are contemporary only with each other: Odysseus and Don Quixote, Rip van Winkle and Shylock, Hamlet and Falstaff, and Sherlock Holmes and—to be sure—Joan of Arc, *La Pucelle.*

It scarcely matters whether one approves or disapproves of such figures; they exist independently of our attitudes toward them, just as they do of the works which portray them. Odysseus, for instance, who in Homer is heroic, admirable, had become by the end of the heyday of Greek classic drama a contemptible trickster and windbag, but remains Odysseus still. And so Joan—even historically ambiguous enough, her sanctity called into question by her association with the vilest ritual sadist, Gilles de Rais, who also lives on in myth as Bluebeard —has divided opinion pro and con down to our own time, without ever ceasing to be herself: a figure of endless fascination and inexhaustible significance.

For those who, in the interest of art and mental health, demand the angelification of the eternal alien, woman, her mythicizing *upward,* Joan remains an object of adoration, however heterodox. The honorable list of her admirers comes immediately to mind: Friedrich Schiller, Bernard Shaw, Jean Anouilh, Eugène Sue, and Mark Twain, dissenters in a Protestant or post-Protestant culture grown too austerely patriarchal to honor the Great Goddess. There have been pious Roman Catholic glorifiers of Joan, too, ever since her second, posthumous trial revoked her condemnation as a witch and prepared the way for her to become a saint; but they seem less interesting somehow, since orthodoxy tends to neutralize myth by turning it into dogma. But the vilifiers of Joan, those driven to mythicize her *downward,* are of at least equal importance and interest, particularly in France, where her official cult, that redeification of woman inside the myth of nationalism, has seemed to some more malign than beneficial to art and sanity alike.

James Joyce, himself an heir of precisely those writers, has provided a clue to the significance of their attack on Joan in an extraordinary little critical essay, which begins as a study of Daniel Defoe but includes before it is through an illuminating series of observations on the development of realism-naturalism (*verismo* is the term Joyce uses, for he wrote it originally in Italian) in modern European literature. "Modern realism," he argues, "is perhaps a reaction. The great French Nation, which venerates the legend of the Maid of Orleans, nevertheless disfigures her through the mouth of Voltaire, lasciviously defiles her in the hands of the engravers of the nineteenth century, riddles and shreds her in the twentieth century with the cutting style of Anatole France. . . ."

But is this not just what Shakespeare, achieving in verse the victory which eluded "English John Talbot" on the field of battle, is doing in *Henry VI, Part I*—disfiguring, lasciviously defiling, riddling and shredding the Maid—though surely not with the same intention as the realists with whom Joyce is concerned. Their attack, no matter how little they may have been conscious of its final implications, was ultimately as an act of aesthetic blasphemy, a denial of the Muse herself, since they were, all of them, in theory as in practice, bent on reinterpreting their art not as a gift of the creative spirit, traditionally felt to be female, but as the pursuit of cold, hard (mythologically speaking, *male*) facts by cold, hard (in fact, male once more) authors. *Le style, c'est l'homme,* they liked to say, or, *Madame Bovary, c'est moi,* which rendered in plain English becomes: "every man his own muse," or, "my heroine is me."

Primarily, Shakespeare is interested, like the Tudor chroniclers on whom he drew and those who sat in the ecclesiastical court which originally condemned the Pucelle to be burned, on making a case for England, or rather against France. But there is in him, too, despite what allegiance he may have felt he owed the old Roman faith of his mother, a Protestant, Puritan, Hebraic, finally patriarchal distrust of Mariolatry in all its forms, any attempt to smuggle into Christianity or patriotic piety homage to the Goddess. For him, in general as well as particular, the virgin is a whore; which is why he, through his mouthpiece Talbot, begins by calling the Pucelle "puzzel," and why he lingers so obscenely over Joan's desperate attempts to escape the fire by claiming pregnancy—though by which of her many lovers she finds it hard to be sure.

In any case, the plea which, in French ignorance, she hoped would save her, in the eyes of English morality doubly condemns her. She begins her confession, "I am with child, ye bloody homicides. / Murder not then the fruit within my womb. . . ." York answers scornfully, "Now Heaven forfend! The holy maid with child!" And when she concludes by crying, "Oh, give me leave, I have deluded you. / 'Twas neither Charles nor yet the Duke I named, / But Reignier, King of Naples, that prevailed," that same interlocutor responds, "And yet, forsooth, she is a virgin pure./ Strumpet, thy words condemn thy brat and thee." From "puzzel" to "strumpet," the English charge remains the same, though the spokesmen shift with the tides of war.

It is not merely the fact of Joan's having been a whore that stirs the fury of English Shakespeare and his English heroes against her ("Break thou in pieces and consume to ashes, / Thou foul accursèd minister of Hell!"). Even more it is the fact of her having claimed to be the total opposite, of having been a liar as well. Like Chaucer, Shakespeare seems to have felt that the three natural gifts of God to women are "Deceite, wepyng, spynnyng" (lies, tears, and skill with the distaff). Unlike Chaucer, however, he could not contain that belief in ironical acceptance, not even in the *Sonnets,* where he makes a show of such containment ("I do believe her, though I know she lies"), and certainly not in the first part of *Henry VI.* Everything about Joan enrages Shakespeare, because everything about her is a lie, an illusion. She enters, for instance, in the guise of a golden girl; but she is revealed, before all the play is played, a swarthy hag in disguise, as Shakespeare has all along suspected every woman is in essence. Joan herself confesses the fact with a kind of pride on first meeting the Dauphin.

> And, whereas I was black and swart before,
> With those clear rays which she infused on me
> That beauty am I blessed with which you see.

It is the Blessed Virgin herself, "God's Mother. . . . in cómplete glory," supreme symbol in the Christian world of divine womanhood, whom she claims as the source of her magical transformation. And, indeed, before that initial encounter is over, a whole gamut of mythological or semi-mythological females has been evoked, from classical antiquity and medieval hagiography as well as the Testaments, Old and New: Saint Katherine, Deborah, the Amazons, the "mother of Great Constantine," "Saint Philip's daughter," and at last the goddess of love herself. "Bright star of Venus, fall'n down on the earth," the Dauphin says toward the scene's end, "How may I reverently worship thee enough?"

Interestingly, of the three saints whom Joan claimed to have seen in visions—Michael, Margaret, and Katherine—only the last is alluded to in Shakespeare's play. Margaret is omitted, perhaps, in order to save the name for Joan's successor as "the English scourge"; and Michael is suppressed, surely, because, along with that other slayer of dragons, Saint George (as already noticed in the florid eulogy by York), he belongs to the other side, which is to say, the male side, Talbot's side. Moreover, Shakespeare may have found Katherine, who was the patron saint of childbirth, ironically appropriate to the final revelation of the Maid's pregnancy, real or imaginary.

In any case, Shakespeare, for all his hostility to Joan, apparently sensed what more sympathetic churchmen have ever since felt obliged to deny, that the Pucelle was, throughout her short life, an adherent of the underground cult of the Great Goddess. This she seems to have believed finally compatible with orthodox Christianity, and at the moment of her sacrificial death, she apparently felt herself to be the avatar of the female force she had worshipped in all innocence and humility. It seems clearly established by the documents adduced at her ecclesiastical trial—a trial uncharacteristically conducted, for its time, without the use of torture or deliberate deceit—that as a child she had been inducted into the ancient rites of the mother, later crushed utterly by a patriarchal church. Certainly, she hung wreaths on the *Arbre des Dames* near her village, around which it was said the *Domines Fatales* were accustomed to gather: "fairies," we have come to call these creatures euphemistically, though "weird sisters" (as Shakespeare named them in *Macbeth*) would be a more accurate translation of their Latin title. Joan was, in short, whether or not also a saint, a witch.

Perhaps we have reached a point in time when once again the word "witch" can be used as something other than a conventional term of abuse or, more confusing still, a name for what does not exist, as in the phrase "witch hunt," meaning the search for an entirely imaginary enemy. Nathaniel Hawthorne represents, in America at least, the beginnings of our long confusions on this score; for in revulsion from the witch hysteria which had swept the community of Salem in the seventeenth century, ending in a series of executions over some of which his own great-great-grandfather presided, he was driven to insist that it had all been paranoia and delusion.

And a hundred years after him, in the wake of the search for "Reds" in high offices led by Sen. Joseph McCarthy, Arthur Miller took up the tale of the Salem witches in a play called *The Crucible.* And this time, once more, they were all portrayed as innocent—*doubly* so, it seemed, since they represented allegorically Communists, whom, as a good liberal, Miller wanted to exculpate completely. At first glance, his play seems to be insisting (in response to McCarthy's paranoiac cry of "Commies everywhere!") that there are not now nor ever have been *any* Communists anywhere, and, by necessary implication, no witches. Indeed, its first audiences seem thus to have understood *The Crucible.* But reading the play at leisure and in light of Miller's own later statements, we see it asserts rather that not everyone called a Communist in a period of repression is one and that, in any case, even those who are, are not what the term means to those who fear and hunt them down.

Obviously, this was true also of the accused witches in Salem, where two dogs were among those finally hanged for sorcery, and where some of the human victims were similarly not criminals but nuisances: nutty old women and half-mad adolescent girls, along with others, male and female, unfortunate enough to have alienated those in power. But over the centuries of witch persecutions, which ended rather than began with Salem, there were, among the thousands accused, many who confessed to being witches, boasted of being witches, in their deepest self-consciousness considered themselves witches, *were*—we must admit, despite a hundred years of pious brainwashing—in some sense, witches. This is, in fact, easier to credit now than it once was, since there are these days a number of otherwise reasonable women plus a handful of men) not at all unwilling to call themselves witches, whether in the interests of black mysticism, practical magic, women's liberation, or some combination of the three.

There have always been self-declared witches at the margins of society, witchcraft providing income and local prestige among the lumpen and an antidote to boredom among a privileged elite. But not until recently has there reappeared a growing sect of witches, propagandizing, proselytizing, committing what seem to alien and unsympathetic eyes atrocities, mass orgies, and ritual murders, in order to establish their identity and express their contempt for the nonwitch world. Once more witchcraft has moved from the occasional Sunday supplement to the daily headlines, becoming, as it was in Shakespeare's day, news and the stuff of living literature.

Perhaps the recent revival of interest in the *Henry VI* tetralogy, particularly *Part I,* owes something to this growing concern with witches. Whatever its cause, that revival is real, for after long years of neglect and critical condescension (along with an attempt to give the play away to other authors), this earliest and still least well known of Shakespeare's history plays has been reinterpreted by the Polish critic Jan Kott and, in a version prompted by his reading, has been spectacularly performed by the Royal Shakespeare Company and at the Stratford Festival in Ontario. A little creaky in the joints from her premature burial, Joan moves across the stage again to conquer, be defeated, and be burned. But as what, for what, even in these new productions, remains unclear, since she must, to make sense at all, be played as a real witch—in a culture just beginning to rediscover what real witches are and what it means to fear them.

What, then, *is* a witch? The recent revival of interest in the occult enables us once more to begin, without seeming either perverse or precious, inside a system of beliefs which considers witches something final and real, rather than symbolic or symptomatic. This system of beliefs assumes that the environment can be altered and human beings influenced by means necessarily and forever outside the realm of science, though the latter boasts of being—at least potentially—total. For the occultist, however, astronomy can never totally subsume astrology; nor chemistry, alchemy. And if certain poisons, for instance, once considered "magical" (magic being what Shakespeare more often called "art" or "the arts"), have been captured for the scientific pharmacopoeia, there stilll remain love philters and, beyond those, amulets and charms, spells to raise the dead, and formulae to make bodies fly.

Unlike the effects of science, which are in theory rational and repeatable, those of magic are by definition mysterious and unique. And for this reason, magic as a whole has been distrusted by the respectable, though from the first it was divided into two categories, white and black, whose means may be the same but whose ends are quite different. White magic aims at achieving goals sanctioned by the legitimate power of the state and the established church; whereas black is dedicated to the subversion of those goals in the interests of others describable in our terminology as "criminal" or "revolutionary" and in theirs as "diabolic" or "satanic." But witches are, of course, precisely practitioners of black magic, servants of Satan. Therefore, when joined in coven, they travesty the rites of the orthodox: celebrating masses on the bare buttocks of women, reciting the Lord's prayer backward, drinking the blood of aborted children from a holy chalice, etc., etc. And in return for such theatrical demonstrations of counterfidelity, they are permitted to see, to kiss the hairy ass of, even to be sexually possessed by Satan (typically, if the medieval confessions can be believed, in anus and vagina at once).

Science, however, being imperialistic by nature, has not been content to let witchcraft thus explain itself, but has sought to explain in its own terms that rival mode of controlling the world. In its brasher early days, science simply dismissed witchcraft as delusory; but since achieving a more sophisticated maturity, it has tried rather to diagnose it, using the terminology of psychiatry in general and psychoanalysis in particular. There are in fact "witches," Freudian analysts begin, which is to say, castrating women of peculiar efficacy and conviction; and, indeed, witches have always been accused of causing impotence and sterility. Meanwhile, other psychiatrists who work with the psychotic rather than the neurotic have been remarking that some schizophrenics, when asked for a self-portrait, draw themselves in the lean and withered form traditionally associated with witches. And they have gone on from this to argue that just such a "deficient body image" may lie behind the common "delusion" of witches that they have escaped gravity completely and can fly through the air to their dark rendezvous.

Jungians, on the other hand, tend to think that witches exist in fancy rather than fact, which is to say, symbolically rather than symptomatically. Men who see witches everywhere, such analysts suggest, are men who have not made peace with the female either in the world, the family, or themselves; and so they discover her, distorted by their fears, as the *vagina dentata,* the phallic mother who would destroy what she has created, consume what she should nurture. And surely the most popular images of the witch—the broomstick protruding from her spread legs (which does not occur at all in Shakespeare) and the beard sprouting from her ambiguous chin (which obsessed Shakespeare)—fit such a reading patly enough. Finally, in any case, all scientific definitions of the witch agree in finding her essentially a woman who in some way challenges the role attributed to her by nature, that is, what males have said is nature.

That there have been and are male witches, many of whom have been, along with women (and, as noted, dogs), persecuted and killed, no one can deny; but to psychoanalysis, these seem finally irrelevant, fellow travelers in a movement which is not quite their own. And with this the historians (makers of myth whose controlling myth is that they too are scientists) in general agree, arguing that what evidence they can find seems to indicate that witches are the remnant of a pre-Christian cult of the Mother, too exclusive to be tolerated by Christianity. Ever ready to assimilate and synthesize, the church proved willing to make some concessions to the female principle, upping the mythological importance of the Blessed Virgin, for instance, so that the patriarchal Trinity of Father, Son, and Holy (sexless) Ghost was virtually replaced by the domestic one of holy mother, holy child, and cuckold-not-quite-father.

Further than this, however, it would not, could not, go, marshaling instead all its forces—philosophical, military, and judicial—to revile, root out, persecute, and destroy, until the scattered survivors of the witch cult no longer knew whom they worshipped, Diana of the Woods, or the Great Buck she hunted, renamed "Satan" by the church; they knew only that what the church called "good" meant death to them. And so, at the solemn moment of initiation, they would recite (reinforcing the fantasies of those who spied or overheard): *"Evil, be thou my good."*

Until Act V of *Henry VI, Part I,* we are left uncertain as to whether Joan is, in this full sense, a witch, a practicing disciple of Satan, or only, as it were, a witch by analogy, a lying and lascivious woman who, in despite of biblical injunctions, has put on the garments of a man. But the third scene of that act removes all of our doubts, beginning with Joan's ritual evocation of her infernal accomplices, in a desperate attempt to turn the tide of war which now runs against her:

> You speedy helpers, that are substitutes
> Under the lordly monarch of the North,
> Appear and aid me in this enterprise.

and reaching a quick climax with their appearance. The "Fiends" enter, but they do not talk, as if Shakespeare were not yet able to imagine a voice and a style for such creatures. *"They walk, and speak not,"* say the stage directions. *"They hang their heads." "They shake their heads." "They depart."* Yet before they have left, Joan has betrayed all: her earlier dealings with them ("I was wont to feed you with my blood. . . ."), as well as her willingness at this point to make the final sacrilegious offerings to hell ("Then take my soul, my body, soul and all. . . ."). But nothing helps; for, Shakespeare suggests, in the end hell betrays its most abject servitors. And as the dark spirits exit, York enters to take her prisoner.

It is apparent that Shakespeare's audience shared fully his obsession with witchcraft, for he seems to have felt free to introduce it not only where the subject demands it, as in *Henry VI, Part I,* but also in plays whose sources do not even suggest it. At the same moment, for instance, that he was retelling the tale of Joan and Talbot, he was working up out of Plautus *The Comedy of Errors,* whose setting, without explanation or excuse, he moved to Ephesus: ancient site of the cult of the Black Diana and notorious home of witches, as he himself reminds us in Act I:

They say this town is full of cozenage:
As, nimble jugglers that deceive the eye,
Dark-working sorcerers that change the mind,
Soul-killing witches that deform the body. . . .

Throughout, he complicates the relatively simple erotic tone of his original with suggestions of the supernatural, so that, for example, turning away a courtesan who has confused him with his twin, Antipholus of Syracuse cries, a little improbably:

Avoid then, fiend! What tell'st thou me of supping?
Thou art, as you are all, a sorceress.
I conjure thee to leave me and be gone.

It is the whore-witch confusion which we have noticed in the case of Joan, played out this time as farce, to be sure, but somehow serious, even sinister, all the same.

Moreover, that audience seems to have had a longing actually to see the ministers of Satan on the stage; and Shakespeare, for his own reasons, apparently felt more than a mere craftsman's pleasure in providing the shudder they sought. Indeed, in *Henry VI, Part II,* he goes out of his way to write a subplot to the story of Suffolk's evil love for Queen Margaret, which allows him to include in his script a full-scale conjuring scene. The play has scarcely started, indeed, before we overhear Eleanor, Duchess of Gloucester, persuading a go-between (who reveals himself almost immediately as a double agent suborned to betray her) to solicit the aid of "Margery Jourdain, the cunning witch, / With Roger Bolinbroke, the conjurer." And, in short order, witch and magician have arrived; it is deepest night, and the magic begins: *"Here they do the ceremonies belonging, and make the circle;* BOLING-

BROKE *or* SOUTHWELL *reads,* 'Conjuro te,' *&c. It thunders and lightens terribly. Then the* SPIRIT *riseth.*"

Called only a "Spirit" in the stage directions and the dramatis personae, though addressed as "Asmath" by the witch Margery Jourdain, that satanic creature answers the ambitious Eleanor's questions about the future of the kingdom with just such riddling answers as the weird sisters later give to Macbeth: "The Duke yet lives that Henry shall depose; / But him outlive, and die a violent death"; "By water shall he die and take his end"; "Let him shun castles. / Safer shall he be upon the sandy plains. . . ." It all seems, as a matter of fact, another preliminary sketch for the great witch scenes of the later tragedy; and Eleanor herself, a pale foreshadowing of Macbeth's terrible queen, consumed with a similar lust for power and the throne. But she disappears quickly from the play, apprehended, as Asmath departs, by the same York who took Joan prisoner. And at her trial, her accomplices are sentenced to death by burning and strangling, she to exile on the Isle of Man—which Shakespeare must have known for the traditional home of witches and their favorite familiar, the Manx cat.

It is a long way, however, from the first historical tetralogy, with its general justification of Tudor rule, to *The "Royal Play" of Macbeth* with its specific glorification of James I: a celebration of his therapeutic royal touch, an apology for his theory of divine right, and especially, an exploitation of the witch terror he had unleashed against the coven who, he claimed, had called up storms to drown him before the name of king was duly his.* But that terror had apparently started to abate by the time Shakespeare was ready to write *Macbeth,*

* One senses in the literature of the time some hints that the witches' plot against James focused the response of women and lovers of women to the court of homosexual sycophants about to replace Elizabeth's household of gallant courtiers. But it is, perhaps, easy to overread such suggestions in knowledgeable retrospect.

so that witches were beginning to seem more chic than truly frightening. And in that play, there is consequently much that is conventional or trivial, along with touches of genuine horror.

Even the scenes undoubtedly written by Shakespeare seem always on the verge of shifting from satanic to grotesque to fully comic, especially toward their endings:

> By the pricking of my thumbs,
> Something wicked this way comes.
> Open, locks,
> Whoever knocks!

And those added by Middleton or whomever, no doubt in response to popular demand for still more witchery, are frankly masquelike and operatic, less evocations of hell than occasions for making song and dance of its terrors.

The real witch of the play—beside whom the others seem illusion and theater, mere "bubbles" of the earth—is, of course, Lady Macbeth herself. A parricide in her own deepest consciousness, she begins by saying of the King, "Had he not resembled / My father as he slept, I had done 't," and looking back on his murder, cries in madness, "Yet who would have thought the old man to have had so much blood in him?" But she is doubly, trebly a witch, being also an "unnatural" woman, impatient with the traditional limitations of her sex ("Come, you spirits / That tend on mortal thoughts, unsex me here. . . ."), and finally a bad mother besides, quite as in the Jungian analysis of the witch archetype.

"How many children did Lady Macbeth have?" those who used to be called the "new critics" once impertinently asked, mocking the willingness of certain old scholars to treat dramatic characters as if they had real biographies outside the works which contained them. Yet far from being a joke on anyone, the question is essential to understanding a play whose sources insisted that Lady Macbeth be sterile, whereas

Shakespeare's myth of evil woman required that she had children to whom she could be shown refusing maternal love, all, in fact, that is traditionally symbolized by "milk." How that word, that image, haunts the closing scenes of Act I, a sinister leitmotif in Lady Macbeth's mouth. It seems merely a casual metaphor when (speaking of the husband who seems to her less manly, more womanly than herself) she muses, "Yet I do fear thy nature. / It is too full o' the milk of human kindness / To catch the nearest way." But it becomes actualized, personalized as, invoking the spirits of darkness, she offers them the sustenance that belongs by right only to the children of her flesh. "Come to my woman's breasts, / And take my milk for gall, you murdering ministers. . . ."

One of the standard charges against witches was that they suckled evil spirits, so that a "supernumerary teat" was taken in the witch trials to be prima facie evidence of guilt. But Shakespeare is more concerned with who is refused the gift of mother's milk than with who is offered it, and for him therefore the climax does not come until the last scene of the opening act, when Lady Macbeth imagines denying her own human child the breast she has offered to the ministers of hell.

> I have given suck, and know
> How tender 'tis to love the babe that milks me.
> I would, while it was smiling in my face,
> Have plucked my nipple from his boneless gums
> And dashed the brains out. . . .

As the play is structured, then, in terms of symbol as well as plot, Lady Macbeth functions not as just another witch, but as the sole substantial reality behind the shadow play of stage convention, hallucination, and delusion represented by the weird sisters and Hecate, whom Middleton added to their ranks. She and they never appear on scene together, so that a single actor-actress might well play, as the dream meanings of the play demand, both Macbeth's queen and one of the witches (in a movie version, all three), her face distorted from beauty to horror in their triple mirror and her chin bearded as if in answer to her prayer to be unsexed.

The witches, mythographers have taught, are three to begin with because all forms of the Great Goddess must be so: three Fates (but "weird" means "fate"), three Graces, three Norns, or sometimes three times three, as in the nine Muses. "Thrice to thine, and thrice to mine," Shakespeare's shadow-witches chant, "And thrice again, to make up nine. / Peace! The charm's wound up." But three (or three times three) is the number of the "charm" because in the beginning woman was perceived as triune in her relationship to man, whom first she bore, next embraced in love, and last of all, laid out when he was dead. The mythological names for her three roles are Hera, Aphrodite, Persephone: mother, mistress, and queen of the underworld.

In Shakespeare, however, the first two functions blur into the third; bad mother and lying whore are indistinguishable from each other and the queen of hell, since they are witches all three. This is why the weird sisters are triple but without distinction in *Macbeth;* and that is also why, in that terrible scene of *Richard III* in which Queen Margaret, Queen Elizabeth, and the Duchess of York gather together, the second two are portrayed as mere shadows of the first, who, we suspect, will disappear when she leaves the land which has never really been hers.

> A dire induction am I witness to,
> And will to France, hoping the consequence
> Will prove as bitter, black, and tragical.

And what else is there for her to do, outfaced by a bad son worse even than the worst of mothers, one who before he could be denied the teat had already bit it?

But leaving England, Queen Margaret does not leave Shakespeare's deep imagination, since she is the prototype—more than poor, silly Eleanor, more even than Joan—for all those wicked stepmothers, who, whether they are like her called witch or not, do witches' work in the plays from *Titus Andronicus* to *Cymbeline.* Quite obviously, the real power of this archetype is released when Shakespeare comes closest, in the terror of his beginnings or the dreamy wisdom of his final work, to the fairy-tale sources of his sources, those nightmares of desertion and cannibalism born in the Black Woods. But there is something of Margaret as well in the more complex women of the great tragedies, even Hamlet's mother, perhaps, and surely in Goneril and Regan, those concupiscent and undutiful daughters whom foolish Lear made stepmothers to his old age.

All are "antiwomen," subverters of the role assigned to them by men who seek to naturalize their strangeness to a patriarchal world. York, that most relentless of enemies to witches, finds the words for Margaret—and by extension all her descendants—in *Henry VI, Part III:* "Women are soft, mild, pitiful, and flexible— / Thou, stern, obdúrate, flinty, rough, remorseless." And earlier he had found a metaphor as well, berating her for her "tiger's heart wrapped in a woman's hide"—a line infamous enough to have been used against Shakespeare in an attack on his "plagiarism" by a pair of professional dramatists annoyed at competition from a mere player. It is hard to know how large a role was played by accident as opposed to malice in turning his most ferocious antifemale metaphor against one who all his life sought to deny the "woman's part" in himself. But there seems an apposite irony in this early revelation of what Shakespeare guarded like a guilty secret.

Sometimes, to be sure, he makes the dark lady his spokesman, a surrogate self, as he did with Venus in *Venus and Adonis* and, most notably, with Cleopatra, of whom it is fair to say with Wyndham Lewis that she represents "the author

. . . in love with Antony." And one can even subscribe to his further generalization that Shakespeare's "sentimentality . . . was directed to other men and not toward women." Yet to conclude that "whether Homer was written by a woman or not . . . Shakespeare was" is to simplify both the poet's ambiguous sexuality and his ambivalent attitude toward it to the point of falsification.

Shakespeare *is* finally a "shamanized man," as Lewis contends, a magical sex-shifter, which is to say, a kind of witch. But from the start he calls upon his magic not to evoke what is most womanly in himself, but to exorcise what is dark and female in favor of what is benign and male. One of his strategies is to invert his own desire to play the "woman's part" and project it onto some unnatural mother, some queen who would be king (like Lady Macbeth or the second wife of Cymbeline), and then to bring her to despair and suicide. Another is to permit some sufficiently modest maiden *temporarily* to assume a boy's disguise and even to win in it some foolish lady's heart, so long as that "boy" unmasks at last to accept a girl's happy ending.

There is, in fact, always the possibility of another turn of the screw (as we noted in discussing the Epilogue to *As You Like It*), since boy actors invariably played the roles of girls. Inside the main action, however, it is girls who act boys and not vice versa. Falstaff's transvestism in *The Merry Wives of Windsor* is an apparent exception. But his disguise as "the fat woman of Brentford" and his subsequent beating as a "witch" is a joke on the whole business of sex-shifting, as befits a play made to order for so equivocal a queen as Elizabeth. "By yea and no," says Sir Hugh Evans, making sure we get the point, "I think the 'oman is a witch indeed. I like not when a 'oman has a great peard." Only once, in the case of Ariel, does Shakespeare present centrally and seriously a male character who assumes female roles. But Ariel is a spirit of air and fire only, as well as a boy-actor, which is to say, half human, disembodied.

In any case, *The Tempest* is a play in which witchcraft is at last redeemed by being made white and male instead of black and female. And what remains in Prospero of Joan has been transmuted into Ariel—a creature able to act Ceres or even a Harpy, but not Venus, who is, in fact, banned from his master's magic stage. Cleopatra, on the other hand, represents a mythological midpoint between "Mars's hot minion" Venus and the faithful Ariel, since like the former she remains still a mouthpiece for a passion which Shakespeare knew foredoomed but could not deny. She, therefore, speaks her most moving words only when her love is dead, his death experienced like a final detumescence.

> Oh, withered is the garland of the war,
> The soldier's pole is fall'n. Young boys and girls
> Are level now with men. The odds is gone,
> And there is nothing left remarkable
> Beneath the visiting moon.

And she cannot restore "the odds" by becoming herself "remarkable," until he has immolated her femininity to the male principle, clutching to her childless breast the image of her serpent self, and disavowing the fertile mud of Egypt, the Yin, which is to say, the female, elements of earth and water. "I am fire and air. My other elements / I give to baser life," she cries before her end. Yet, even denying what is most grossly witchlike in herself, she seems a woman still—no disembodied spirit. A little earlier she has foreseen in horror the travesty of herself by some "squeaking" actor who will "boy my greatness / I' the posture of a whore." And determined now to be no longer a "whore" at all, she dreams herself first a Roman wife ("Now to that name my courage prove my title!") and then a mother, a good mother giving that milk which Lady Macbeth refused ("Peace, peace!" she cries, "Dost thou not see my baby at my breast, / That sucks the nurse asleep?").

In *The Tempest,* however, the bad mother returns to haunt

Shakespeare—an unrepentant witch, this time with a demon child. True, she is killed off before the action proper starts; but though a ghost only, she has a name, Sycorax, and a black history that Prospero, the white magician, cannot cease rehearsing. It is from him, in fact, that we learn of her banishment from her native Algiers "for mischiefs manifold and sorceries terrible" and discover that she might well have been burned like Joan, except that "for one thing she did / They would not take her life." This is somewhat circumspectly expressed, but clearly what saved Sycorax from the stake, permitting her to die in another world, was precisely the plea that failed in Joan's case, the plea of pregnancy.

Unlike Joan, however, she bears the child she pleads in her own behalf, not in metaphor, as Joan breeds Margaret, but in fact. And what she leaves behind her is a New World stranger, a male "Indian with the great tool," who represents for Shakespeare, as we shall see, a pole of otherness so remote that beside it France and woman seem scarcely strange at all.

Henry VI, Part I, on the other hand, is a play without any mothers, since Joan, witch though she may be, bears no resemblance to such dark maternal figures as Sycorax or Lady Macbeth or the evil Queen of *Cymbeline.* Nor is she even, like Margaret is until the birth and death of her son, a kind of base Iseult, who, before she enters the scene, has already won an ignoble Tristan's heart and doomed that of an effeminate King Mark to break. It is to Paris rather than Tristan that her lover, Suffolk, actually compares himself in the play's last speech, making her by implication a fatal Helen, and France a new Greece at war with British Troy.

But Joan falls out of this mythological pattern as well, for though she names three possible fathers for her perhaps-imaginary child-to-come—the Dauphin and Alençon, as well as Reignier, King of Naples—on scene she makes love to no one and betrays no one except her father and herself. She is, that is to say, a daughter-witch, whom Shakespeare has imagined not as a decrepit hag whose treason to her sex a beard declares, but as a beautiful young woman who might well be a beardless boy. And her denial of all that is "soft, mild, pitiful, and flexible" in herself is revealed by the sword she wields with such success. Later in his career, Shakespeare will learn to make runaway girls in boy's clothing seem lovable, even when they buckle a man's weapon to their sides. But he will never let them use that weapon with any skill, much less defeat with it a male champion like Talbot.

But Joan is by definition (which is to say, in patriotic myth) a successful warrior as well as a perfidious Frenchwoman and a witch, so that her battlefield transvestism, unlike, say, Portia's assumption of "the lovely garnish of a boy," must be rendered as a final horror rather than a redeeming grace. And, in any case, becoming a warrior, she proves herself a bad daughter, her father's enemy, which constitutes for Shakespeare the worst of treasons. "This argues," York says at one point, speaking of Joan's denial of her origins, "what her kind of life hath been — / Wicked and vile. . . ." And one cannot doubt that Shakespeare concurs.

She had begun modestly and piously enough, introducing herself to the court of France with the declaration: "Dauphin, I am by birth a shepherd's daughter." But just before her death, she gives her English captors a totally different account of her origins, a seeming bald-faced lie. That lie can be read, as we have already surmised, as a higher truth, a ritual affirmation of her faith in the Great Goddess, whose avatar she feels herself to be at the point of sacrifice.

> First, let me tell you whom you have condemned:
> Not me begotten of a shepherd swain,
> But issued from the progeny of kings,
> Virtuous and holy, chosen from above
> By inspiration of celestial grace
> To work exceeding miracles on earth.

And for one moment she sounds like the female Antichrist: a daughter of the Heavenly Mother, even as Jesus was Son to the Heavenly Father.

Her earthly father, however, can read all this only as filial impiety, for when he cries in pity, "Ah, Joan, sweet daughter Joan, I'll die with thee," she screams back at him in rage:

> Decrepit miser! Base ignoble wretch!
> I am descended of a gentler blood.
> Thou art no father nor no friend of mine.

And when he begs, "Deny me not, I prithee, gentle Joan," she answers brusquely, "Peasant, avaunt!" Then turning to the English bystanders who plead on his behalf ("Graceless! Wilt thou deny thy parentage?"), she says accusingly, "You have suborned this man / Of purpose to obscure my noble birth."

Such actual apostasy to a living sire no theoretical allegiance to a maternal deity can justify, especially in a patriarchal world in which the Goddess's proper names cannot even be spoken. It is to "our Lady gracious," "God's Mother," "Christ's Mother" that Joan, in the beginning, attributes her special powers, using, that is to say, her Christian pseudonyms. And when the Dauphin calls her "Bright star of Venus," she turns away in silence, having already declared, "I must not yield to any rites of love." In the end, however, no holy name at all is on her cursing tongue, only satanic epithets, "darkness . . . death . . . mischief and despair. . . ." We must, therefore, accept as just the judgment York makes after her final exit, "Thou foul accursèd minister of Hell!"

Though the vilest of all Shakespeare's undutiful daughters, perhaps, Joan is by no means the last. Indeed, there is scarcely a play in the canon in which daughters do not betray or seem to betray their fathers. Sometimes, indeed, those fathers are portrayed as deserving betrayal (like Shylock); and their daughters go to a happy ending scot free. But more often, even those girls who cross their fathers for the purest love must die (like Juliet and Cordelia and Desdemona), since to refuse, like Joan, to "kneel down and. . . . stoop" for the paternal blessing is to remain in some vestigial sense a witch. And the grim biblical injunction never ceases to ring in Shakespeare's head: "A witch shall be put to death!"

Only in his final plays was Shakespeare able to conceive girls on whom the shadow of Circe does not fall. Issued Athene-like from the male head rather than the female womb, such pure daughters of the father redeem the whole world which threatens them, proving at last saviors more potent even than those motherless sons whom earlier Shakespeare had believed the sole redeemers. In *Cymbeline,* in fact, the two principles of salvation become one, Imogen marrying Leonatus, the man not born of woman. But first the witch mother must die by her own hand, and Imogen, along with her two brothers, must be reborn of the father. "O what am I?" Cymbeline cries in joy and anguish, "A mother to the birth of three? Ne'er mother / Rejoiced deliverance more." A new heaven and a new earth have been created in Cymbeline's tent by a "a piece of tender air," a "virtuous daughter," who, kneeling as Joan would not, invokes her father's blessing.

But all this lies for Shakespeare at the moment of writing *Henry VI, Part I* still in "the seeds of time." And Joan, in any case, has denied the possibility of such transcendence by persisting in her filial apostasy to the last. She is therefore cursed from the stage not only by her enemies but by him who begot her:

> Kneel down and take my blessing, good my girl.
> Wilt thou not stoop? Now cursèd be the time
> Of thy nativity! I would the milk
> Thy mother gave thee when thou suck'dst her breast
> Had been a little ratsbane for thy sake!
> Or else, when thou didst keep my lambs a-field,
> I wish some ravenous wolf had eaten thee!

And finally, her death sentence is confirmed by that voice which speaks for Shakespeare with greater authority than any judge, priest, or commander in the field—the voice of that rejected father crying:

> Dost thou deny thy father, cursed drab?
> Oh, burn her, burn her! Hanging is too good.

SONNET 20

A woman's face with Nature's own hand painted
Hast thou, the master-mistress of my passion,
A woman's gentle heart, but not acquainted
With shifting change, as is false woman's fashion,
An eye more bright than theirs, less false in rolling,
Gilding the object whereupon it gazeth,
A man in hue, all hues in his controlling,
Which steals men's eyes and women's souls amazeth.
And for a woman wert thou first created,
Till Nature, as she wrought thee, fell a-doting,
And by addition me of thee defeated
By adding one thing to my purpose nothing.
    But since she pricked thee out for women's pleasure,
    Mine be thy love, and thy love's use their treasure.

II

The Jew as Stranger: or

"These be the Christian husbands."

If Shakespeare's first historical tetralogy had ended with Joan's condemnation, to turn from it to *The Merchant of Venice* would seem a transition in tone, perhaps, but not in theme. Its last words, however, are not a father's curse but Suffolk's prediction that "Margaret shall now be Queen, and rule the King; / But I will rule both her, the King, and realm." And though he comes quite soon to grief, before the next three plays are done, the cast of maidens with whom the chronicle began has been replaced by wives and widows and, especially, mothers. *The Merchant,* on the other hand, remains throughout a motherless play, in which not being, but getting, married is the theme.

The absence of mothers seems, in fact, to symbolize for Shakespeare the difference between the world of high comedy or romance and that of real history or tragedy. True, he wrote, both early and late, comedies in which mothers play a role—*All's Well That Ends Well,* for instance, as well as *Cymbeline* and *The Winter's Tale.* But in these, the shadow of maternal treachery falls across his sunlit lovers, and a certain troubled note reveals an uneasiness not present in the motherless *Twelfth Night, As You Like It,* and *The Merchant* itself. Not that the latter plays lack all melancholy, but its weight is different, since the problems of fathers and children prompt it; and fathers in Shakespeare are more often betrayed than betraying.

There are fathers a-plenty, in fact, in *The Merchant of*

Venice: Shylock and Old Gobbo, who are alive and on scene; plus Portia's father, who though recently deceased remains a moving force by virtue of his last will and testament; and finally, Antonio, a self-appointed foster father, however equivocal in the role. And each is, in some sense, deceived by his own "child." The father of Launcelot Gobbo is mocked in jest by his foolish son; Antonio is brought by his beloved Bassanio almost to the point of death and then left to stand alone. Similarly, the two daughters seek to outwit their fathers: Jessica fleeing the house of Shylock with his gold, Portia subverting the ritual test by which her father had sought to preserve her virginity. Both re-enact, that is to say, the filial apostasy of Joan, though being good witches, they betray, like Bassanio, for marriage's sake, not for hell's; and like him, therefore, they go at the last act's close, not to burning, but to bed. Their endings are not quite as blissful or unambiguous as they may seem at first, but are played, it should be noticed, without the baleful presence of Shylock. If, indeed, we would remember him at the play's close, we must bring him on, in the playwright's despite, from the wings of imagination.

The Merchant of Venice is undeniably, *among other things,* a play about a Jew: a comedy written at a moment when a quite uncomic court scandal involving a Jewish physician had stirred the passions of a community which, having scarcely any other Jews on whom to vent its wrath, demanded, on the stage, symbolic scapegoats. Shakespeare was persuaded to create such a figure against, one suspects, his own deepest instincts, for there is no other Jewish character in all his plays. And even the word "Jew" is used only in casual insults or allusions, as in the witches' recipe in *Macbeth:* "Liver of blaspheming Jew, / Gall of goat and slips of yew. . . ." Forced to it, he sought to dignify the theme by turning the melodramatic confrontation of Christian innocents and a Jewish bugaboo into an allegorical contest between Old Testament principles and

New. The opposing poles are specified everywhere in the text: law versus grace, justice versus mercy, an-eye-for-an-eye versus forgive-ye-one-another—all reaching a climax in the operatic duet which pits the coloratura of Portia against Shylock's basso profundo.

But Shakespeare touches on more complex matters as well, evoking what theologians have called the mystery of the casting away of Israel: the curse presumably self-imposed by the chosen people in rejecting the Messiah. Certainly, when Shylock cries, "My deeds upon my head!" we are expected to remember Shylock's ancestors saying of Jesus, "His blood be on us, and on our children." And when he insists on the inviolability of the bond he makes with Antonio, Shakespeare must surely intend to suggest a parallel to Israel's dependence on the letter of God's covenant with Abraham, even after the Crucifixion: "for because thou hast done this thing, and hast not withheld thy son . . . in blessing I will bless thee, and in multiplying I will multiply thy seed as the stars of the heaven . . . and thy seed shall possess the gate of his enemies. . . ."

We cannot, however, without distorting the meaning of the play fail to take into account Shylock's quite unscriptural, though very Jewish, comment on the behavior of Bassanio and Gratiano in the court of law: "These be the Christian husbands." It is a phrase which underlines what a reading of the dramatis personae alone should have made clear: that if *The Merchant of Venice* is on one level a play about Jewish contumacy, on another, perhaps more important in the whole context of Shakespeare's work, it is about Christian wiving. It deals in fact with *three* Christian marriages, a triple happy ending which leaves not one but *two* merchants of Venice—the first, a hated Jew, the other a beloved "ancient Roman," almost equally alien to the world of the play—bereft of all they hold most dear. "Which is the merchant here," Portia has asked earlier, revealing the ambiguity of the title as well as the unsuspected kinship of Antonio to Shylock, an ambiguity and kinship which we cannot help recalling as the six paired lovers exit toward bed hand in hand, leaving the real merchant to a loneliness he dare not deplore.

The Merchant of Venice is, moreover, not just about wiving, but—in a phrase from *The Taming of the Shrew,* to which it has some unnoticed resemblances—about wiving it "wealthily." It is, in short, a play in which Eros and Mammon are closely intertwined, both embodied in girls as golden (and as devious) as any heiress pursued by a Scott Fitzgerald hero. But for Shakespeare's Bassanio and Lorenzo, unlike the Great Gatsby, such girls are not pursued in vain, since each of these aristocratic privateers gets daughter and ducats, the fairy princess and the hoard, which in Shakespeare's version is guarded by no dragon, no beast in fact more ferocious than a dead or impotent father. How easy it is for them to succeed, these dandies who not only absurdly style themselves Jasons but even more absurdly triumph like Jasons in their quite unheroic world. In that world, men's weapons are not steel, but gold; and the un-hero prepares for his expedition not by building a ship and gathering to him a crew of fabulous warriors, but by touching one friend for the price of a new doublet and hose and by persuading another to come along and amuse his lady's maid.

In such a world, in which no blood is ever really shed and only the villain even draws a knife to whet in comic impotence on his boot sole, women prove inevitably the better men; and the sole "Daniel come to judgment" turns out to be a female trickster disguised in lawyer's robes. "In such a habit," she has earlier said to her accomplice as they prepare to assume the garb of men, "they shall think we are accomplishèd / With that we lack." The verb is one Shakespeare uses for putting on the accoutrements of war, as in the Prologue to Act IV of *Henry V,* which speaks of "the armorers, accomplishing the knights"; and the implicit analogy brings to mind Joan girding on her armor to do battle among men, though the meanings here are erotic only.

Yet finally the phrase seems apropos in a play where not Portia alone, but all three female characters put on "the lovely garnish of a boy," pretending thus to be fully accomplished in another sense, that is, fully phallic, sexed like men; but, of course, they know (and we know) that only the pretty boys who lean on them are really "pricked . . . out for women's pleasure." Here Shakespeare does not seem to want us (as he does in both *As You Like It* and *Twelfth Night*) to fall out of the illusion, realizing that boy actors play the parts of what seem girls pretending they are boys; but even the limited ambiguity he permits sets us to remembering once more the last six lines of Sonnet 20.

> And for a woman wert thou first created,
> Till Nature, as she wrought thee, fell a-doting,
> By adding one thing to my purpose nothing.
> But since she pricked thee out for women's pleasure,
> Mine be thy love, and thy love's use their treasure.

Surely they were in his mind, too, writing *The Merchant of Venice,* since the word "use," with its variants "usance" and "usury," lies at the very center of the play. Only two of its customary Elizabethan meanings are evoked here, however: "employment" and "interest on a loan." Quite repressed—as it is not in the sonnet or, as we have remarked earlier, in *Measure for Measure*—is its third sense of "sexual enjoyment." Indeed, the language of *The Merchant of Venice* is, for Shakespeare, extraordinarily chaste, particularly when Antonio speaks, so that, though the melancholy merchant, were he given to writing poems of love at all, might well have echoed the sentiments of Sonnet 20, he would not have made the pun on "prick."

Yet it is a favorite, for instance, with his opposite number,

Mercutio, who, like him in so many ways, still manages to spare himself the pain of someone else's happy ending by dying before his beloved friend is quite Juliet's. Speaking of the pangs of love to that friend, in any case, Mercutio advises him to "prick love for pricking"; and merely asked the time, he answers, "the bawdy hand of the dial is now upon the prick of noon." But Mercutio is loquacious on any subject and bawdy on most; whereas Antonio, on the topic of love at least, is taciturn to the point of muteness, responding only, when asked by that indistinguishable pair of bores, Salarino and Salanio, whether he is in love, "Fie, fie." We do have, however, a somewhat longer example of his laconic prose on record: a letter to his friend in which oddly, suggestively, all the key words that cluster at the end of Sonnet 20 fall together (except, of course, for "prick"), but which, though it begins "Sweet Bassanio," ends as dryly as an office memo: "Notwithstanding, *use* your *pleasure*. If your *love* do not persuade you to come, let not my letter." (The italics are mine.)

In any case, there is some point in trying to repossess *The Merchant of Venice* by reading it as if it were Antonio's play: the play of one too much a merchant to be a tragic hero and trapped for all his tragic implications in a comedy where Spartan reticence is as little at home as Roman virtue or Jewish piety. No wonder he ends by falling quite out of the play, whose course of action he cannot at any point control by rhetoric or wit. True, he proves capable of overcoming the Jew's bloody plot against his interest-free existence, but only with the aid of his friend's woman, who ends by demanding with high eloquence "use" in love as Shylock has in trade. Shakespeare seems, finally, to have felt dissatisfied with the fate of Antonio in this play, though Antonio himself declares early on his resigned acceptance of his role: "I hold the world but as . . . a stage where every man must play a part, / And mine a sad one." And so Shakespeare revives him to walk the stage a second time in *Twelfth Night.*

Shakespeare kept certain other characters alive through a continuous series of plays, like Margaret in the first tetralogy, and had even, at royal request, resurrected the dead Falstaff in *The Merry Wives of Windsor.* But in no other case except Antonio's did he permit a figure imagined for one fable to reappear in another, preserving his name, his life-style, his habits of loving, though deprived of all memories of his past, like an amnesiac or a transmigrated soul. Revived thus in *Twelfth Night,* Antonio is transported from the world of Venice-Belmont—which is to say, a world constantly in motion between reality and dreams—to that of Illyria—which is to say, a world of dream alone, where wish and not necessity spins the plot of a comedy whose subtitle, after all, is *What You Will.*

In Illyria, Antonio, though still dependent on the sea for his living, has not only escaped the countinghouse for actual shipboard but has been given a new prehistory as a naval hero. In that land of wish, therefore, he who was, according to the first cast of characters, "Antonio, a merchant of Venice," is labeled instead, "Antonio, a sea captain, friend to Sebastian." Moreover, as seems appropriate to a play whose characters can be doubled or split so that conflicting desires may be reconciled, he is followed in the cast by *another* "Sea Captain," without a name, further identified as a "friend to Viola," since Viola and Sebastian, being sundered twins, each sure the other is dead, must be rescued by different heroic mariners.

Only thus can they make the double marriage at the end which leaves *two* lonely saviors—two Antonio's, as it were—to stand in double loneliness outside their bliss. The otherwise anonymous Sea Captain, however, does not survive the second scene, in which he provides Viola (as well as the audience) with necessary information about Illyria, then helps her assume the disguise of a boy so that she can enter the service of the Duke, exiting on the line, "Be you his eunuch, and your mute I'll be."

He is, in fact, even better than his word, for he not only never speaks but never even appears again, though he is remembered for his "gentle help" at the point when, toward the action's close, Viola is about to doff her "masculine usurped attire." "I'll bring you to a captain in this town," she says, "where lie my maiden weeds. . . ." And we have the impression that Shakespeare has, at the last possible moment, remembered him, even as he has forgotten his more active double, Antonio. Antonio, at any rate, though present in the flesh, has himself at this juncture become a "mute," speaking not a word through nearly two hundred lines of recognition and reversals, embracings and declarations of eternal love.

And God knows what the actor does who is playing his equivocal part—simply melt into the scene like one more bystander, or try somehow by stance and gesture (but *how?*) to indicate what becomes clear at this point to the reader: that Antonio is not what he may have seemed at first, another actor in the dream play, but rather its "shamanized" dreamer. As such he no longer has a function on stage, where he is represented by the two surrogates of his bisexual desire: Olivia, the female whom brother Sebastian tells, "You are betrothed both to a maid and man," and Duke Orsino, the male who himself tells sister Viola (invoking—inevitably—Sonnet 20 yet again), "You shall from this time be / Your master's mistress."

Antonio is given no such ritual tag of recognition, only a few words of puzzlement and wonder at the dream miracle, which provides, when all seems lost, precisely what the poet who portrays the "woman's part" in Shakespeare had joyed to find and wept to lose in the *Sonnets:* a young man as beautiful as a twin sister might have been in boy's disguise, but "accomplished" in what Viola at one point almost confessed she lacked. "Pray God defend me!" she has cried, faced with the prospect of a duel. "A little thing would make me tell them how much I lack of a man."

She is, however, rescued just in time by Antonio, who, once more like the poet of the *Sonnets,* would have had to insist, had he overheard her, that even if nature had added what she lacked, it would have been to his purpose "nothing." But he also knows, what Shakespeare had apparently learned since: that no one can have love's "treasure" without its "use" and that, therefore, neither Sebastian, who is "pricked . . . out for women's pleasure," nor Viola, who, like Ophelia, has "nothing" between her legs, can provide him a happy ending. Consequently, he speaks no words of love but only of confusion when both stand separately before him. "An apple, cleft in two, is not more twin / Than these two creatures," he says, then asks, "Which is Sebastian?" and is dumb.

Before that point, however, Antonio has enacted—inside the good dream which all the other actors share—what amounts almost to a play within the play, a nightmare subplot of his own. When we meet him first on stage, he is declaring, as we gather he has declared a thousand times, his devotion to the boy he has rescued from "the breach of the sea." "If you will not murder me for my love," he says rather grimly, "let me be your servant. . . . come what may, I do adore thee so. . . ." However abject, he is ineffectual, for the boy, though duly grateful, is a little cool, revealing his longing to move on to new adventures and new loves after three months during which (as Antonio tells us later) with "No interim, not a minute's vacancy, / Both day and night did we keep company."

Sebastian, at any rate, does take off; and they meet again shortly only because Antonio has dogged his footsteps. Overjoyed, the older man presses on him money to buy what "toy" he will, but Sebastian answers briefly, "thanks," and suggests they do some sightseeing! We are shown, in short, the small daily tortures of such a relationship, as we are not in the *Sonnets* or even in *The Merchant of Venice*. But this time the anxious lover, as his beloved boy should know, has a price on his head and is, in fact, caught before very long by the Duke's officers. "This comes with seeking you," he says resignedly to one he thinks his own Sebastian and, therefore, asks—with profound apologies—for some of his own money back. His supposed friend, however, turns out to be Viola in her boy's disguise, which is to say, a girl, a stranger who thinks him mad.

And, indeed, he is almost maddened by what he takes to be Sebastian's ingratitude, railing at his supposed friend—as he is hauled off to prison—quite as Shakespeare had railed at his in the bitterest of the *Sonnets:*

This youth that you see here
I snatched one half out of the jaws of death,
Relieved him with such sanctity of love,
And to his image, which methought did promise
Most venerable worth, did I devotion. . . .
But oh, how vile an idol proves this god!
Thou hast, Sebastian, done good feature shame.
In nature there's no blemish but the mind;
None can be called deformed but the unkind.

Then summoned before the Duke himself in Act V, he continues to bewail the betrayal of his pure love, the "witchcraft," he is moved to call it, of an unfaithful boy:

His life I gave him and did thereto add
My love, without retention or restraint,
All in his dedication. For his sake,
Did I expose myself, pure for his love,
Into the danger of this adverse town, . . .
Where being apprehended, his false cunning,
Not meaning to partake with me in danger,
Taught him to face me out of his acquaintance,
And grew a twenty years' removèd thing
While one would wink—

The presumed betrayal is, of course, revealed by a plot reversal to be nothing but a "mistake," a confusion of identities; but on the level of myth and dream, the pain of rejection is real and irremediable, followed in the text not by forgiveness but by bewilderment lapsing into silence. "Which is Sebastian?" Antonio may well ask; and for him the question is never resolved, however sure the Duke and Olivia finally are. He is, in effect, struck dumb by a riddle of identity which love itself, not his at any rate, cannot transcend. And Shakespeare abandons him at this point, not even putting into his mouth such a blustering exit line as the one with which the play's other odd man out departs, Malvolio's threat to the triumphant world of hedonists, high and low, who have made a fool of him: "I'll be revenged on the whole pack of you."

Since hatred and distrust of self are Antonio's chief motivations, he cannot even imagine revenging his indignities; but Malvolio, moved throughout by love of self, knows that all who do not share his grand passion are the enemy. He is, therefore, as absolute for vengeance as Shylock himself—foil to the first Antonio as Malvolio is to the second—feeling himself chosen above the Gentiles, which is to say, all people of the world outside his tribe of one. It is, in light of all this, tempting to press the analogy between Shylock and Malvolio even further; and were the latter as clearly the "Puritan" he is sometimes called as Shylock is a Jew, the analogy would hold up all the way.

He does intermittently, it is true, represent the principle of repression in a play of holiday release; and the lubricity which feeds his censoriousness is revealed when, reading what he takes to be a love letter from Olivia to him, he says, "By my life, this is my lady's hand. These be her very C's, her U's, and her T's; and thus makes she her great P's." Shakespeare's editors long resisted granting what by now is clear to everyone, that, in comic inadvertence, the "Puritan" begins by spelling out the female equivalent of "prick" (a word which Shakespeare tends to conceal even more circumspectly in puns) and that he ends by encouraging us to imagine the stately Olivia crouched down to piss.

But though Malvolio is also, like the Jew, a self-declared enemy of music—he is characterized by Sir Toby Belch, whose concert he has interrupted, as one who believes that because he is "virtuous, there shall be no more cakes and ale"—Shakespeare will not permit us to identify him completely with the sect just then launching its long campaign against cavalier frivolity. Maria, a spokesman generally to be trusted, at first says of Malvolio, "Marry, sir, sometimes he is a kind of Puritan," which is qualified enough; but she ends by deciding, "The devil a Puritan that he is, or anything constantly, but a timepleaser; an affectioned ass . . . so crammed, as he thinks, with excellencies, that it is his grounds of faith that all that look on him love him."

Yet we do somehow take him, though by fits and starts, as a symbol of Puritanism and its threat, in the name of business and bourgeois good sense, to the cult of unthrift and pleasure by which Shakespeare's beloved aristocrats live, so that we shudder for an instant at his departing threat to return in vengeance, imagining him coming back in the guise of Oliver Cromwell. But a moment's reflection assures us that, reborn, he will rather be the butt of some Restoration comedy, one more pretentious clown who does not know his place.*

Beginning thus with Antonio, and setting the play in the context of the *Sonnets* and *Twelfth Night,* we have a chance at least of escaping the limitations imposed on us by a general

* Or are these merely two readings of the same archetypal figure, after all, the revolutionary being inevitably reread as the *bourgeois gentilhomme* in a time of reaction? Malvolio remains, in any case, a fascinatingly ambiguous character, more illuminatingly paired with Iago, perhaps, than with Shylock. Between them, at any rate, Olivia's steward and the Moor's ancient define the proper province of the fool or clown, since if Malvolio represents a fool who does not know his "place," Iago stands for one who has been denied his.

familiarity with the text, which breeds not contempt but blissful incomprehension. *The Merchant of Venice* is surely one of the most popular of Shakespeare's works, but by the same token, perhaps, one of the least well understood. The common error which takes the "Merchant" of the title to be Shylock is symptomatic of a whole syndrome of misconceptions about a play which few of us have ever really confronted, so badly is it customarily annotated, taught, and interpreted on the stage and so totally does the Jew now dominate its action. The play has captured our imagination, but Shylock has captured the play, turning, in the course of that conquest, from grotesque to pathetic, from utter alien to one of us.

And why not, since the Jew is, to begin with, an archetype of great antiquity and power, a nightmare of the whole Christian community, given a local habitation and a name by Shakespeare, so apt it is hard to believe that he has not always been called "Shylock," has not always walked the Rialto. The contest between him and the play's other characters—Antonio, for instance, that projection of the author's private distress, or Portia, that not-far-from-standard heroine in male garb—is as unequal as that between mythic Joan and historic Talbot in *Henry VI, Part I.* Even the sort of transformation he has undergone is not unprecedented in the annals of theater. Molière's "Misanthrope," for example, was converted much more quickly, in less than a generation, rather than over nearly two centuries, from absurd buffoon to sympathetic dissident. But Molière's margin of ambivalence toward Alceste was greater by far than Shakespeare's toward Shylock, and a major revolution in taste and sensibility had begun before he was long dead.

Shakespeare, on the other hand, though not without some prophetic reservations about the wickedness of Jews, had to wait two centuries or more before such reservations had moved from the periphery to the center of the play. To be sure, the original entry in the Stationers' Register for 1598 refers to the play as "a booke of the Marchaunt of Venyce, or otherwise called the Jewe of Venyce"; and by 1701, Lord Lansdowne had quite rewritten it as *The Jew of Venice.* But even at that point, the appeal of Shylock was not so much pathetic as horrific and grotesque. It took three generations of nineteenth-century romantic actors to make the Jew seem sympathetic as well as central, so that the poet Heine, sitting in the audience, could feel free to weep at his discomfiture. The final and irrevocable redemption of Shylock, however, was the inadvertent achievement of the greatest anti-Semite of all time, who did not appear until the twentieth century was almost three decades old. Since Hitler's "final solution" to the terror which cues the uneasy laughter of *The Merchant of Venice,* it has seemed immoral to question the process by which Shylock has been converted from a false-nosed, red-wigged monster (his hair the color of Judas's), half spook and half clown, into a sympathetic victim.

By the same token, it proved possible recently to mount a heterodox production of *The Merchant* as an anti-Semitic play within the larger play of anti-Semitic world history—by enclosing it in a dramatic frame which made clear to the audience that the anti-Semitic travesty they watched was a command performance put on by doomed Jewish prisoners in a Nazi concentration camp. The play within a play turned out in this case to lack a fifth act, since the actor-Shylock "really" stabbed a guard with the knife he whetted on his boot; and that same actor spoke all his speeches in a comic Yiddish accent, except for those scant few lines in which Shakespeare permits the Jew to plead his own humanity. But none of this seems as important finally as its renewed insistence on what everyone once knew: that the play in some sense celebrates, certainly releases ritually, the full horror of anti-Semitism. A Jewish child, even now, reading the play in a class of Gentiles, feels this in shame and fear, though the experts, Gentile and Jewish alike, will hasten to assure him that his responses are irrelevant, even pathological, since "Shakespeare rarely 'takes sides' and it is certainly rash to assume that he here takes an unambiguous stand 'for' Antonio and 'against' Shylock. . . ."

It is bad conscience which speaks behind the camouflage of scholarship, bad conscience which urges us to read Edmund Keane's or Heinrich Heine's Shylock into Shakespeare's lovely but perverse text, as it had almost persuaded us to drop *Henry VI, Part I* (which means, of course, the Pucelle) quite out of the canon. And which finally is worse: to have for so long forgotten Joan, or to persist in misremembering Shylock? In either case, we have, as it were, expurgated Shakespeare by canceling out or amending the meanings of the strangers at the heart of his plays.

The problem is that both of these particular strangers, the woman and the Jew, embody stereotypes and myths, impulses and attitudes, images and metaphors grown unfashionable in our world. Not that we have been emancipated from those impulses and attitudes, whatever superficial changes have been made in the stereotypes and myths, the images and metaphors which embody them; but we have learned to be ashamed, *officially* ashamed of them at least. And it irks us that they still persist in the dark corners of our hearts, the dim periphery of our dreams. What is demanded of us, therefore, if we would find the real meaning of these plays again, is not so much that we go back into the historical past in order to reconstruct what men once thought of Jews and witches, but rather that we descend to the level of what is most archaic in our living selves and there confront the living Shylock and Joan.

Obviously, it is easier to come to terms with such characters on the "enlightened" margin of Shakespeare's ambivalence. We are pleased to discover how much he is like what we prefer to think ourselves, when, for instance, he allows Shylock a sympathetic apology for himself: "Hath not a Jew eyes? Hath not a Jew hands, organs, dimensions, senses, affections, passions? Fed with the same food, hurt with the same weapons, subject to the same diseases, healed by the same means, warmed and cooled by the same winter and summer as a Christian is? If you prick us, do we not bleed? If you tickle us, do we not laugh? If you poison us, do we not die?"

And we are similarly delighted when Shakespeare lets him for an instant speak out of deep conjugal love: "It was my turquoise, I had it of Leah when I was a bachelor. I would not have given it for a wilderness of monkeys," or when Shakespeare permits him to rehearse the list of indignities he has suffered at Antonio's hands:

> Signior Antonio, many times and oft
> In the Rialto you have rated me
> About my moneys and my usances.
> Still I have borne it with a patient shrug,
> For sufferance is the badge of all our tribe.
> You call me misbeliever, cutthroat dog,
> And spit upon my Jewish gaberdine. . . .

But we must not forget that immediately following that first speech, Shylock is crying "revenge" and vowing that he will practice "villainy," and that scarcely has he spoken the second, when he is dreaming that he will "have the heart of" the Christian merchant. True, he bows and fawns and flatters throughout the third, but in a tone so obviously false, it could fool no one but gullible Antonio. And we would do better, therefore, to face that in ourselves which responds to the negative, which is to say, the stronger, pole of Shakespeare's double view: the uneasiness we feel before those terrible others whom we would but cannot quite believe no longer alien to us and all that we prize.

Women seem to give us even more trouble in this regard than Jews, for all of us have been brainwashed against the "second sex" by poetry of highest power and ribaldry of the widest popular appeal. Surely, then, it is the fear of something responsive in ourselves which makes us unwilling to grant, or quite remember, that Shakespeare, unlike those self-declared defenders of the female from Friedrich Schiller to Jean Anouilh, could really, *really* have traduced the symbol of what is best in woman by mocking the sole saint besides Francis of Assisi to have survived the contempt of a secular age. To this very day, even those who otherwise find the bourgeois apotheosis of women a slight more offensive than outright vilification prefer to think of Shakespeare, quite like the most simple-minded of his nineteenth-century admirers, as the creator of a gallery of good women, or rather of good girls. Did he not, they argue, echoing Mrs. Jameson and Charles Lamb, create the gentle Juliet and Rosalind, as well as the long-suffering Cordelia and Desdemona—and, to be sure, the doughty but delicate Portia herself?

How actresses have always loved that sympathetic part; but not actresses alone, for lovers of Shakespeare still too anti-Semitic to make Shylock into the hero of the play, have given it to Portia, whom they typically remember urging the claims of Christian mercy on the heartless Jew. What they forget is that, like Joan, Portia, too, is an enemy of fathers, and that, like Joan, she puts on male garb; but unlike her French counterpart, she is presented as no threatening stranger. She is rather portrayed as always and everywhere at home: in Belmont, where she recites the litany of her prejudices into the ear of her maid, and in Venice, where, disguised as "a Daniel come to judgment," she acts out in a ritual of Jew-baiting not only her own anti-Semitism, but that of all the other major characters in the play.

She constitutes, in short, the focal center of a play which contains an almost exhaustive catalogue of the stereotypes bred by Elizabethan xenophobia: the stranger-hater *par excellence*, secure in the midst of a protected Establishment. She is as "supersubtle" a Venetian as Desdemona herself, but blonde as the fair youth, which symbolizes her virtue and her worth, not Italian black, which stands for evil, or even Titian red, which would seem ambiguous. And Shakespeare makes it clear that she is not just blonde in appearance like the witch, Joan. Nor is she merely bewigged like those fashionable deceivers granted by the wigmaker's art the "golden . . . dowry of a second head" —on whom Bassanio oddly reflects before opening the right casket and assuring himself her hand, her portrait seeming to him, at the moment of his triumph, to be graced with "a golden mesh to entrap the hearts of men / Faster than gnats in cobwebs."

But where do they come from, these insidious metaphors of rifled graves and insects trapped, so inharmonious with the lovely music of the scene? They represent no *arrière-pensée* of her accepted lover, but rather an irrelevant intrusion of Shakespeare's own marginal ambivalence, the residue of the anti-feminist rage that moved him when he wrote *Henry VI* and subverted his attempt this time to write a play in which not the daughter but the father would be a stranger. What Bassanio himself believes, he has unequivocally declared to Antonio on the eve of setting out to woo and win her: "her sunny locks / Hang on her temples like a golden fleece. . . ." And Antonio does not gainsay him. Portia is, in fact, so unchallenged, so secure in the golden heart of her little world, which, as long as the play lasts, seems the great world's center, that she can mock every upstart alien who comes in quest of her.

How much like Célimène she sounds, the *médisante* of Molière's *Le Misanthrope,* as one by one she shoots down all the suitor-strangers whom, one by one, Nerissa sets up as targets for the fire of her wit: the horse-mad Neapolitan ("Ay, that's a colt indeed. . . . I am much afeard my lady his mother played false with a smith"); the frowning County Palatine ("He hears merry tales and smiles not. . . . I had rather be married to a death's-head with a bone in his mouth. . . ."); the all-too-adaptable French lord ("God made him, and therefore let him pass for a man. . . . He is every man in no man"); the inarticulate baron of England ("He hath neither Latin, French, nor Italian. . . . He is a proper man's picture, but, alas! who can converse with a dumb show?"); the cowardly Scot (". . . he borrowed a box of the ear of the Englishman and swore he would pay him again when he was able"); the sodden young German ("When he is best, he is a little worse than a man, and when he is worst, he is little better than a beast. . . . set a deep glass of Rhenish wine on the contrary casket, for if the Devil be within and that temptation without, I know he will choose it").

It is not merely that each is in his own way inadequate as a suitor, absurd as a man, but that each, including the Englishman (who proves also a stranger in Belmont, that earthly paradise of absolute belonging), performs his national stereotype—at least so Portia assures us, who never see them—as if on purpose to deserve her scorn. But doing so, they please the audience as well, which knows in advance, but is tickled to be reminded, which foreigner will be mad for horses, which for drink; which will be affected, which supersober, which dumb.

Beyond these half-dozen wooers dismissed, as it were, off stage, we see two actually on scene, in a kind of double introduction to the lucky third, Bassanio. And one of these, as might well be expected in a time when the Armada was still a living memory, is a Spaniard who is largely allowed to damn himself out of his own mouth, talking boastfully of "merit" and "honor," then making, as he must, the wrong choice and exiting with cries of self-reproach. "Did I deserve no more than a fool's head? / Is that my prize?" The second, however, quite unexpectedly turns out to be a Moor, a black man, obviously intended to represent the absolute pole of otherness; and to him Shakespeare gives more space than to any of the other aspirants to Portia's self and fortune, except for Bassanio.

He is mentioned to begin with at the climax of the scene

of ticking off the suitors, though, in his case, it is not some stereotypical flaw in character, but his "complexion," which is to say, his skin color, that Portia holds against him, sight unseen: "If he have the condition of a saint and the complexion of a devil, I had rather he should shrive me than wive me." When Morocco actually appears in the next scene, he proves to be, in fact, dignified and sympathetic—a little grandiloquent, perhaps, but not emptily bombastic like the Spaniard. And his first words are a plea against precisely the kind of prejudgment Portia has made. "Mislike me not for my complexion," he says, "The shadowed livery of the burnished sun, / To whom I am a neighbor and near bred. . . . / I would not change this hue, / Except to steal your thoughts, my gentle Queen."

It is one of those noble apologies which Shakespeare permits even the most theoretically ignoble of his outsiders when they speak of what they love, quite like the splendid passage on music and dreams he will bestow on Caliban. Yet most admirers of the play scarcely remember Morocco's words, which seem to contribute nothing to the central encounter between Portia and the Jew. But James Fenimore Cooper, at least, realized the sense in which archetypally the black prince and the Jewish usurer are one, representing the best and worst side of the non-European stranger. And so in *The Last of the Mohicans,* he links them by identifying his noblest savage (Moor plus Jew becoming in his mythic arithmetic Indian) with the former, and his most ignoble with the latter, quoting the black prince's plea on his title page and vindictive tags from Shylock at the head of his bloodiest chapters. Unlike Portia, however, Cooper was willing to treat his Morocco figure with pathos rather than contempt, clearly regretting his failed marriage with a white girl, though not finally permitting it. It is as if he sensed in Shakespeare certain reservations in this regard not shared by his heroine and wanted to make them manifest.

Portia herself, in fact, seems for one moment moved by

Morocco's plea to distrust the promptings of her own dearest prejudices and grant that one black on the outside might inwardly be "fair."

> . . . if my father had not scanted me,
> And hedged me by his wit, to yield myself
> His wife who wins me by that means I told you,
> Yourself, renownèd Prince, then stood as fair
> As any comer I have looked on yet
> For my affection.

We remember, however, not only what she has said of the Prince earlier but also her opinion of the other suitors so that we catch the equivocation of her phrase: "any . . . I have looked on yet." Moreover, at this point, we have realized that Portia is a courteous liar as well as *médisante;* and yet we surmise beneath her courtly dissimulation the presence in Shakespeare's preconsciousness of possibilities he was later to realize in *Othello:* the accomplished marriage of a "supersubtle" Venetian lady to a noble Moor, with all the attendant joys and woes.

But he will not let it happen here, and, in another (his final) scene, the Prince of Morocco takes and fails the ritual test, choosing the wrong casket because he still must learn that "all that glisters is not gold," and winning as his award not the "angel in a golden bed" he dreamed, but only a *memento mori,* a death's head to remind him that "gilded tombs do worms infold." And once he has left the scene, Portia speaks the concluding couplet, re-echoing the contempt with which she began.

> A gentle riddance. Draw the curtains, go.
> Let all of his complexion choose me so.

She is through now with all her foreign wooers, through with the sham her father's will compels, and ready to accept Bassanio, who alone is really "fair" and of her own kind. She had, in fact, approved of him at first sight, declaring to Nerissa, who mentions him favorably even before the testing of the Spaniard and the Moor, "I remember him well, and I remember him worthy of thy praise."

There is only one stranger in *The Merchant of Venice* whom Portia does not vilify in great detail, and that is—disconcertingly—Shylock, the Jew. But surely this is because Shakespeare assumed that his characteristic faults were already known to everyone, as well as exposed in the plot, and that therefore there was no need to itemize the catalogue: usuriousness, avarice, lust for vengeance, and hostility to music, masquing, and young love. For all of this, in Shakespeare's day, the unmodified generic epithet "Jew" would serve; and so Portia calls Shylock either "Jew" vocative, when they are face to face, or else, in the distancing nominative, "the Jew," turning her back on him to discuss him with her fellow Christians as though he were a creature in another realm of being.

What she leaves unspecified, though not unsuggested, is, in any case, screamed out by Gratiano, who provides throughout the courtroom scene a kind of antiphony of abuse to her pious plain song. "This currish Jew," he amends her unmodified epithet, for instance; and earlier in the scene, he had expanded the metaphor, making a little lyric of his hate.

> Oh, be thou damned, inexecrable dog! . . .
> Thy currish spirit
> Governed a wolf who, hanged for human slaughter,
> Even from the gallows did his fell soul fleet,
> And, whilst thou lay'st in the unhallowed dam
> Infused itself in thee, for thy desires
> Are wolvish, bloody, starved, and ravenous.

Gratiano, indeed, speaks for three: taking away the task of particularized vilification not only from Portia but also from Bassanio, his friend and almost master, to whose not-quite Don

Quixote he plays not-quite Sancho Panza. Sometimes Bassanio seems troubled by the manners of his more candid alter ego, warning him at one point that he is "too wild, too rude, and bold of voice." This is, however, while Bassanio is still courting Portia and feels the need of circumspection. And, in any case, he hastens to reassure Gratiano that his excesses are not really evil, only undiplomatic, a premature giveaway of what, beneath the show of courtesy, they both really stand for, what as husbands it will be proper for them both to reveal. Both, finally, are one—along with Lorenzo, Salanio, and Salarino, splittings of a single, charming, feckless, and insolent young man; and their quarrels are family quarrels, arguments about how certain kinds of behavior might appear to outsiders, which "in such eyes as ours appear not faults. . . ."

Gratiano's speech seems in retrospect not just the climax, but the keynote of a whole chorus of anti-Jewish abuse in which many other voices joined: a chorus in which the leitmotif is "dog" and its variations. And Shakespeare, we remember, seems to have been no dog lover at all, reserving his canine metaphors for destructive women, cringing courtiers, and the most treacherous of his villains. Antonio himself has used that word in insult before the action of the play begins, as we learn from Shylock, in whom it continues to rankle. He can hardly keep his tongue away from it, in fact, referring to it over and over in his first conversation with Antonio. "You call me misbeliever, cutthroat dog. . . . And foot me as you spurn a stranger cur. . . . 'Hath a dog money? Is it possible / A cur can lend three thousand ducats?' . . . another time you called me dog. . . ." The effect is odd, finally, Shylock's intended ironies cutting the wrong way, so that the audience ends feeling he is self-condemned, branded a "dog" out of his own mouth, rather than out of Antonio's, who on scene only answers quietly, "I am as like to call thee so again. . . ."

Nor does Shylock leave it at that, insisting later, when he has Antonio at his mercy, "Thou call'dst me dog before thou hadst a cause, / But since I am a dog, beware my fangs." This time, Antonio proves as good as his word, even upping the ante from "dog" to "wolf," as he addresses the court. "You may as well use questions with the wolf, / Why he hath made the ewe bleat for the lamb. . . ." It must have been an especially effective epithet at the moment, reminding Shakespeare's audience of the pun implicit in the name "Lopez" or read into it at least by those eager to make clear how appropriately it was borne by the Spanish-Jewish doctor to Elizabeth, who had just been executed for treason.

Meanwhile, Salanio and Salarino—those echoers of fashion and each other—take up the theme, referring to "the dog Jew" and "the most impenetrable cur." Indeed, the range of insults for Jews seems pitifully limited in Venice. The Duke himself, it is true, manages "stony adversary" and "inhuman wretch"; but generally, if it is not "dog," it is "Devil." So Salanio once more speaks of "the Devil . . . in the likeness of a Jew." Even that dullest of Shakespearean clowns, Launcelot Gobbo, describes his old master at one point as "the very Devil incarnal"; and the lovely apostate Jessica makes the same point by implication, speaking of how she found "our house is hell. . . ."

Like all forms of obscenity, the abuse bred by prejudice is notably monotonous, so that reading over the anti-Semitic tirades of *The Merchant of Venice,* one thinks somehow of Bédier's comment after years of editing the fabliaux (those rhymed dirty jokes of the Middle Ages, themselves based on vilification of women and clerics) about "the incredible monotony of the human obscene." There are, to be sure, a wide range of possible inflections of obscenity; and Shakespeare's play constitutes, as it were, a little anthology of these: the note of dignified contempt in Antonio, Bassanio, and Portia; the note of tender self-hatred in Jessica; the note of endearing imprecision in Gobbo; the note of passionate self-indulgence in Gratiano, becoming secondhand chic in Salanio and Salarino.

It is, however, the sense of a repetitiveness verging on obsession which remain with us—revealing finally how deep the roots of anti-Semitic horror go at all levels of the society which Shakespeare portrays.

And, indeed, the clue to what lies at those roots is provided by the very terms of abuse; for "devil" plus "dog" or "wolf" add up to "ogre," a symbol of great mythic potency: the male equivalent of the witch-mother, and like her associated with the murder or eating of children. The witch, as we have seen, represents in one of her aspects (appearing also in Shakespeare as the witch-daughter) the evil mother, who cannot bear to leave alive outside herself the maturing daughter whose beauty she feels a challenge to her fading charms. To think, for instance, of the wicked Queen in *Cymbeline* is to be reminded of the stepmothers and witches, sometimes split and sometimes joined, in such ancient tales as "Hansel and Gretel" or "Snow White." In Shakespeare, however, another dimension is added, since his cruelest mothers dream rape rather than cannibalism, whetting the lust of their spoiled sons against the hated stepdaughters.

The ogre, on the other hand, stands for the evil father, who seeks to swallow down his son, thus ingesting the male strength he has sired lest it destroy and succeed him. But in his war against time, the ogre-father, unwilling to yield his privileges to anyone, seeks also to become his own son-in-law by keeping his natural daughter for himself. The twin threat of the ogre is, therefore, cannibalism and incest, cannibalism to the son and incest to the daughter. But this constitutes a double process of life-denial which, archetypally, is endless, since even the sons born of the daughter must be eaten, the daughters of the daughter possessed before they fall into the hands of the other—and so (ogres being immortal) with the children of those children, and their descendants to the end of time.

Insofar as the *The Merchant of Venice* tells the story of

the "merry bond," it is concerned with the threat of the ogre to the son. Insofar as it tells that of the three caskets, it deals with his threat to the daughter. And in both, it evokes archetypal patterns which lie far beneath Shakespeare's conscious mythologizing of his own life, patterns that came to him, as they continue to come to us, out of sources deeper than literature or waking experience—those old wives' tales we can scarcely distinguish from our dreams. In those tales and dreams, creatures much like Shylock, though still without a proper name, not even "Jew," rise to confront us. Half devil and half wolf they seem, which is to say, like the Devil of popular imagination, not-quite-humans in almost human form and, like the wolves of travelers' chronicles, eaters of human flesh.

It is the Duke of Venice who sums up the first aspect of Shylock, calling him "a stony adversary" (but the Hebrew word for "adversary" is "Satan") and "an inhuman wretch"; and doing so, he has in effect, already condemned him by finding him nonhuman, something else. Similarly, Gratiano qualifies him as a dog run wild ("wolvish, bloody, starved, and ravenous"), though it is Shylock himself who seems earlier to have insisted on making the cannibalistic nature of his hunger for human flesh quite clear. "I will feed fat the ancient grudge I bear him," he declares of Antonio near the beginning of the play; and the metaphor is reinforced a few lines later when he remarks, even more inadvertently it would seem, to Antonio, who has just entered, "Your Worship was the last man in our mouths." Before the scene is through, he has also said to Bassanio, brushing aside his worries about the pound of flesh his friend has offered to forfeit should he fail to meet his loan, "A pound of man's flesh taken from a man / Is not so estimable, profitable neither, / As the flesh of muttons, beefs, or goats. . . ."

It seems overreading, perhaps, to insist that some notion of eating human flesh is already implicit in such a casual butcher's list. Yet two acts later, that shadowy implication becomes an explicitly cannibalistic metaphor when Shylock, in response to Salarino's query, "Why, I am sure if he forfeit, thou wilt not take his flesh. What's that good for?," answers, "To bait fish withal. If it will feed nothing else, it will feed my revenge." And this, the grimmest of these threats, it should be noticed, is followed almost immediately by the noblest of his apologies, which asks, among other things, if a Jew is not "fed with the same food . . . as a Christian is?"

But, of course, Shylock does not actually eat Antonio, does not even really want to eat him, except maybe in dreams, even though he does want him dead, feeling him—along with all his friends and doubles—as rebellious Christian sons, who, in seeking to destroy Judaism, have turned against the father of Jews and Christians alike, the patriarch, Abraham. As a matter of fact, even metaphors of eating disappear from the text in Act IV, which marks the climax and end of the bond plot, being replaced by the image of the threatening father with a knife, a special variant of the ogre archetype derived not from fairy tales, but precisely from the story of Abraham and Isaac in the Scriptures of the Jews.

Meanwhile, both father-son myths are being hard beset by a cognate myth, known in its folk-tale form as "the ogre's daughter": the story of a girl who betrays her own inhuman father, sometimes letting him be killed, always permitting the stealing of his treasure—and all for the sake of a human hero, with whom she afterward tries to flee back to his world. It is a tale best remembered these days as the Grimm brothers have reproduced it in "Jack and the Beanstalk," in which version the daughter has been transformed into the wife of the giant cannibal, to obscure the incestuous nature of their connection. But in *The Merchant of Venice,* the archetypal daughter remains at least a daughter, though the incest motif is camouflaged in other ways.

Two ogre's daughters, in fact, two female betrayers of the father, appear in this play, whose dreamlike logic, having already splintered the human rival to the monster-father into several fragments, also splits the treacherous daughter into Portia and Jessica. Each functions, as the names indicate, in a separate mythological world: the one classical or Greco-Roman, the other biblical or Hebreo-Christian—the two complementary traditions, in short, which made the mind of the Renaissance.

It is easy to identify Jessica as the ogre's daughter, considerably less so to realize that Portia plays a similar part. But a clue is given early by a reference to Shakespeare's favorite source book of classical mythology, Ovid's *Metamorphoses.* Toward the end of the first scene of Act I, Bassanio, pressing Antonio for a loan so that he can court Portia in proper style, passes from praise of her blonde beauty to the evocation of a mythological parallel to his quest.

> And her sunny locks
> Hang on her temples like a golden fleece,
> Which makes her seat of Belmont Colchos' strond,
> And many Jasons come in quest of her.
> O my Antonio, had I but the means
> To hold a rival place with one of them. . . .

Moreover, after Bassanio has got "the means"—borrowed for him by Antonio on the security of "the bond"—and has chosen the proper casket of the three, Gratiano completes the identification with the myth of Colchos by crowing, "We are the Jasons, we have won the fleece."

But if Bassanio is archetypally Jason, then Portia must be Medea, which is to say, "the cunning one," a witch, however favorable she may be to the hero, and, as a witch, an enemy to fathers. It is a role in which it is hard to imagine Portia, and yet there are close analogies between her actions and those of her ancient prototype. Medea's own father, Aeëtes, had set for

Jason a triple task which seemed impossible to achieve; but already in love with him, Medea helped him pass the test by magic. And just so, Portia, by the only kind of witchcraft Shakespeare will permit in *The Merchant of Venice,* the spell of song, helps Bassanio solve the triple riddle posed by the "will" of her dead father.

It is well to be clear about the nature of the task Portia's would-be husbands were asked to perform, as well as the penalties imposed for failing it. Nerissa describes it first as a "lottery that he hath devised in these three chests of gold, silver, and lead—whereof who chooses his meaning chooses you. . . ." And the Prince of Morocco clarifies the matter further by reading aloud the riddling inscriptions on all three.

> The first, of gold, who this inscription bears,
> "Who chooseth me shall gain what many men desire."
> The second, silver, which this promise carries,
> "Who chooseth me shall get as much as he deserves."
> This third, dull lead, with warning all as blunt,
> "Who chooseth me must give and hazard all he hath."

But it is left to Portia to explain the penalty for choosing wrong, which is, "Never to speak to lady afterward / In way of marriage."

The triple riddle, with its three clichés, seems not especially hard to solve; though behind it readers have always sensed a more absolute enigma, the riddle of the riddle, which Shakespeare seems not himself to have quite understood. Many famous puzzle-solvers, including Sigmund Freud, have tried to guess the meaning of the three caskets. Some suggest that all three represent female sexuality, which to the "wrong man" means death; some, that, like the three daughters in *King Lear* or such fairy tales as "Cinderella," they are meant to illustrate nothing more recondite than the Christian paradox that the last shall be first. Others, however, have suggested that they are therapeutic rather than homiletic, a parable meant to exorcise the fantasy of preadolescents that their unworthy siblings are preferred and they are cast off like hated stepchildren.

In *The Merchant of Venice,* however, that parable blurs into the even more terrifying tale of the sleeping princess, who can be awakened only by her lover's kiss, once he has penetrated the maze in which her father's possessiveness has immured her. And that maze, like the riddle which is its alternative form (surely this is what the ban on future marriages signifies), threatens castration to those who do not make it through.

Being, however, witch as well as bewitched, Medea as well as *belle au bois dormante,* Portia provides her lover with the clue he needs to find her and avoid unmanning. It is all there in the "magic" she has sung to him.

> Tell me where is fancy bred,
> Or in the heart or in the head?
> How begot, how nourished?
>   Reply, reply.
> It is engendered in the eyes,
> With gazing fed, and fancy dies
> In the cradle where it lies.
>   Let us all ring fancy's knell.
>   I'll begin it.—Ding, dong, bell.

Not only the spell of the music, which, as everywhere in Shakespeare, resolves discord and dispels terror, but the words, too, do the trick: the reiterated end rhymes in "ed" of the first stanza, echoed in the word "fed" in the very midst of the second, and reinforced by the allusion to death on which the whole closes. They move Bassanio to make—on the rim of consciousness where the "magical" occurs—associations with the unspoken words "dead" and "lead" and thus to realize that the casket in which his golden girl is "locked" is a coffin, where she lies, as if wrapped in lead, until he revives her. "Turn you where your lady is," reads the "gentle scroll" inside the leaden box, "and claim her with a loving kiss." Only so can "the will of a living daughter" triumph over the "will of a dead father" (the play on the word "will" hints at the theme of incest foiled), and only so can Jason have, as the Medea archetype demands, the Golden Fleece.

But like Medea, Portia is involved with more fathers than one—with three in fact. Her ancient prototype had first renewed Aeson, the good father of her lover, Jason, then tricked to his death Pelias, his wicked uncle, which is to say in archetypal terms, his bad father. And so Portia, reversing the order, first redeems (or seems to, there being a quibble here) Bassanio's good father, Antonio, who declares in gratitude, "Sweet lady, you have given me life and living," then tricks into a catastrophe as near to death as the ground rules of comedy will allow, the bad father, Shylock. "You take my life / When you do take the means whereby I live," the Jew declares before his final exit, then dies to the action as his intended victim moves toward the happy ending he would have foiled. Portia, however, never overtly makes the identification of herself with Medea—in part, perhaps, because Shakespeare consciously was reluctant to draw a parallel between so sympathetic a heroine and the descendant of the archwitch Circe.

He therefore portrays her as, in her own eyes at least, the passive victim of one generation's male villainy awaiting deliverance by the male heroism of another; though this completely contradicts what happens in the play. "Go, Hercules!" she cries to the quite un-Herculean Bassanio as he stands musing over the three caskets. "Live thou, I live. With much more dismay / I view the fight than thou that makest the fray." That we do not feel the whole scene as travesty is a tribute to Portia's magic and her maker's, for if Bassanio's view of himself as Jason is absurd, her own self-image is doubly so. Jason, at least, depended for his triumphs on the women who loved him, as Bassanio depends on Portia and on the "woman's part" in Antonio; but the fights of Hercules were real and bloody and won without the help of anything but his own miraculous strength.

Nonetheless, thinking of her lover thus enables Portia to see herself as "the virgin tribute paid by howling Troy / To the sea monster," which is to say, to claim archetypal kinship with Hesione, whom Hercules rescued after the treachery or cowardice of her untrustworthy father had condemned her to death. "I stand for sacrifice," she declares, not only making clear her conviction that her father's last will has condemned her to a living death but also identifying herself with all other girls offered up by kingly fathers for great causes which those daughters neither understood nor wished to. Iphigenia comes especially to mind, bound to the altar by Agamemnon eager to be off to Troy, that archetype of the Hellenic world closest to the Hebrew myth of the sacrifice of Isaac.

But Jessica, the Jew's daughter, toward the close of her moonlit duet with Lorenzo at the opening of Act V names the name that neither Bassanio nor Portia had dared utter. Theirs is the first happy ending we are shown, after Shylock's disappearance from the stage, but it is qualified by a gentle melancholy which impels them to linger over the sorrows of lovers long dead as well as to utter presentiments about their own future. Such melancholy is not rare in this bitter comedy, in which Antonio enters confessing that "such a want-wit sadness makes of me / That I have much ado to know myself." And Portia's first words are: "By my troth, Nerissa, my little body is aweary of this great world." But its causes are elsewhere more clearly specified. Portia is sad because she fears she will never marry; and Antonio, because he knows he never can. But what moves Jessica in the first hours of her honeymoon to recite a litany of mythic tales from Ovid and Chaucer all involving death and betrayal?

It is Lorenzo who begins by invoking Troilus at the moment when he "sighed his soul toward the Grecian tents, / Where Cressid lay that night"—lay, as his listeners know, with false

Diomede. But it is Jessica who says, bringing the mythic catalogue to a close:

> In such a night
> Medea gathered the enchanted herbs
> That did renew old Aeson.

She evokes, to be sure, the most benign of all the achievements of "the crafty one," an act of white magic; but doing so, reminds us of the darker aspects of Medea's story: her betrayal of two fathers and Jason's deception of her. Jessica, however, is no Medea figure, though she has begun by gilding herself "with some moe ducats" stolen from her father for the sake of her lover, who, remembering that moment, says:

> In such a night
> Did Jessica steal from the wealthy Jew,
> And with an unthrift love did run from Venice. . . .

But she has been purged by suffering to a touching gentleness and leaves the scene no witch at all, only a fearful wife. She has been transformed from the Ovidian version of the ogre's daughter into a variant medieval in origin and Christian in essence: the Jew's daughter, or more precisely, the Jew's faithless daughter, which is to say, God's faithful servant.

The archetype of the menacing Jewish father with the knife and the blessed apostasy of his daughter is created by grafting onto a pre-Christian folk tale elements derived from the official mythology of the Christian church, though much altered in the course of popular transmission. More specifically, it represents an attempt to translate into mythological form the dogmatic compromise by which Christianity managed to make the New Testament its Scripture without surrendering the Old, and in the course of doing so, worked out ways of regarding the Jews simultaneously as the ultimate enemy, the killers of Christ, and the chosen people, with whom God made the covenant, the bond (this is the meaning of "testament"), under which all who believe in Jesus as the Christ are saved.

At the heart of the Old Testament, however, stands the figure of the patriarch with whom that covenant was first sealed, and who, for its sake, first circumsised his son (as his heirs under the new covenant do not), then tied him to the altar as a sacrifice. "And Abraham stretched forth his hand, and took the knife to slay his son." It is an image which has haunted Europe for nearly two millennia: the original Jew, bearded and ancient, raising aloft the threatening blade as Isaac, whom the rabbis taught was thirty years old or more, but whom the imagination of Christianity has made a child, watches from the altar in submissive silence. But Abraham is connected also with the New Testament, the new covenant, in which patriarchal rigor is replaced by maternal mercy; the symbol of that mercy, Mary herself, on learning her destiny, evokes his name. According to Saint Luke, at least, that chosen Jewish maiden, standing belly to belly with her long-barren cousin, Elizabeth, both of them miraculously pregnant, says, "My soul doth magnify the Lord. . . . For he has regarded the low estate of his handmaiden. . . . He hath holpen his servant Israel, in remembrance of his mercy; As he spake to our fathers, to Abraham, and to his seed for ever." That is to say, she declares herself a daughter of Abraham, an inheritor of the covenant, and in due course, circumcises her son on the eighth day, as the first Jewish father did his.

Even those Christians with little or no knowledge of the web of exegesis that was spun around these texts—beginning with Paul's Epistle to the Romans ("to the end the promise might be sure to all the seed; not to that only which is of the law, but to that also which is of the faith of Abraham; who is the father of us all. . . .")—have been dimly aware of their filial relationship to Judaism. Yet to such minds, the myth of Mary's virginity seems to mean that though herself in one sense Jewish, she does not belong to her Jewish father, much less to his impotent surrogate, her Jewish husband, but only to her Christian sons. Archetypally, that is to say, she exists as no one's wife, but as an eternal daughter-mother, purged at once of the evil embodied in her ancestry and in the act by which all humans are conceived—a being utterly female without being human: Pearl of Great Price, Rose without Thorns, Burning Bush, Star of the Sea. So sublimated, however, the female principle cannot be imagined as acting in human affairs, only on them; and this posed a problem for the earliest Christian mythmakers.

In the first Christian folk tales embodying such myths, therefore, only the evil Jewish father and the Gentile child he threatens really exist in time and on earth; the Jewish mother-daughter intervenes from the eternal heavens. The tale, for instance, which Chaucer puts into the mouth of his Prioress is typical in this regard, representing, indeed, the form in which the archetype possessed the mind of Europe for almost a thousand years, beginning, it would seem, around A.D. 500, and reaching the peak of its popularity between 1200 and 1400. At this point, the original anti-Semitic child-murder story—born of the confluence in the popular mind of much half-remembered scriptural stuff: the sacrifice of Isaac, the massacre of Hebrew infants by the Pharaoh, the death of the Egyptian first-born, the slaughter of the innocents, the execution of Christ at the high priest's instigation—had been transformed into a "miracle of the Virgin." And as such it enjoyed its greatest vogue. Industrious Chaucer scholars have discovered nearly thirty contemporary analogues, and in Chaucer's own retelling, along with William Wordsworth's modern Englishing, it continues still to charm and terrify quite-sophisticated readers.

In *The Prioress's Tale,* the archetypal calamity befalls a seven-year-old Gentile boy, whose way to and from school takes him every day through the town's "Jewerye." At first, he is not molested or menaced, until he learns from an older friend a hymn in praise of the Virgin, *Alma redemptoris,* which he insists on practicing aloud under the very windows of the Jews. And they are so infuriated by this tribute to an apostate daughter of Abraham that they, prompted by the "serpent Sathanas" in their hearts, hire a Jewish murderer, who with the archetypal knife cuts the boy's throat to the "nekke boon." To conceal the crime, they throw his body in a privy, where "thise Jewes purgen hire entraille"; but he continues to sing his song, since God's Mother, whom he has adored, has put a magic "greyn" upon his tongue that will not let him cease until his corpse is found and his assailants apprehended, torn apart by wild horses, and then hanged.

Those assailants are described as Jews, both the actual assassin and the cabal of plotters who hired him, but nowhere are we reminded that "Cristes mooder" was a Jew as well; for the point of the tale, like that of the courtroom scene in *The Merchant of Venice,* is to make the symbolic equations: Jew equals murderer; Christian equals "welle of mercy." And to clinch the point, the final stanza evokes a more recent incident in England itself, the murder of the boy Hugh of Lincoln, whose case—true to myth, however fictional—is also memorialized in a child's ballad.

> O yonge Hugh of Lyncoln, slayn also
> With cursed Jewes, as it is notable,
> For it is but a litel while ago,
> Preye eek for us, we synful folk unstable,
> That, of his mercy, God so merciable
> On us his grete mercy multiplie,
> For reverence of his mooder Marie.

In that ballad, however, an actual Jewish girl appears—"The Jewe's Daughter," in fact, of its subtitle—though only as the accomplice of her father, the beautiful bait in his terrible trap.

By the time Shakespeare was dreaming Shylock and Jessica,

there had begun to grow both in him and in his audience a longing—unsatisfied by either *The Prioress's Tale* or "Sir Hugh, or The Jewe's Daughter"—for a representation of the female principle in Jewish form more human than the Blessed Virgin, yet, unlike the Jew's daughter of the ballad, benign and on their side: a good Jewish daughter of a bad Jewish father, in short. And Shakespeare's Jessica is the first distinguished embodiment of this secularized archetype after Abigail, daughter of Barabas, in Marlowe's *The Jew of Malta,* who, however, flees to a convent rather than a Christian husband.

The Jewish angel of mercy brought down from heaven has flourished ever since in English and American literature: as the Rebecca of Scott's *Ivanhoe,* for instance; the Ruth of Melville's long poem *Clarel;* even as Trilby, perhaps, in the popular novel called by her name. In deciding the fate of such latter-day descendants of Jessica, however, their authors have tended to follow Scott's model rather than Shakespeare's; which is to say, they have not finally allowed the marriages with the Gentile heroes to take place, no matter how angelic the heroines may be. In all such writers, however, the steep contrast between father and daughter, which Shakespeare and Marlowe sensed as central to the myth, continues to prevail; and what inhibits the possibility of the happy ending is the shift of anti-Semitism in the nineteenth century from a religious to a "racist" base, as science ousts theology. Yet no racist's Jew is more terrible, more absolute in his obduracy than Shylock—unmatched even by Marlowe's contemporary Jew of Malta, who seems too bad to be true, a caricature of the fears that fostered him. Among later nightmare versions of the Jew, Dickens's Fagin comes closest in archetypal power to Shakespeare's Shylock, though he moves through a fable without daughters, only adopted sons. Still, in him the smiler with a knife returns, disguised as a nineteenth-century English fence, but essentially the specter that had haunted Christendom for centuries in all its authentic horror and splendor and absurdity.

Shylock, on the other hand, is portrayed as a "usurer," a lender of money on interest rather than a receiver of stolen goods, as is appropriate to his time. In point of fact, Jews (though not only Jews) were usurers during the many hundreds of years when they were forbidden by Christian law to practice other trades and professions. But Jews alone were identified as usurers pure and simple, rather than as men who, like the Medici or dukes of Norwich, happened to have grown rich in that theoretically forbidden way. Even in Chaucer's poem, the offhand equation Jew equals usurer is assumed, an axiom from which the corollary follows that Jew equals killer: "a Jewerye, / Sustened by a lord of that contree / For foule usure and lucre of vileynye. . . ."

But there is mythological as well as historical justification for this, since archetypally the Jew does not exist at all, not even for himself, until he has made his covenant with God, a bond or contract involving promises to be kept, with rewards and penalties contingent on their performance or nonperformance—quite like a promissory note signed to secure a loan. The link, that is to say, which joins together scriptural and legal notions of the bond, identifying both with nascent capitalism, exists in fact and fantasy alike; and this connection Shakespeare exploits with great effect, moving from market place to the Bible and back again in the exchanges between Antonio and Shylock at the beginning of the play.

There is no meeting of minds between these two, who confront each other from across a time barrier which is also the border between two mythologies: the Jewish merchant already in a mercantile future, in which God's promise to his people will be ironically fulfilled; the Christian merchant clinging to a feudal past, in which that people was excluded and despised. Shylock begins by raging to himself against Antonio, who "in low simplicity / . . . lends out money gratis and brings down / The rate of usance. . . ." What is an accusation for him, however, is a boast for Antonio, who says, entering, "I neither lend nor borrow, / By taking nor by giving of excess. . . ."

Yet the importunities of Bassanio have forced him to ask for a loan on Shylock's customary terms, and Shylock welcomes the opportunity to give a little lecture on the propriety of interest, with appropriate scriptural citations. All this proves too much for Antonio, however, who, whatever necessity compels, would like to believe that piety is on his side; and so he interrupts Shylock, crying out:

> Was this inserted to make interest good?
> Or is your gold and silver ewes and rams?

Shylock answers, dryly, "I cannot tell. I make it breed as fast." But his little joke inspires only horror in Antonio, who, quite orthodoxly, considers thriving on "a breed for barren metal" a sin against human industry, nature, and ultimately God himself.

All this, however thematically important, turns out to be beside the immediate point, since this time Shylock wants no "usance" at all to be written into the bond, only (in what he calls "a merry sport") a promise that if repayment is not made on time, Antonio will forfeit "an equal pound / Of your fair flesh, to be cut off and taken / In what part of your body pleaseth me." And with this shift from "barren metal" to living flesh, we have moved back to that other, more archaic set of associations with the bond, moved back to circumcision and Father Abraham.

Long before the old Jew with the knife has been turned into the usurer, the precapitalist threatening disruption to the medieval *oecumene,* he was felt as a menace to something dearer to the deep psyche than the priority of land over money, a threat to manhood itself. Certainly, with the coming of full capitalism, an economy in which everyone from the great industrialist to the housewife with her small savings in the bank profited by interest, the terror of the Jew is not allayed; and that terror has survived into the era of postcapitalism in countries where the state has become the only usurer.

The Protocols of the Elders of Zion, the Beiliss case,* the Nazi extermination and calumnies of Streicher, the continuing campaigns of vilification and persecution in Poland, the Soviet Union, and the Arab world, as well as in the more genteel West—these represent an unbroken, perhaps endless, chain. Even yet the ghost of Father Abraham has not been laid, and Father Abraham, in the nightmares of the simple Christian, who does not awake from them simply by ceasing to go to church, has become the castrating papa: the performer of the first circumcision and the would-be, the almost-sacrificer of the son blending into a single figure forever whetting on his boot sole a knife to cut away the chunk of living flesh he claims for his patriarchal due.

Small wonder, then, that everywhere in the popular Christian literature of Shakespeare's day—in the *Gesta Romanorum, Il Pecorone* of Ser Giovanni Fiorentino, Anthony Munday's *Zelauto,* the ballad of *Gernutus, the Jew of Venice,* even in Alexandre Sylvaynes' *Orator* (presumably a collection of moral debates rather than of fiction)—the mythic theme recurs, and that all these books not written originally in English were translated to feed the hunger which Shakespeare's and Marlowe's Jewish plays, as well as Gosson's lost *The Jew,* tried to appease.

* The false accusation of child murder against Mendel Beiliss in the year 1911 shook the entire liberal world in those now irrecoverable days before Hitler when single victims still somehow managed to count. Beiliss was finally exonerated but his name has become proverbial, in the Jewish community at least.

Tales of flesh promised or surrendered for a boon are found in the myths of all times and places, and in the Christian era they are often associated with witchcraft, as in the case of Joan of Arc, who, according to Shakespeare, declares to her familiars, "I'll lop a member off and give it to you. . . . My body shall / Pay recompense if you will grant my suit," then goes on to promise even more, "Then take my soul, my body, soul and all. . . ." More typically, however, the Renaissance separated the offer of the soul from the bond of flesh, associating the first exclusively with Satan, the second with that minor devil, the Jew. Both female witchcraft and Jewish usury, on the other hand, reflect the male Gentile's fear of loss of potency; and, in this sense, the paranoia behind the myth of the merry bond, like that which motivates the myth of the satanic pact, reveals a hidden truth, since paranoiacs, as Freud once disconcertingly reminded us, never entirely lie. Judaism *has* unmanned the Gentile world, insofar as Jewish morality, transmitted via Christianity, limits and controls the free sexuality presumably enjoyed by men in pre-Christian Europe. It is that morality which the pagan undermind of Europe imagines holding a knife to its genitals, and the consequent resentment which male Europeans feel, but cannot confess, against their own church they project back upon the mythic founder of it all: old Father Abraham.

That Shakespeare identified Shylock with the archetypal Abraham there seems no doubt, for he puts the patriarchal name into the merchant's mouth right from the start. "This Jacob from our holy Abram was." Shylock reminds Antonio in the midst of his casuistical defense of usury; and a little later, just after proposing the merry bond, he cries out in ironical dismay, "O Father Abram, what these Christians are. . . ." The phrase prepares for the later, more serious cry, "These be the Christian husbands," which is itself followed by a last reference to Jessica, whose name was surely suggested to Shakespeare by the Iscah of Genesis, daughter of Haran, who is brother to Abraham. "I have a daughter," Shylock says, "Would any of the stock of Barrabas / Had been her husband rather than a Christian!" Shakespeare had found the name Barrabas in the same New Testament context from which Marlowe borrowed it for his Jew, taking it (since he did not know its etymological significance, "son of the father") to mean "thief" and "murderer," the murderer, in fact, whom the perfidious Jews chose for Passover amnesty in preference to Jesus.

At this point, Shylock seems more Jephthah than Abraham, the daughter's enemy rather than the son's, though Jessica stands not for "sacrifice" (in the end she gains all, loses nothing), but for everything in the Judaic tradition which represents gentleness as opposed to rigor, love as opposed to justice, the right hand as opposed to the left, and as such is thought to be worthy of good fortune in the Christian world. "Gentle Jew," she is called in one place, and the pun on "Gentile" is intended. There is, therefore, a kind of truth in Salarino's mocking response to Shylock: "There is more difference between thy flesh and hers than between jet and ivory, more between your bloods than there is between red wine and Rhenish."

But it is also true, as Jessica herself insists to Launcelot Gobbo, that however alien "to his manners," she is undeniably a "daughter to his blood." And when that clown asks her to hope that she is "not the Jew's daughter," she can only answer in melancholy jest, "That were a kind of bastard hope, indeed. So the sins of my mother should be visited upon me." No, her only legitimate "hope" is to be saved by her husband, who, as she tells Gobbo, "hath made me a Christian"; which is to say, she can only be saved by elopement and apostasy, by what must seem to her father filial rebellion: "My own flesh and blood to rebel!" To rebel against a very devil, however, can only be construed as virtuous, even if that devil is a father and one thinks, as Shakespeare did, that filial impiety is among the worst of sins.

The myth of the ogre's daughter, in any case, provided Shakespeare with a way out of the trap into which he felt himself betrayed each time he turned to comedy, which in his time—and always, it would seem, at its most popular—demands at its close marriage, which means the abandonment of fathers by daughters they are apt to love too well. But (as in *Henry VI, Part I* and the *Sonnets*) Shakespeare's personal mythology considered not marriage but male friendship the redeeming sentimental relationship and the denial of the father the equivalent of damnation. Once he had abandoned the relatively loose, essentially nonmythic structures of the sonnet sequence and chronicle play—structures which in themselves imposed no archetypal overview—he found himself, therefore, in trouble. Especially the New Comic mode, that benign version of the Oedipal conflict inherited from Plautus and Terence, implied (as Northrop Frye has convincingly demonstrated) a kind of overmyth, to which the submyths implicit in particular plots had to be accommodated.

It is fascinating to watch Shakespeare, from the time of *Love's Labor's Lost,* struggling against the mythological imperative that boy must get girl and that the older generation must be frustrated in desires which at first Shakespeare does not even suspect may be incestuous. In that freest of his early comedies, he begins, as we have already observed, by subverting the dream of a homosexual utopia so that, it would appear (though he supplies in the text reasons biological and theological as well), the conventions of New Comic theater can be honored. But he cannot quite compel himself to end in a quadruple marriage. The death of a king intervenes, the "will of a dead father" inhibiting the intended course of four courtships; and, as Berowne mournfully declares: "Our wooing doth not end like an old play. / Jack hath not Jill."

Later, his inherited comic plots no longer permit so evasive an un-ending, and he provides for his audiences the scenes of love triumphant which they demand—establishing, however, certain ground rules of his own to mitigate the Oedipal implications he could not abide. Though daughters can sometimes deceive fathers with impunity in his comedies, sons never can; nor can wives ever betray their husbands—only seem to. Yet even inside these self-imposed parameters, he appears not to have felt quite at ease, haunted always by the sense that those who defied their fathers even in love's name deserved to die. The archetypal story corresponding to that sense he found, like so much else, in Ovid: in the tale of Pyramus and Thisbe, who, deceiving their parents, found only death by moonlight, executing themselves as if in error, but really in response to exigencies they never understand. It is a myth which obsessed Shakespeare throughout the early part of his career, apt to surface in his mind whenever he imagined, for whatever reason, a scene lit only by the moon.

In *Titus Andronicus,* for instance, the first and most improbable allusion occurs; Martius, finding the bloody corpse of Bassianus, is moved to say, "So pale did shine the moon on Pyramus / When he by night lay bathed in maiden blood." The last is put into the mouth of Jessica, in an idyllic scene whose opening words are, "The moon shines bright."

In such a night
Did Thisbe fearfully o'ertrip the dew,
And saw the lion's shadow ere himself,
And ran dismayed away.

And in the most moon-drenched of all Shakespeare's plays, *A Midsummer Night's Dream,* the Ovidian story of bootlegged love come to grief is travestied by bumpkins all the way to its bitter end, though "Moonshine" through some confusion has left the scene early and "Thisby" must, therefore, kill herself in the dark.

> Come blade, my breast imbrue.
> And, farewell, friends.
> Thus Thisby ends.
> Adieu, adieu, adieu.

Laughing, we do not notice that meanwhile, in the main plot, Hermia, who has like Thisbe defied her father, survives the madness of the night to win his forgiveness and her own true love. And this, indeed, may have been Shakespeare's intent in making a burlesque of Ovid's tale the play within the play.

How different the effect in *Romeo and Juliet,* in which the Ovidian myth, with little changed except the names, becomes the main plot, the tragedy of "star-crossed lovers"—or rather, a foiled comedy, a comedy gone wrong. Those who do not understand all this worry much about why the two lovers have to die, Shakespeare having perversely (they argue) blurred the motivation provided by his Italian and his English sources. It is, however, the myth which kills them finally: the myth misunderstood by those who first turned Pyramus and Thisbe to Romeo and Juliet, but understood by Ovid long before and by his Elizabethan alter ego afterward, the myth which insists, in New Comedy's despite, that every marriage makes a father weep and that for those tears the price is blood.

With *The Merchant of Venice,* however, Shakespeare seems to have exorcised that archetypal ghost at last by substituting for Ovid's bloody fable the happy-ending folk tale of the ogre's daughter, in which the death of Thisbe becomes a cadence in a lovers' serenade. In this play, therefore, Jack hath his Jill three times over, as Shakespeare lets his three pairs of lovers move inexorably toward marriage, only insisting, by way of ritual purgation, that each of the three girls first pass as a boy. But how perfunctory the sex-shifting remains, perhaps because Shakespeare is still scarcely aware of what it means or, maybe, rather because he wants this time for once to have his women triumph *as women,* though in boy's clothing. There seems, indeed, something almost willfully perverse, even self-punishing, about the conclusion of *The Merchant of Venice,* a sense of the poet grimly denying the impulse in himself which had resisted New Comedy. It is almost as if he had lost his original innocence, realizing simultaneously the incestuous dream which motivates his stage fathers and the equivocal nature of his own erotic mythology.

He did not do full justice to the former until the time of *Pericles, Prince of Tyre,* but he exposed the latter quite candidly through Antonio, especially in that courtroom swan song in which the merchant for once nearly becomes a poet.

> I am a tainted wether of the flock,
> Meetest for death. The weakest kind of fruit
> Drops earliest to the ground, and so let me.

Antonio, however, does not die in fact; for this is comedy, and no father may be killed on scene—except symbolically, of course. So Portia's life-denying father is killed a second time to free his daughter from a death in life, and Shylock is killed by conversion-confiscation to be reborn a Christian, baptized like a newborn babe, the holy water canceling out his *brith,* the seal of the covenant in his flesh.

But Shylock is not reborn, dying to Shakespeare forever when he ceases to be "the Jew,' as his absence from Act V reveals. Yet it is not Christianity which kills him, in this play in which no self-styled Christian really goes to church—only Shylock to his synagogue. When Portia, for instance, says at one point that she is betaking herself to a monastery "to live in prayer and contemplation . . . until . . . my lord's return," the "lord" of her equivocal phrase is her lover on earth not her God in heaven; and she is again lying, as in the early casket scenes.

Indeed, she is almost always lying (her most triumphant scene a sustained web of prevarication), when she is not performing character assassination, talking courtly smut, or indulging in empty platitudes. Such platitudes are, indeed, themselves a form of lying, or at least of glossing reality with pieties too familiar to be taken quite as truth. The famous speech on mercy, for instance, delivered in the midst of a scene whose end is vengeance and whose means deceit, is a case in point. Yet critics of Shakespeare, unable to grant the poet a range of irony beyond their own, insist on taking seriously (they fall into the same trap with Polonius on borrowing and lending and with Ulysses on degree) such saccharine banalities as: "It is twice blest; / It blesseth him that gives and him that takes. / 'Tis mightiest in the mightiest." Nor do they even balk at those silliest lines of all, spoken just before the release of sheer bawdry which ends the play: "How far that little candle throws its beam! / So shines a good deed in a naughty world."

We must not be deceived by what Portia says; neither her morality nor her deepest faith are Christian. What moves her —and what kills Shylock—is hedonism, the pleasure principle. Similarly, what Belmont and gallant Venice alike hold against the Jew is not so much his usury, much less his denial of Christ, but his puritan austerity and his insistence that men are finally *accountable.* When, leaving his house, he turns to warn his daughter:

> What, are there masques? Hear you me, Jessica.
> Lock up my doors, and when you hear the drum
> And the vile squealing of the wry-necked fife,
> Clamber not you up to the casements then,
> Nor thrust your head into the public street
> To gaze on Christian fools with varnished faces,
> But stop my house's ears, I mean my casements.

Let not the sound of shallow foppery enter
My sober house.

he is expressing a distaste not just for music and public festival but for the whole code of conspicuous consumption and the ethics it implies. And how could one to whom the Law is all condone a world in which everyone forgives in advance the profligacy of everyone else (of his *own kind,* of course) and no one is held accountable for anything.

But such a code is as incompatible with Roman honor as with Jewish thrift, and so Antonio—whom Bassanio describes as "one in whom / The ancient Roman honor more appears / Than any that draws breath in Italy"—must also go down before it. Being, however, a Roman rather than a Jewish father, he is also a lover rather than a killer; and so he does not confront the pleasure principle head-on in rage, but strives to accommodate to it, compromise with it, even subsidize it with his hard-won capital. In the end, of course, nothing avails. But how he struggles before that end—how Shakespeare struggles for him: that advocate of an austere Uranian love, for whose sake the older lover educates to manliness the boy he adores, and in whose name he is prepared to die, though he knows he cannot ask as much in return, since that boy must rather die to him by marriage. There is not even a proper symbol for his connection with Bassanio in a play in which all other relations are represented by some outward and visible sign. But Antonio attempts to pre-empt for that purpose the ring, an effort doomed from the start, since the ring, by long tradition, stands for marriage and for female sexuality itself.

Nonetheless, for lack of an alternative, the ring, as the play moves from the fourth into the fifth act, comes to stand for Antonio's efforts to hang on to his "son," as the bond had stood for Shylock's efforts to destroy him and the three caskets had symbolized the mortmain of Portia's father. Giving that ring to Bassanio first, since it is hers to begin with, Portia says: 'Myself and what is mine to you and yours / Is now converted. . . . I give them with this ring. . . ." It is an anticipation of the wedding ceremony in which the golden girl and all her golden dowry will be converted from the Golden Fleece into what Gratiano calls "a hoop of gold . . . whose posy was / For all the world like cutler's poetry / Upon a knife, 'Love me, and leave me not.' " But a "hoop" means a restraint; while the word "knife" inevitably evokes the threat of castration. And we are left wondering how the free gift, the longed-for prize, has thus become a fetter, a menace.

The answer is obvious, foreknown. Even in the world of the pleasure principle, love turns to marriage as youth fades toward age; and the marriage contract contains a restriction, a penalty analogous to those written in a dead man's will or a Jew's bond: forsaking all others, *or else.* And how can the free association of Uranian love, bound by no bond, threatening no forfeiture, compete with so exclusive a commitment? For a brief moment, it has seemed possible to Antonio that he and Portia might somehow share his friend ("Mine be thy love's, and thy love's use their treasure"), as, carried away by the pathos of the courtroom scene, Bassanio boasts: "But life itself, my wife, and all the world. . . . I would lose all . . . here to this devil, to deliver you."

This Roman sentiment, however, sets Portia in her disguise to muttering, "Your wife would give you little thanks for that. . . ."; and it prompts Shylock to cry out, as we have earlier remarked, "These be the Christian husbands." For Antonio, it seems more than he had looked for—a happy ending, in fact, after which all else would be anticlimax. Later, therefore, when Portia, playing the lawyer, which is to say, another male, tempts her husband to part with the ring, which, as a woman, she had bade him keep as long as he would keep her love, he is emboldened enough to plead:

> Let his deservings and my love withal
> Be valued 'gainst your wife's commandment.

He puts it wickedly enough: "my love" against her "commandment," affection against mere duty; and it seems to work, bringing him a momentary triumph which Portia does not easily forgive him. Yet it is for him only a delusive victory, since the "boy" who gets the ring is really she, a good witch, who, possessing the only real power in the play (her dream, we know by now, not Antonio's, motivates the plot), gets everything. And there is one more thing which she desires: real revenge for that seeming victory, which in the final scene, she has.

At home again in Belmont, she receives Antonio coolly, even her customary sham of courtesy withheld, until he has, step by step, apologized, recanted, set things right. At first, she quite ignores him, speaking of him in the third person, as if he were not there, while she quibbles with Bassanio on the word "bound": "You should in all sense be much bound to him, / For, as I hear, he was much bound for you." And to this, Antonio, sensing her resentment, answers, "No more than I am acquitted of." It is apparently the right tack, for she bids him welcome at last, though briefly as well as belatedly, then hurls herself into the quarrel about "the ring," already begun by Gratiano and Nerissa: a quarrel which reaches its climax when she and Bassanio swap impassioned speeches, in each of which that obsessive word ends a line five times. "If you did know to whom I gave the ring," is the leitmotif of his; "If you had known the virtue of the ring," of hers.

It is all, of course, pure farce, though only Portia realizes the fact; but it is, for her, farce without a purpose: a burlesque lover's quarrel intended partly as erotic foreplay, partly as a way to even her score with her rival, Antonio. And at last, he rises to the bait, observing in his grave voice, more appropriate for melodrama than burlesque, "I am the unhappy subject of these quarrels," to which she answers, still not quite satisfied, "Sir, grieve not you. You are welcome notwithstanding." And he, who has understood her tenor from the start, does not fail to notice the residual bitterness of that final word, making, during the next interval of their comic bickering, his full recantation.

> I once did lend my body for his wealth,
> Which, but for him that had your husband's ring,
> Had quite miscarried. I dare be bound again,
> My soul upon the forfeit, that your lord
> Will never more break faith advisedly.

It is a speech in which every word counts, though one usually scanted by directors eager to get to the final reconciliations.

"I dare be *bound* again," Antonio says, picking up the word on which Portia had played at the beginning of the scene, and taking us back once more in memory to the original merry bond. Then he continues with "my *soul* upon the forfeit," as if to make quite clear that Portia, like some super-Shylock, will not be contented with a pledge of flesh—out of a sense perhaps that he and Bassanio, eschewing the body, love soul to soul: "my soul upon the forfeit, that your *lord*"—not *"my* love," notice, or *"my* friend," but "your lord / Will never break faith advisedly." This is much, but still, apparently, not enough; for Portia wants the full, the overflowing, measure of revenge. "Then *you* shall be his surety," she insists, forcing him to place the ring once more on his beloved's finger, to give the bridegroom away. "Here, Lord Bassanio," he intones ritually, marrying them, as it were, the second time, "swear to keep this ring." And even to his friend's face now, it is "sweet Bassanio" no longer, but "Lord Bassanio," since, like the long-suffering "I" of the *Sonnets,* he has been taught his place.

There is, however, yet another turn of the screw, as Portia, finally satisfied, grants the defeated Antonio a second semblance of a happy ending. His ships have all come in after all, she assures him, though only she has known until that moment, and he is rich once more. "Sweet lady," he says in his final speech, knowing enough by now not to offend a witch, "you have given me life and living. . . ." And his words seem the very opposite of Shylock's valedictory cry of despair, "You take my life / When you do take the means whereby I live," until we remember that long before, he had told Salarino, ". . . my merchandise makes me not sad." And we suspect it cannot make him joyous either.

In any case, the very last words of the play are not his but Gratiano's, who in their first exchange had spurned Antonio's melancholy, crying, "Let me play the fool." And as the fool, he caps the bawdry to which all four lovers turn after Antonio's recantation and the girls' disclosure of their trick. Cuckoldry is the subject of their jests, since, pretending anger at their husbands' presumed infidelity with the rings, the threat of such betrayal is what had first risen to their minds. Indeed, it seemed thus inevitably to rise to Shakespeare's whenever (as we shall see in *Othello*) he let a comedy run on beyond the marriage that is its natural end. In *Love's Labor's Lost,* in fact, even without the final pairing off, that consequence is projected in a song.

> Cuckoo, cuckoo! Oh, word of fear,
> Unpleasing to a married ear!

In Gratiano's closing couplet, however, not only is the fear of cuckoldry evoked but the final meaning of the ring is revealed, in an allusion to a dirty joke known to almost everyone in Shakespeare's audience and preserved to this very day in a fabliau called "Hans Castorp's Ring." "Well, while I live I'll fear no other thing," Gratiano says, preparing to take his bow, "so sore as keeping safe Nerissa's ring." And the understanders in the pit must have roared with laughter, remembering how in Hans's dream, the Devil slipped a magic ring on his middle finger, promising that so long as he wore it, his wife could never betray him, and how, awaking, Hans found that finger up her cunt.

SONNET 138

When my love swears that she is made of truth,
I do believe her, though I know she lies,
That she might think me some untutored youth,
Unlearnèd in the world's false subtleties.
Thus vainly thinking that she thinks me young,
Although she knows my days are past the best,
Simply I credit her false-speaking tongue.
On both sides thus is simple truth suppressed.
But wherefore says she not she is unjust?
And wherefore say not I that I am old?
Oh, love's best habit is in seeming trust,
And age in love loves not to have years told.
    Therefore I lie with her and she with me,
    And in our faults by lies we flattered be.

III

The Moor as Stranger: or "Almost damned in a fair wife. . . ."

Othello is one of the oddest of Shakespeare's plays and, therefore, one of the most difficult to interpret, not only because of its equivocal tone but also because of its anomalous structure, which, in fact, determines and explains that tone. In the theater, we are carried along from beginning to end of the action by what seems a single, unbroken rhythm; but in reading the play, we can scarcely fail to notice that it is actually *two* plays, intricately linked together yet finally quite separable. Critics, however, seldom trouble to call this to our attention, finding it perhaps too obvious, and somehow irrelevant. But it is hard to begin talking about *Othello* at all without taking into account that fact that it consists of a one-act comedy followed by a tragedy in four acts: the first, owing little or nothing to Shakespeare's Italian source, the *Hecatomithi* of Giraldi Cinthio; the second derived largely from Cinthio, though also continuing and reflecting ironically upon the first.

The two differ in setting as well as genre, since the first takes place in what we are meant to feel as the untroubled center of Christendom and the second, on its embattled borders—which is to say, the first in Venice, the second in Cyprus. That Venice is, moreover, disconcertingly familiar to anyone who has recently read *The Merchant of Venice:* a place in which money is power and men rise in the world by wiving it "wealthily." "Faith," says Iago of Othello early in the comic one-acter, at a point when the Moor has just eloped with a rich senator's only daughter, "he tonight hath boarded a land carrack. / If it prove lawful prize, he's made forever." Nor are we surprised when the silence of that night is broken (since in such a city, theft is feared beyond all offenses) by the cry of alarm: "Thieves! Thieves! Thieves! / Look to your house, your daughter and your bags!"

We are reminded of Shylock's similar clamor in the streets of Venice: "Justice! The law! My ducats, and my daughter! / A sealed bag, two sealed bags of ducats. . . ." Yet it is no comic-horrific Jew who responds to the alarm this time, but a "most reverend" signior, Brabantio, the father of Desdemona: the very opposite of an alien and outsider, more like what we imagine Portia's father to have been than what we know of Shylock. Except, however, for that substitution of a Gentile father for a Jew, the cast of characters in the comic prelude to *Othello* is remarkably like that in *The Merchant of Venice*. Three parallels suggest themselves at the outset: Desdemona for Portia, Michael Cassio for Bassanio, Othello for the Prince of Morocco; and a fourth seems more and more probable as we move deeper and deeper into the text: Iago for Gratiano.

The name "Gratiano" actually recurs in the play, given to a supernumerary who does not appear until the last act, in which he announces the death of Brabantio, to whom he is a brother and kind of double. But it is Iago who speaks with Gratiano's voice: the rough and hearty tone of a man among men, determined always to be "honest" at whatever cost. To be "honest" in this sense, however, means to speak a truth which always somehow hurts a little—or, in Iago's case, a lot, since he is a Gratiano turned bitter for reasons we shall have occasion to examine later. Yet the speech of Gratiano to Antonio, for example, in the first scene of the earlier play, could be transferred to Iago without a change.

I tell thee what, Antonio—
I love thee, and it is my love that speaks—

It seems the ancient's typical opening gambit, and like him, Gratiano moves from such protestations of affection to denigration, assuming (and assuming all men assume with him) the worst possible motives for everything:

> There are a sort of men whose visages
> Do cream and mantle like a standing pond,
> And do a willful stillness entertain,
> With purpose to be dressed in an opinion
> Of wisdom, gravity, profound conceit,
> As who should say "I am Sir Oracle,
> And when I ope my lips, let no dog bark!"

But though the major characters are alike in both plays, their relationships to each other are drastically altered—almost as if Shakespeare had said to himself: *Let's try that Venetian fable again, but this time let's turn everything upside down.* And the root of it all is that Portia-become-Desdemona chooses "a tawny Moor" over Cassio, who has inherited Bassanio's role: she chooses the suitor most alien to her, the utter stranger, rather than the one most like her in age, breeding, class, and "complexion." But in doing so, she leaves Cassio, who had presumably grown up assuming that such a marriage was in the cards for him, a foot-loose bachelor to menace married men and, by the same token, makes Othello, who for years avoided marriage as a "circumscription" to his "unhousèd free condition," an uneasy husband. It is as if this time the white witch had charmed herself out of the leaden casket into the golden one, where the proud, rhetoric-drunk African, knowing no rules of the social game beyond self-respect, can discover her and make her his bride.

As in *The Merchant of Venice* (but not in the tragic portion of *Othello*), it is female magic which spins the plot in the comic first act; or, in Iago's terms, it is "witchcraft" rather than "wit," which is to say, male intelligence, that moves events inexorably toward the fairy-tale happy ending. Brabantio is in one respect quite right, then, when he insists throughout the early scenes that the marriage of his daughter to the Moor could only have been brought about by "foul charms," "chains of magic," "spells and medicines"; but he is quite wrong when he accuses Othello of being the "practicer / Of arts inhibited and out of warrant." No father, in any case, finds it easy to think his own child a witch; but Brabantio is further confused by his belief that the "arts" which have presumably "corrupted" his daughter must be black arts, suitable only to one himself black enough to be a devil. Iago, however, knows better; and though skeptical about the genuineness of any witchcraft, he attributes the seeming magic that has made the improbable match not to the Moor but to Desdemona, of whom he says later on:

> She that so young could give out such a seeming
> To seel her father's eyes up close as oak—
> He thought 'twas witchcraft—

Merely to understand who the witch is, however, is not enough; and until the end of Act I, Iago cannot manipulate events, try as he will. He can rouse Brabantio and play on his deepest fears of miscegenation, his pride, even the repressed incestuous wishes that have troubled his sleep before the first alarm ("This accident is not unlike my dream," the old man says still half asleep); but he is unable to stop the marriage or turn the rulers of Venice against the Moor. As long as she remains a maiden, Desdemona remains in charge: a virgin "jewel" and "warrior," half Blessed Mary, half Athene—in any event, a figure of magical power and prestige, far different from the passive, whimpering Griselda she will become once she is a wife and has left her native Venice for the sea-marches of Islam. There neither she nor Cassio will thrive, her courtly witchcraft, like his courtly charm, powerless in a camp of armed men where "wit" alone can cope with drunken brawls and casual whores. There Iago comes into his own, turning even the magic of conjugal love—whose symbol is the handkerchief a gypsy wove, "dyed in mummy which the skillful / Conserved of maidens' hearts"—into a web that strangles her.

But so long as she remains at home, her maiden will prevails. Though Othello makes the beautiful speeches, it is she, not he, who carries the day against her father, topping his Lear-like challenge ("Do you perceive in all this noble company / Where most you owe obedience?") with a Cordelia-like definition of her divided loyalties.

> To you I am bound for life and education,
> My life and education both do learn me
> How to respect you, you are the lord of duty,
> I am hitherto your daughter. But here's my husband,
> And so much duty as my mother showed
> To you, preferring you before her father
> So much I challenge that I may profess
> Due to the Moor my lord.

And to this, her father can find no answer except farewell: "God be with you! I have done."

Similarly, it is Desdemona who, in the name of what she calls "my downright violence," first pleads for permission to go with the Moor to Cyprus, rather than be left behind as a mere "moth of peace." Clearly, she has earned the unorthodox happy ending, her heart's honeymoon in the midst of war; and the good wishes of her native state go with her, as an otherwise unidentified "First Senator" says, "Adieu, brave Moor. Use Desdemona well." No trace of the sinister undermeanings of the verb "use" seems to remain in this second valedictory. And though her father adds a warning note before the council breaks up for good ("Look to her, Moor, if thou hast eyes to see. / She has deceived her father, and may thee"), at first we do not take him quite seriously.

It is more like the exit line of some spoilsport or stranger, unreconciled to his discomfiture, than that of a father in a comedy making his peace before the final bow; and we expect it to have no more consequence within the play than, say, Malvolio's departing threat in *Twelfth Night*. But the play is not over, for when all the "DUKES, SENATORS, OFFICERS, *etc.*" have exited, followed by Othello and Desdemona, there remain on the stage two conspiratorial figures, hushed, waiting for the others to be gone so they can speak. And the first word we hear is the name "Iago" uttered by his gull, Roderigo. The point is clearly established by the dramatic strategy; Iago has inherited not merely the playing space but also the control of the action. Indeed, Othello says as much before his own exit in the casual words, "Honest Iago, / My Desdemona must I leave to thee."

We learn immediately how odd a choice this is for one to make who a moment before has cried of his beloved, "My life upon her faith!"; Iago proceeds at once to make clear his view of the passion which joins them. It is to Roderigo—who thinks he loves Desdemona, too, and despairs of ever attaining her—that he speaks, crying that "this that you call love. . . . is merely a lust of the blood and a permission of the will," and advising him, "therefore put money in thy purse," as if adultery could be bought with time and gold, quite like marriage in the world of Portia and Bassanio.

He then goes on to describe the special frailty of this particular match, marshaling all the *idées reçues* he shares with Roderigo and his audience about blacks ("These Moors are changeable in their wills"), young wives of older men ("She must change for youth"), and the unviability of mixed marriages. "If sanctimony and a frail vow," he concludes, "betwixt an erring barbarian and a supersubtle Venetian be not too hard for my wits and all the tribe of Hell, thou shalt enjoy her." He does not yet pick up the parting words of Brabantio, saving them for Othello ("She did deceive her father, marrying you. . . ."). But they continue to ring still in our ears at the act's end: a last, convincing argument against the stability of the happily-ever-after on which the Moor has bet his life—and Desdemona's, too, though he has not said as much.

Before the play is over, at any rate, Shakespeare will have made explicit the paradox which the marred endings of certain comedies from *Love's Labor's Lost* to *The Merchant of Venice* had, as we have noticed, all along implied: for marriage to occur, a girl must abandon her father, and that abandonment necessarily implies revealing capacities for deceiving men which terrify her husband forever, making assurance in marriage impossible. Behind the conventional happy ending of New Comedy, therefore, lies a potential disillusion which the genre itself cannot contain, yielding to farce when the consequence is cuckoldry, tolerated or ignored, and to tragedy when it is adultery, discovered and bloodily revenged.

Which is it to be in *Othello?* we are left wondering as the one-act New Comedy achieves a marriage but no end. And, at first, it seems as if only gross burlesque can follow, since Beauty this time has run off not with Prince Charming but with the Beast. Throughout the opening scenes, Iago, who yearned to turn it all to farce even before the abortive happy ending, has harped upon this theme, describing Othello as a "black ram . . . tupping your white ewe," "a Barbary horse" about to mount a girl. Tupped or "covered" by such a thick-lipped animal, Desdemona, too, becomes (in Iago's mind and mouth) a beast; the act of love which joins them, "making the beast with two backs." She herself may dream that within the seeming beast she loves there is a hidden god whom that love will reveal, but her story is destined to be no retelling of the Cupid and Psyche myth, in which what begins as suspicion and grief and seeming death ends as peace and harmony and life renewed. Shakespeare is still a long way from the mythic view which reimagines Desdemona as Hermione and sets her at the redemptive center of the tragicomic *Winter's Tale.*

His Italian source (the *donnée* from which all else follows) requires her brutal death—an ending whose harshness Shakespeare may mitigate a little but will not change in essence. *The girl must die:* so much he knows, and yet cannot help complicating the causes of that death by making her bestial lover an aged one as well ("an old black ram" is Iago's whole epithet), though for this there is no warrant in Cinthio. For the Italian novelist, what separates his lovers and dooms their marriage is threefold: *la natura, il cièlo,* and *la modá della vita;* but for Shakespeare, there is a fourth disparity added to race, religion, and manners: lack of "sympathy in years." Most productions of the play tend to make Othello younger than he is and Desdemona's father older, yet they must be and should be made up to look nearly the same age, since it was as Brabantio's friend that the Moor was first invited to their house, and since his elopement must seem in all respects a caricature of the father's incestuous dream.

Certainly, Othello is aware that he is far from young; indeed, he boasts of it in an almost perverse way when, pleading for permission to have Desdemona accompany him to Cyprus, he carefully explains:

I therefore beg it not
To please the palate of my appetite,
Nor to comply with heat—the young affects
In me defunct—and proper satisfaction,
But to be free and bounteous to her mind.

He is not, to be sure, publicly declaring himself impotent (though there is an odd ambiguity in his phrasing), merely asserting that his passions have been moderated by time. Yet there is something a little ridiculous, potentially farcical, about his statement; for what, we are tempted to speculate, can possibly happen which is *not* comic when a young girl has chosen to induct her into the pleasures of sense an aging and tired barbarian who boasts he has married her "to be free and bounteous to her mind."

Shakespeare has dealt before with the subject of lovers mismatched in age, and, indeed, it seems his private obsessions which make the theme central in a story which came to him without it, modifying the character of Othello into a kind of covert self-portrait, himself as aging nigger. In the *Sonnets,* the subject of "crabbèd age and youth" is typically an occasion for humor, as in the wry close of Sonnet 138, which Jaggard picked to open *The Passionate Pilgrim:*

> But wherefore says my love that she is young?
> And wherefore say not I that I am old?
> Oh, love's best habit is a soothing tongue,
> And age, in love, loves not to have years told.
>   Therefore I'll lie with love, and love with me,
>   Since that our faults in love thus smothered be.

or in the more rollicking verses (perhaps not even Shakespeare's) on the same theme that Jaggard included as well, as if to clinch the point:

> Youth is full of sport, age's breath is short;
>   Youth is nimble, age is lame;
> Youth is hot and bold, age is weak and cold;
>   Youth is wild, and age is tame.
> Age, I do abhor thee; youth, I do adore thee.

As we enter Act II of *Othello,* then, the age-old farce of January and May—that archetypal projection of male insecurity, given classic form by Chaucer in *The Merchant's Tale* —threatens to be reborn; but Shakespeare will not let it happen on stage, having, in fact, a deep distaste for the comedy of cuckoldry. Nonetheless, inside the Moor's head (and Iago's, too, for in this respect they are one) that farce is played over and over: a nightmare and a dirty joke which Othello ends by taking for reality. Indeed, it is the essence of this joke that it purports to be the revelation of reality, the fact of betrayal behind the façade of seeming faith. It represents the "reality," however, of males only, so that while Othello is tangled in his bad dream, Desdemona is dreaming quite another, in which she is not May but Griselda, being tested—however cruelly and irrationally—in preparation for the second, the wife's, happy ending, which, unlike the first, the maiden's, cannot debouch in tragedy or sheer burlesque.

These complementary mythic fantasies seem linked not by chance or whim but necessarily and essentially: the male nightmare of unmerited betrayal and the female dream of patient suffering rewarded, each entailing the other. Certainly, they do so also in Fragment IV of *The Canterbury Tales,* in which the Clerk, who has just told the story of Patient Griselda, yields to the Merchant, after an Envoy linking their two tales. That Envoy begins with the melancholy announcement that "Grisilde is deed, and eek hire pacience," then ironically admonishes all living wives to take care lest they inadvertently provide some other clerk the occasion for "a storie of swich mervaille / As of Grisildis pacient and kynde," and concludes by urging them to torment their husbands without mercy or fear.

> Ne dreed hem nat, doth hem no reverence,
> For though thyn housbonde armed be in maille,
> The arwes of thy crabbed eloquence
> Shall perce his brest, and eek his aventaille.
> In jalousie I rede eek thou hym bynde,
> And thou shalt make hym couche as doth a quaille.

It is hard to know how much Chaucer Shakespeare had read and how well, but certainly he knew the fabliaux and folk tales, along with the sermons and popular tracts on marriage which had fed the earlier poet's imagination. And, indeed, he could just as well have learned from his own domestic difficulties or from his observation of those of others the ironic link between the sentimental melodrama of the abused wife and the pornographic farce of the betrayed husband. To be aware of so much, however, implies an awareness, too, that the jokes men make upon women may ultimately prove jokes on themselves. And some such awareness surely sustains the undercurrent of black hilarity which runs beneath the surface tragic flow of *Othello*.

There have, in fact, always been critics acute enough to sense that though notably weak in its intentionally comic scenes, Othello everywhere comes perilously close to—if it does not, indeed, go over the edge of—being unintentionally comic. Such critics, however, have generally been considered too irreverent and benighted to be taken quite seriously, though Thomas Rymer, at least, the father of all anticultist Shakespearean criticism, provides a real clue to the double tone of *Othello,* which is finally even more confusing than its much-discussed "double-time." Writing in 1693 that the audiences of *Othello* "must deny their senses to reconcile it to common sense," Rymer was presumably not just expressing an eccentric dissent from everyone else, but registering a substantial minority opinion which cannot be dismissed as mere silliness.

Unmodified "common sense," however, can go as comically wrong as Rymer thought Shakespeare had, so that, for instance, Rymer can miss entirely the point of the infamous handkerchief; namely, that its very essence is its insignificance, that any trifle could have been endowed, under such circumstances, with magic enough to eventuate in death. And we smile at him a little condescendingly, reading: "Had it been Desdemona's garter, the sagacious Moor might have smelled a rat; but the handkerchief is so remote a trifle, no booby, this side of Mauritania could make any consequence from it." When, on the other hand, he goes on to observe: "There is in this play some burlesque, some humor and ramble of comic wit . . . but the tragical part is, plainly, none other than a bloody farce," we are forced to pause and consider.

How else, indeed, can the scene of Othello's epileptic fit be played (to cite just one example) except as sinister farce? The audience must be encouraged to laugh, however bitterly, at the actor in blackface (Othello *must* be played so, since to give the part to an actual black man is to blur the point), rolling his eyes, writhing on the floor, and crying, "Pish! Noses, ears, and lips. Is 't possible?—Confess?—Handkerchief?—Oh, devil!" Otherwise, they will feel their temptation to snicker (and who can resist it?) as irrelevant, outside the intended tone of the play. Nonetheless, we cannot accept Rymer's judgment without qualification, since it tends to suppress one half of the paradoxical reaction to *Othello* which alone does it justice, quite as most modern interpretations of it tend to cancel out the other half. Difficult as it is, we must keep both parts of the paradox intact: the fable of *Othello* is incredible and yet we believe it; the events of *Othello* constitute a "bloody farce," and yet we respond to them with the tragic shudder.

Really to understand our own double reaction and the play's double tone, we must first understand more clearly just what *Othello* burlesques. And to do so we must begin by analyzing a term whose definition we tend to take for granted —begin by asking what, *in this particular drama,* is meant by "jealousy," since the meanings of that word are not always and everywhere the same in the body of Shakespeare's work. We are likely to put *Othello* in the context of *Cymbeline* and *The Winter's Tale,* which also deal centrally with the theme of irrational and unjustified "jealousy"; but in the two later plays, that absurd passion is entirely subdued to the mood and structure of comedy. And this somehow seems right, righter than the case of *Othello;* for there is something essentially comic about a jealous husband—the sense that his anguish, whether justified or not, is a fitter occasion for laughter than for tears.

And yet, as *Othello* reminds us (and the two comedies do not), the consequence of that anguish for the suspected wife may be bloody, even mortal. We must think of *Othello* then, as the sole drama of Shakespeare which exploits both the comic and tragic possibilities of jealousy to the full, the only work in which he confronted the paradox, implicit in male notions about female marital infidelity, that jealousy simultaneously creates a comic situation for men and a tragic one for women. And whether that paradox is itself comic or tragic is left equivocal in *Othello* when that play is properly acted or read.

Othello is, in any event, a play not about the jealousy of one man but about jealousy in general. Unlike, therefore, *The Winter's Tale,* it contains no study in depth of the psychic mechanisms which underlie that special form of paranoia; and to try to understand Othello's motivation in such terms is to miss the point totally. In *The Winter's Tale,* on the other hand (as I. A. M. Stewart has convincingly argued), Leontes is clearly, almost clinically, portrayed as the victim of unacknowledged homosexual desires directed toward his old friend Polixenes. These impulses he disguises as nostalgia for the "innocence" of their childhood, which Polixenes, sharing his covert passion, describes for both of them.

> We were as twinned lambs that did frisk i' the sun,
> And bleat the one at the other. What we changed
> Was innocence for innocence, we knew not
> The doctrine of ill-doing, nor dreamed
> That any did. Had we pursued that life, . . .
> we should have answered Heaven
> Boldly "Not guilty," the imposition cleared
> Hereditary ours.

And when the Queen objects, "By this we gather / You have tripped since," he answers, giving the game away:

O my most sacred lady!
Temptations have since then been born to 's. For
In those unfledged days was my wife a girl,
Your precious self had then not crossed the eyes
Of my young playfellow.

Polixenes's presumably courtly banter with the Queen is in this sense a disguised flirtation with her husband. But Leontes, not understanding this and totally unable in any event to deal with his own response, projects it out onto his wife, as she stands holding in her hand that hand that no longer clasps his in boyish "innocence."

Too hot, too hot!
To mingle friendship far is mingling bloods.
I have *tremor cordis* on me. My heart dances,
But not for joy, not joy.

In *Othello,* however, there is no suggestion of any similar homosexual projection on the part of the Moor, though there are equivocal hints of a repressed passion between males turned destructive, rather like the relationship more frankly treated by Herman Melville in *Billy Budd.* That ambivalent passion, however, belongs to Iago and is directed not toward Othello, but toward one whom Othello has preferred to him, Michael Cassio. Of him, Iago says at one point, speaking to Roderigo, "He hath a daily beauty in his life / That makes me ugly. . . ." But this represents only the most superficial aspect of a complex feeling whose secret depths he reveals in casual metaphors and flights of lying fancy. Asked, for example, the cause of the drunken brawl between Cassio and Montano, he begins with what seems a totally unmotivated erotic simile: "Friends all but now, even now, / In quarter and in terms like bride and groom / Divesting them for bed." He picks up the image of sexual consummation when he recounts to Othello an imaginary dream of Cassio's:

I lay with Cassio lately,
And being troubled with a raging tooth,
I could not sleep. . . .
In sleep I heard him say "Sweet Desdemona,
Let us be wary, let us hide our loves."
And then, sir, would he gripe and wring my hand,
Cry "O sweet creature!" and then kiss me hard,
As if he plucked up kisses by the roots
That grew upon my lips. Then laid his leg
Over my thigh, and sighed, and kissed. . . .

The presumable point is to convince the Moor of his wife's unfaithfulness and Cassio's (whose death Iago lusts for more passionately than hers), but there is surely some warrant for reading his words as a betrayal of his own dreams, which knowingly he would not have admitted even to himself. Real or fancied, in any case, such glimmerings of homosexuality belong not to the main plot of *Othello* but to a peripheral action never fully developed. They may provide, in fact, some clues to the long-vexing problem of Iago's "motiveless malignity," but they scarcely help us to understand the Moor.

To find a more helpful model, we must turn from *The Winter's Tale* to *Cymbeline,* in which Posthumus Leonatus is ravaged by a kind of jealousy of his chaste wife, Imogen, which seems at first glance rather more like Othello's than did Leontes's, having its base in mythology rather than psychology, which is to say, in certain commonplaces about the nature of women. Even in plot details, the two plays are similar, Posthumus, for example, being also victimized by a suggester at his ear, called Iachimo, which means, of course, "little Iago." But in *Cymbeline,* the absurdity of the situation is mitigated because the case which Iachimo makes is circumstantial and convincing enough to put no strain on our credulity. And, in any case, like *The Winter's Tale* but quite unlike *Othello* the fable of *Cymbeline* only seems to allow the killing of a wife, permitting Imogen in fact Griselda's happy ending, in which her rejection by the husband turns out to represent not his damned fall but only a blessed test of her.

Posthumus, who had cast her off, reviled her, and plotted her murder, in the last scene of the last act strikes her to the earth, taking her in male disguise for a presumptuous boy (but when had he known her really?); yet rising, she clasps him in her arms and says in total submissiveness, "Why did you throw your wedded lady from you? / Think that you are upon a rock, and now / Throw me again." And only then does he, having meanwhile been blessed by Jove in all his paternal glory, declare his final faith: "Hang there like fruit, my soul, / Till the tree die!"

Earlier, however, he had recited the famous litany of woman's faults, marshaling on the occasion of what he believed to be his betrayal just such an array of antifeminist clichés as haunted Othello's madness.

> All faults that may be named, nay, that Hell knows,
> Why, hers, in part or all, but rather all.
> For even to vice
> They are not constant, but are changing still
> One vice, but of a minute old, for one
> Not half so old as that. I'll write against them,
> Detest them, curse them. Yet 'tis greater skill
> In true hate to pray they have their will.

It is, however, mothers rather than wives who are the real butts of this slander, though at its heart there lurk queasy images of Imogen being possessed by the "yellow Iachimo," who, the self-torturing Posthumus imagines, "like a full-acorned boar . . . Cried 'Oh!' and mounted. . . ." But the leitmotif has been set earlier by the phrase, "We are all bastards. . . ."; and the play's happy ending, which permits the "resurrection" of Imogen, demands the death of her stepmother, Cymbeline's evil Queen. It is an odd conclusion, in which, the shadow of the mother once lifted, utopia is established: two sons and a daughter reborn of their father, and that reborn daughter joined again to the one man in the world not born of woman. What will happen when Imogen herself becomes a mother is a question that we are not permitted to ask. We know only that she has survived a war and her husband's anger, though not without the intervention of the gods, to whom at the play's end the smokes of thanksgiving ascend.

Not so in *Othello,* in which not grace but gravity has triumphed, and the earthbound survivors go off to tell the story: "This heavy act with heavy heart relate." *Othello* is, in short, a play in which no one is forgiven, except the dead—as opposed to *Cymbeline,* in which all who survive are pardoned, even Iachimo, and in which, besides the mother, only the son of the mother, the rapist, Cloten, dies. Iachimo, indeed, expects his death, kneeling and asking Posthumus for the *coup de grâce.* "Take that life, beseech you," he prays, as "heavy conscience" bends his knee. And it is Shakespeare's "heavy conscience" that speaks in him, just as it is Shakespeare's hard-won ability to forgive himself which answers through Posthumus. "The power I have on you is to spare you, / The malice towards you to forgive you. Live. . . .

In *Othello,* however, it is Shakespeare's bad conscience which has the final word, the bad conscience not only of all in himself which the black stranger symbolized but of his whole culture: the Renaissance, in which he lived; the Middle Ages, which shaped it; and the modern West, which is the heir of both. What cues that bad conscience is, to begin with, men's awareness that women are the victims of a marriage system in whose making they had no voice and a double standard concerning chastity on which they were never consulted. And it is aggravated by the suspicion that women, being conscious of those indignities, are eager for the kind of revenge which is always in their power, the revenge of adultery, and that, in any case, they cannot keep those marriage vows which male idealism and selfishness in strange concert invented, but which have always striven in vain against the hairy beast between their legs: the *animal avidum generandi.*

In *Othello,* such views are aired quite explicitly over and over, chiefly by Iago, who quite believes all the antifeminist platitudes he uses to entrap the Moor. To Othello, he speaks in deadly earnest; and if he lies, he does not know it.

> In Venice they do let Heaven see the pranks
> They dare not show their husbands. Their best conscience
> Is not to leave 't undone, but keep 't unknown.

To Cassio, he suggests such readings of womankind more insidiously: for Cassio, in speaking of Desdemona at least, plays the complimentary game of courtly praise, so that their conversation is, as it were, in two different languages. And yet we should remember when Cassio speaks that adultery is the end of courtly love, as well as the ribald theme of the fabliaux. "She's a most exquisite lady," Cassio says of Desdemona. To this Iago answers, "And, I'll warrant her, full of game," which Cassio then translates to, "Indeed she's a most fresh and delicate creature." This Iago takes not as a check but only as an invitation to a new tack: "What an eye she has! Methinks it sounds a parley to provocation." "An inviting eye," Cassio agrees, but hastens to add, "and yet methinks right modest." It is only on the subject of a highborn lady, however, that their views are so disjunct; speaking of Bianca, a Cypriot prostitute in love with Cassio, they talk the same language, since to both she is a "caitiff," a "customer," a "monkey," "another fitchew."

To Iago, they are all "fitchews": the island whore, his own wife, his noble mistress; nor does he hesitate to generalize about the sex even to the latter, for this is the "honesty" on which he prides himself—not being what he seems, perhaps, but saying what he thinks all the same. To Desdemona, however, in that odd wit combat held on the quayside just before Othello's arrival in Cyprus, he affects a mocking tone rather than an earnest or insidious one. "Come on, come on," he retorts when she objects to his calling his own wife a shrew:

> You are pictures out of doors,
> Bells in your parlors, wildcats in your kitchens,
> Saints in your injuries, devils being offended,
> Players in your housewifery, and housewives in your beds.

And when she calls him "slanderer," he glosses his own words: "You rise to play, and go to bed to work." It is a challenge she cannot resist, the sort of word match she presumably grew up playing, so that, though the occasion seems unsuitable for levity, she excuses herself half aside ("I am not merry, but I do beguile / The thing I am by seeming otherwise"), then begins to parry as he continues to thrust.

At first her tone is light and paradoxical, as he pretends his is; but after proposing for his witty denigration a conventional-enough list of female character types (the woman "fair and wise," "black and witty," "fair and foolish," "foul and foolish"), she describes the model of female excellence she obviously hopes herself to be: "one that in the authority of her merit did justly put on the vouch of very malice itself." And he responds in his longest rhymed epigram, saving the sting for the couplet which is its tail:

> She was a wight, if ever such wight were. . . .
> To suckle fools and chronicle small beer.

Desdemona may know very well, and indeed she has already said, that this and his other quips ". . . are old fond paradoxes to make fools laugh i' the alehouse"; but when she turns to Michael Cassio for support (taking him by the hand in a gesture of mild coquetry as customary to her as the badinage itself),

Cassio turns out to be on Iago's side, saying, with three fingers to his lips to allay the sting, "He speaks home, madam."

And at this moment, the trumpet announces Othello, who before long will be giving his assent to those "alehouse" paradoxes, though in barbarian earnest rather than courtly jest. Indeed, he needs no Iago to teach him the conventional calumnies of woman. They are all there in his head, picked up in the same army camps where Iago himself had learned them—so that we must believe the latter when he says in belated self-justification, "I told . . . no more / Than what he found himself was apt and true."

Othello is in the end more Iago's collaborator than his victim, more his alter ego than his collaborator, because both (unlike Desdemona or Cassio) could neither reject the conventional slanders of women nor exorcise them in jokes and courtly play. Forced to reconsider his exemption of Desdemona ("My life upon her faith!") from the generalizations about female frailty to which he otherwise subscribes, he falls back into the standard sort of calumny.

> Oh, curse of marriage,
> That we can call these delicate creatures ours,
> And not their appetites! I had rather be a toad
> And live upon the vapor of a dungeon
> Than keep a corner in the thing I love
> For others' uses. Yet, 'tis the plague of great ones,
> Prerogatived are they less than the base.
> 'Tis destiny unshunnable, like death.
> Even then this forkèd plague is fated to us
> When we do quicken.

Being Othello, which is to say, one too much "loving his own pride and purposes" (Iago is right in describing him so, as he is most often right about what is worst in men) to take himself less than seriously, he affects a tragic and grandiloquent tone. Yet what he speaks are precisely the banalities about cuckoldry and the special susceptibility of the great intended "to make fools laugh i' the alehouse."

But it is the function of "alehouse" laughter to exorcise what is darkest and dirtiest, most unmanageable and destructive, though secretly prized and protected in the soul—everything, in short, which "honest Iago" betrays, the dark side of his age's ambivalence toward honor, chastity, self-control, and loyalty. It is not easy for Shakespeare to say—and perhaps he could not, at this point, have confessed it except in a play as out of control as a dream—that we all must, if we are not to be destroyed by our deep resentment of what we deeply believe, give a "place" to one able to speak on behalf of thoughts "vile and false," as Iago does to Othello.

> Who has a breast so pure
> But some uncleanly apprehensions
> Keep leets and law days, and in session sit
> With meditations lawful?

But what *is* that "place"? Iago himself declares, in an early speech, that proven merit and "old gradation" recommend his promotion to a lieutenancy, an office at the right hand—or perhaps, rather, the left—of the governor general; but the military metaphor does not finally suffice. No, it is Desdemona who more properly identifies his function, casting him instinctively in the role of clown, fool, privileged jester, thus revealing to us all what Iago has in common with the Touchstone of *As You Like It* or the gloomier Feste of *Twelfth Night.* And we remember that the name of the character in *The Merchant of Venice* to whom he provides a dark analogue, "Gratiano," was in the *commedia dell'arte* a conventional title for the zany or buffoon. But Iago no longer inhabits the festive world of Touchstone and Feste or Gratiano, the sunny comic clime in which the lovers whom the jester mocks move inevitably all the same toward their appointed marriages.

The world of *Othello* is instead one in which the fool does not flourish, the poor "Clown," for example, listed in the dramatis personae, exchanging a few feeble "quillets" which Cassio in one scene and with Desdemona in another, then disappearing from the action, *spurlos versenkt.* And why not, since Iago can be intentionally wittier and the Moor seems destined to be unintentionally more absurd, though neither of their parts, we may be sure, was played by the official funnyman of Shakespeare's company. Moreover, Shakespeare seems at this stage of his career to have been having deep trouble with the conventional fool of the Elizabethan theater, whom earlier he had been willing to give not just whole juicy scenes but even the final word, as he did with Puck, that apotheosized jester of *A Midsummer Night's Dream,* or Feste, who, when all others have exited, sings his melancholy prevision of what will follow their happy endings.

> But when I came, alas! to wive,
> With hey, ho, the wind and the rain,
> By swaggering could I never thrive,
> For the rain it raineth every day.

At the time he was writing the major tragedies, however, along with such bitter not-quite-comedies as *Troilus and Cressida or Measure for Measure* ("bloody farces," both of them, quite like *Othello* itself), Shakespeare seems to have been driven, first, to make the jester more involved participant than mere antiphonal chorus and, second, to kill him. Even in *Lear,* for instance, that celebration of the sanity of madness and the wisdom of folly, the Fool, as we learn in a scant sentence spoken by the old king, has somehow died before the fable is quite over. "And my poor fool is hanged!" says Lear; and we scarcely know whether it is, in fact, the jester he means or that other speaker of antiphonal truth, his youngest daughter, Cordelia. Indeed, the two never appear on stage together, and may well have been played by the same actor, for practical if not symbolic reasons. In *Hamlet,* on the other hand, the royal jester,

Yorick (who, perhaps for this very reason, has proved immortal), has died before the play begins, as if to signify that the legitimate critic of the rightful king cannot survive his master—and dying, leaves the son to play the fool in the court of the usurper or in the graveyard with subordinate Clowns: "Where be your gibes now? Your gambols? Your songs? Your flashes of merriment. . . . Not one now, to mock your own grinning?"

In the dark demicomedies, however, the process is at a different stage (earlier? later? it is hard to be sure), for in them, the fool has been stripped of his motley, which is to say, his official role and diplomatic immunity, so that when Thersites, for example, scolds the blustering bullies of *Troilus and Cressida,* they scold back. Even in the cast of characters, he is listed not as a clown or fool, but as "a deformed and scurrilous Grecian," having as little legitimacy as anyone else in a world which needs no underground critic to qualify values in which no one really believes. Certainly, no one can gainsay him when he cries, "Lechery, lechery! Still wars and lechery! Nothing else holds fashion," or says of the particular war which has brought him to Troy, "All the argument is a cuckold and a whore. . . ."

Twice death threatens him as the action moves toward its bloody and pointless end: once when he confronts Hector, greatest of King Priam's legitimate sons, and once when he meets in the midst of battle Margarelon, "a bastard son of Priam." Each time, however, he saves his skin by turning his scorn upon himself, mocking, as it were, the very principle of satire. To Hector, he declares, "I am a rascal; a scurvy railing knave; a very filthy rogue"; and to Margarelon, "I am a bastard too. . . . a bastard begot, bastard instructed, bastard in mind, bastard in valor, in everything illegitimate." And with that he has dismissed himself to silence, leaving it to Pandarus, the "broker lackey," traitor, and bawd, to tell the final dirty jokes which follow hard on Hector's death.

In *Measure for Measure,* however, the two return as one, the bawd and fool coalesced in Lucio, whom the dramatis personae calls simply "a fantastic." But once more we are in a world without order, a world whose ruler has, for unconvincing reasons, deposed himself. And Lucio addressing that "Duke of dark corners" in disguise, as fools have traditionally addressed kings, gets no traditional response, no lofty counter-quip and condescending gift of gold. "The Duke," he says, not knowing of course to whom he is talking, "I say to thee again, would eat mutton on Fridays. He's not past it yet, and I say to thee he would mouth with a beggar though she smelt brown bread and garlic." And to this the Duke can only mutter, "No might nor greatness in mortality / Can censure 'scape. . . . What king so strong / Can tie the gall up in the slanderous tongue?"

But as he planned to deal with lechery through his vice-regent, Angelo—thus unleashing all the absurd sorrows of the plot—he plans to deal with slander: by punishing excessively what he himself knows he cannot ban. At any rate, when, at the play's climax, he discloses his identity, he sentences the "fantastic" first to marry a whore whom he has got with child, then to be "whipped and hanged," and only remits the second pair of penalties out of a sense that for Lucio, "marrying a punk . . . is pressing to death whipping, and hanging." "Slandering a prince," he says in humorless righteousness, "deserves it."

If the Duke of *Measure for Measure* proves himself powerless to deal with mockery by any means except repression, so also does Othello, who seems, in fact, even more like that puritan double of the Duke, the "precise" Angelo, whom Lucio describes as "a man whose blood / Is very snow broth, one who never feels / The wanton stings and motions of the sense. . . . when he makes water, his urine is congealed ice." After all, the Moor has spoken of himself in pride, much as Lucio speaks of Angelo in slander, boasting his very love for Desdemona free of "appetite" and "heat." How can he be expected, then, to give the "obscene jester" his due, having denied him even at a marriage, which of all human occasions seems most to demand his presence. Banned, however, from military councils and courts of law and bed itself, the Iago principle of cathartic mockery turns diabolical, since in mythological terms the fool denied becomes that vice or devil he was to begin with—unritualized, unsocialized, malefic.

But the Devil is, by definition, invisible, evasive; and so the man possessed by him sees him everywhere except where he truly is, in himself, at his own side. Certainly that is the case with Othello, who fails until the very last moment to recognize his demon in Iago or Iago in himself, but thinks he has discovered him in the "hot, and moist" hand of Desdemona, whom Shakespeare's sources confusingly had named "dis-demon" or "evil spirit." "For here's a young and sweating devil here, / That commonly rebels," he says at the point when "jealousy" has become to possess him completely. And we notice the insistence of the double "here" (as if to say, in *you,* not me; your *hand,* not my head), as well as the evocation of her denied father in the word "rebels." But the "cause" is not in Desdemona, as Emilia, even before she knows the demon's true name, insists, answering her mistress' protest, "I never gave him cause," with the commonplace, "They are not ever jealous for the cause. . . .'Tis a monster / Begot upon itself, born on itself." And to this, Desdemona can only answer, "Heaven keep that monster from Othello's mind!"

She prays in vain, of course, since the "monster," the vice stripped of motley now dressed in green, not only drives Othello but blinds him as well. "It is the cause," he says three times over preparing to smother Desdemona, "it is the cause, my soul. . . . It is the cause." But what his "cause" amounts to in the end is that her palm is moist, which is to say, she sweats, his angel *sweats*—and may be presumed, then, being as human as any other lady, to desire in marriage something more, or less, than one "free and bounteous to her mind." All this, however, Iago might have told Othello, had he let Iago play the proper fool, sealing him to himself as a comrade-clown, a Sancho Panza. Certainly, he had told as much to the equally bedazzled and even stupider admirer of Desdemona, Roderigo, who had described her in terms more suitable for the Blessed Virgin, as "full of most blest condition." "Blest fig's-end!" Iago had answered. "The wine she drinks is made of grapes. If she had been blest, she would never have loved the Moor. Blest pudding!"

More is involved, however, in Othello's predicament than just his fictional fate. Indeed, the very shape of the play is at stake, since Shakespeare, like Othello, is possessed by the spirit which he denies, by irrational elements in himself which escape his control even as the ancient escapes Othello's. Fail to write the disruptive fool into your plot—the play appears to be saying, in its author's despite—and the devil that fool becomes will write his own plot, dictate his own tone, impose his own obsessive themes. So Iago writes *Othello* from the beginning of the second act to the midpoint of the final scene of Act V, when the Moor recognizes that the devil he thought he perceived in Desdemona's hand and in Cassio (who in turn thought he had found it in the wine bottle) actually resides in Iago, *is* Iago.

Thereafter, it is as a full-fledged devil, with all the appropriate mythological attributes, that Othello addresses or refers to him. "I look down toward his feet, but that's a fable," he says, stabbing at his former ancient. "If that thou be'st a devil, I cannot kill thee." Then a moment later, he says to Cassio, "Will you, I pray, demand that demidevil? / Why he hath thus ensnared my soul and body?" "Demidevil" is more accurate than "devil," since Iago constitutes only one half of the satanic monster of which Othello is the other half, as he never explicitly acknowledges. But perhaps even the implicit recognition is enough, for at this point the Moor can at last ask pardon of the much-maligned Cassio; and the Iago principle is forever silenced, declaring cryptically, "Demand me nothing. What you know, you know. / From this time forth I never will speak word."

By this time, however, Iago has won a victory which neither his own silence nor the torture and execution due to follow can ever quite impugn. Not only has he caused, directly or indirectly, the deaths of Desdemona, Emilia, Roderigo, and finally Othello himself but even more damagingly, he has imposed his world view on the play and us, sustaining in particular his charges against womankind. First the males embroiled in his plot have repeated over and over his "alehouse" slanders, until even if they had not begun as platitudes, they would have achieved that status within the play. Moreover, the play's other women have seemed to verify those platitudes in action, before being hustled off to jail or summary death.

Emilia is most important in this regard, being not only wife and, in some sense, fit partner to Iago, but also maid-in-waiting and foil to Desdemona, rather like Nerissa in *The Merchant of Venice*. But Emilia is first and last an untamed shrew, who begins by turning her tongue against her husband ("Sir," Iago says to Cassio, "would she give you so much of her lips / As of her tongue she oft bestows on me, / You'd have enough") and ends by using it to lash Othello, whom she calls—granted by circumstances the privileged position of a court jester—a "murderous coxcomb." And in between, she functions as a bawd, not only in the destructive fantasy of Othello but also in the creative imagination of Shakespeare, which here as elsewhere comes so close to the Moor's paranoia.

"Leave procreants alone and shut the door," the Moor says mockingly to Emilia as he moves toward the moment of his fatal embrace, "Cough, or cry hem, if anybody come. / Your mystery, your mystery." And we tend to reject his charge, remembering Emilia's faithfulness to her mistress and her role in exposing her husband's plot. But if she does not really play the "mystery," the trade of bawd, she seems to possess the instincts of a procurer at least. What else are we to make, for instance, of the scene just before the absolute catastrophe, in which she appears to be tempting poor Desdemona by evoking the charms of a newly arrived young Venetian, Lodovico. "A very handsome man," she insinuates, undressing her mistress, her tone quite like that of the Nurse at a similar point in *Romeo and Juliet.* "I know a lady in Venice would have walked barefoot to Palestine for a touch of his nether lip."

Then, a moment later, she is pooh-poohing Desdemona's assertion that there surely can be *no* woman who would betray her husband even "for the whole world," her cynicism growing ever stronger as Shakespeare plays it dialectically against her mistress's naïveté. She can think of a dozen, Emilia assures Desdemona, "and as many to the vantage as would store the world they played for." And finally she launches into a full-scale defense of female infidelity as woman's sole weapon in what she takes to be the endless warfare of the sexes, betrayal answering betrayal to the end of time.

> But I do think it is their husbands' faults
> If wives do fall. Say that they slack their duties . . .
> Or else break out in peevish jealousies,
> Throwing restraint upon us, or say they strike us, . . .
> Why, we have galls, and though we have some grace,
> Yet we have some revenge. Let husbands know
> Their wives have sense like them. They see and smell
> And have their palates both for sweet and sour,
> As their husbands have. . . .
>   And have not we affections,
> Desires for sport, and frailty, as men have?
> Then let them use us well. Else let them know
> The ills we do, their ills instruct us so.

If in some ways, her bitterness and cynicism remind us of her husband's; in much more important ways, they are different. She speaks from the point of view of the oppressed rather than the oppressor and finally, therefore, sounds more like Chaucer's Wife of Bath, or even Shylock. Exploited outsiders tend to resemble each other strangely, so that women and Jews fall together not only in Shakespeare but in the imagination of the Western world as a whole. And this, indeed, is the point of an infamous little critical essay on Chaucer called "Was the Wife of Bath Jewish?" For whatever is excessive in her position, in any case, Emilia pays before the play has ended, being stabbed to death by her husband, which is to say, destroyed by the same Shakespeare who let her speak. But Desdemona also dies, though she has abjured revenge against the reigning sex, responding to the final couplet of Emilia's tirade with a considerably more Christian, though rather obscure, couplet of her own:

> Good night, good night. Heaven me such uses send,
> Not to pick bad from bad, but by bad mend!

And lest we think any male in the play exempt from Emilia's charges, Shakespeare provides us as final evidence the maltreatment of Bianca by the third major male character, Cassio. To be sure, only minor indignities are visited upon her before she exits, dragged off to jail; but the culprit in her case is neither "a villain," nor "an extravagant and wheeling stranger," driven half mad by that villain's devices. He is, rather, one whom the dramatis personae describes as "an honorable lieutenant," and of whom we are clearly intended to approve, even at the point when, playing the man among men with Iago, he describes Bianca's pursuit of him and the teasing lies with which he puts her off. She is, of course, no lady, but, as the cast list makes clear, "a courtesan," a whore in love; which is to say, a joke by definition. Her very name, "Bianca," is an irony, apt enough in a "bloody farce," in which the conventional color symbolism of the age is turned upside down.

Why, then, should not Cassio (who knows all the rules of "honorable" discourse, whom to kiss, whose hand to hold, etc.) mock her to make Iago and his audience laugh. "She was here even now," he begins (and Othello, eavesdropping, takes the "she" to mean his Desdemona rather than Cassio's Bianca). "She haunts me in every place. I was the other day talking on the sea bank with certain Venetians, and thither comes the bauble, and, by this hand, she falls thus about my neck—" At this point, Othello is about to explode in rage and shame, and Cassio can scarcely keep from dissolving into laughter—as if the whole scene were an allegory to make manifest the double possibilities of the double standard, moving toward tragedy and farce even within a single play, a single frame. "So hangs and lolls and weeps upon me, so hales and pulls me! Ha, ha, ha!" Cassio says; and Othello, seeing only his gestures, reinterprets, "Now he tells how she plucked him to my chamber. Oh, I see that nose of yours, but not the dog I shall throw it to."

Yet if by their indignities and deaths, the ladies of *Othello* seem to confirm Emilia's charges against men, by their lives and functions, they seem rather to sustain Iago's view of women. Two out of three women in the play not only prove weak and false but also are cast in roles which reflect the conventional slander of their sex: a shrewish bawd and a foolish whore. And that figure becomes three out of four if we choose to count a ghost called "Barbarie"—an odd name really, being not merely a variant form of "Barbara" but also one-half of Iago's insulting epithet for Othello: "your daughter covered with a Barbary horse." "Barbary," Berber, barbarian—it is a fascinating series, not so much irrelevant as displaced and to be solved, resolved, like some riddling conjunction in a dream. In any case, it is the melancholy-bawdy song of Barbarie, who was her mother's maid, that rises unbidden to Desdemona's lips just before her death.

> I called my love false love, but what said he then?
> Sing willow, willow, willow.
> If I court moe women, you'll couch with moe men.

It is a song, the scholars say, in which the speaker was originally a man; but Shakespeare switched the sex of the "I," feeling the need, apparently, of one more victimized woman reflecting on the riddle of falsity answering falsity in love.

Three out of four, then, weak or treacherous, or both, it is an average sufficient to sustain any statistical truth, which, in fact, all commonplaces are, whether slanderous or not: "La donna è mobile"; "Deceite, wepyng, spynning God hath yive / To wommen kyndely, while that they may lyve"; "Down from the waist they are Centaurs"; "Players in your house-wifery, and housewives in your beds." The Iagos of any age tell not lies but such truths as these, *typical* truths; and, typically, they are believed. But Othello is a play about an untypical woman—the fourth or dozenth or one-thousandth case—a miracle of virtue murdered in her unstained bed by one believing falsely what would have been true the other three or eleven or nine hundred and ninety-nine times.

> She that, being angered, her revenge being nigh,
> Bade her wrong stay and her displeasure fly.
> She that in wisdom never was so frail
> To change the cod's head for the salmon's tail.

Precisely such cases breed the misogynist's second convolution nightmare: that driven mad by his fear of woman's unfaithfulness, he will end by taking revenge on one supremely faithful.

And what moved Shakespeare on to that second convolution—after the relatively simple antifeminism of the *Sonnets* and *Henry VI, Part I* and its subtler qualifications in *The*

Merchant of Venice—seems to have been the tensions created in him by reading Giraldi Cinthio. The mythic implications of the tale Cinthio told were so dissonant with those of his own personal mythology that, attempting to reconcile them, he released in his own deep imagination something different from both, something quite new for him. The essential problem is that in Cinthio's story, the wrong person is black and even, in some sense, a witch. But a male black witch is unassimilable to the symbolic system of Sonnet 144, of which the Othello story seems an implicit parody: "the better angel is a woman right fair, / The worser spirit a man colored ill." To be sure, Othello is not "colored ill" in quite the same sense as the dark lady of the *Sonnets,* being what Shakespeare usually calls a "Moor," sometimes an "Ethiope" or even on occasion a "Negro," though he does not use the two latter words in this play.

But Shakespeare's vocabulary and the assumptions which underlie it are confusing in this regard, and it is, therefore, well to understand from the start that though he occasionally refers to Desdemona as "white" (e.g., "that whiter skin of hers than snow"), for him "fair" rather than "white" is the customary opposite of "black." Moreover, the antithesis of black and fair was not associated in his world, as it has long been in ours, with race, or even with what he calls "tribe"—a term he uses not only for Shylock and the Jews but also, quite puzzlingly, for Iago and his ilk, but never for Othello. Speaking of black and fair, he uses instead either "hue" or "complexion," "complexion" being a technical term out of contemporary psychology, meaning originally the mix or blend of humors in an individual. "Mislike me not for my complexion," we remember the Prince of Morocco saying to Portia in *The Merchant of Venice;* and still inside the same vocabulary, Othello cries to Desdemona, "Turn thy complexion there . . . thou young and rose-lipped cherubim— / Aye, there, look grim as Hell!"

But this means that for Shakespeare "black" does not primarily describe an ethnic distinction (though, of course, Othello is meant to be perceived as an African, thick-lipped as well as dusky-hued), but a difference in hue—and temperament—distinguishing from one another even what we would identify as members of the same white race. For instance, in this very play, it is of blondes and brunettes, not Caucasians and Africans, that Iago is talking to Desdemona when he compares a woman "fair and foolish" with one "black and witty." And it is not of skin or hair color at all that the Duke of Venice is thinking when he tries to reassure Brabantio about his daughter's marriage: "If virtue no delighted beauty lack, / Your son-in-law is more fair than black." In this context, "fair" has primarily a moral significance, being felt as the opposite not of "black," though "black" is itself pejorative to Shakespeare, but of "foul," which means both "ugly" and "vile."

The etymological line of descent is clear, since for Shakespeare's contemporaries blonde equals beautiful, and beautiful equals good. But the philosophical sources of this double equation are more obscure, for though the second is undoubtedly rooted in Platonism, the origins of the first are lost on the misty borders of history, perhaps at the point when fair-haired Saxons first conquered the black-haired Celts. The cult of blondeness, however, is equally strong in Italian poets like Petrarch, suggesting beginnings in remoter regions of mythohistory, when Aryan confronted Minyan, perhaps; or in the contemplation of antinomies older than myth itself, like that of day and night.

In Elizabethan usage, at any rate, "fair" is constantly paired with both "foul" and "black," the two sets of antonyms either blended together or ironically played off against each other, as in the leitmotif of *Macbeth:* "Fair is foul, and foul is fair." In *Othello,* the contrast of "black" and "fair" is so central that we tend not to notice how obsessively the other antithesis also occurs: from the moment in Act I when Brabantio charges

Othello with using "foul charms" (associating that word, as in *Macbeth,* specifically with witchcraft) to the point toward the close of Act V when the Moor, no longer quite believing himself, cries of his wife, "Oh, she was foul!" There is scarcely any character in the play to whose lips the word "foul" does not rise in reference to bad weather, drunkenness, slander, magic, adultery, or murder. And there is scarcely any kind of occasion which fails to prompt it, whether it be as frivolous as Iago's bantering exchange with Desdemona ("There's none so foul, and foolish thereunto, / But does foul pranks which fair and wise ones do") or as sinister as that queasy conversation in which Othello charges Desdemona with unfaithfulness. "Or keep it as a cistern for foul toads. . . . O thou weed, / Who are so lovely fair. . . . Was this fair paper, this most goodly book, / Made to write 'whore' upon?" says Othello; and Desdemona answers:

> No, as I am a Christian.
> If to preserve this vessel for my lord
> From any other foul unlawful touch
> Be not to be a strumpet, I am none.

In light of all this, it would be a mistake to think of *Othello* as trading on the kind of horror at the mating of a black male and a white female commonly felt by, say, American audiences of the late nineteenth and early twentieth centuries. *Othello* may, indeed, end with precisely the scene of erotic black-white murder which has haunted the American mind all the way from *The Klansman* to *Native Son,* but its tonalities are different, since the whole notion of miscegenation had not yet been invented. The seeds are there, perhaps even the first sprouts, but only when fostered by "scientific" anthropology can the miscegenation-madness attain full growth. Iago does his best to encourage such notions, but he has no Darwinian theories of evolution or sets of statistics, whether of skull measurements or intelligence scores, to sustain him when he implies that all Moors are lascivious, or suggests that to couple with the Moor is more like being tupped by a beast than being made love to by a man.

True, he can move old Brabantio to rage and terror by prophesying that if the marriage of his daughter to the "Barbary horse" is recognized, his nephews will neigh to him; but the metaphor of bestialization remains a mere figure of speech. And, in general, his "alehouse" slander of blacks is received with considerably less credulity than his unfavorable clichés about women. He seems to be attended to only when he argues that any marriage with an alien is foredoomed, since a girl ought to marry one "of her own clime, complexion, and degree. . . ." This is, however, though Shakespeare attributes it to a character labeled "villain," the very moral which Cinthio had put into the mouth of Disdemona, foreseeing her own terrible fate: "and much I fear that I shall prove a warning to young girls . . . not to wed a man whom nature and habitude of life estrange from us."

The blackness of Othello is, in short, primarily symbolic, signifying not that he is of a lesser breed, but rather one at the furthest possible cultural remove from the girl he loves and who loves him. It is no real surprise, therefore, to discover that Othello was not ethnically "black" at all in the sources from which Cinthio drew his story, which is to say, in the non-mythicized events which lay behind both his account and Shakespeare's. According to them, the deceived and desperate murderer of the most forgiving and virtuous of wives was no displaced African, but an Italian nobleman called "Il Moro," which is to say, "the blackberry," or "the mulberry," because that fruit was inscribed on his coat of arms. It is no mere mistake, however, but the mythmaking instinct of the popular audience which demanded that the destroyer of the most elegant of Patient Griseldas appear in blackface (and she in white, her pallor as much a mask as his swarthiness) in order that they seem as unlike as possible.

Othello is, in fact, the sole one of Shakespeare's strangers to be labeled by that name: "an extravagant and wheeling stranger." And as the epithet makes clear, he is portrayed as forever homeless, uprooted, and on the move, incapable—or at least so his enemies contend—of ever being naturalized. But to Desdemona that is the source of his appeal, lending him the charm of a god come from another world. And, indeed, to her, as to Shakespeare's audience, Africa was a realm as mysterious as Olympus or Hades, a place "of antres vast and deserts idle, / Rough quarries, rocks, and hills whose heads touch heaven. . . . And of the cannibals that each other eat, / The anthropophagi, and men whose heads / Do grow beneath their shoulders."

Moreover, Desdemona dreams, or rather Shakespeare dreams through her, a symbolic marriage of all that Europe and Africa mythically mean: civilization and barbarism, courtesy and strength, belonging and freedom, Beauty and the Beast; or, in classical terms, Diane and Ares, which is to say, the virgin and the warrior, the absolute poles of masculinity and femininity. So long as the marriage holds, it signifies a miracle, a *discordia concors* in the flesh. And when it fails, it represents, by the same token, the eternal impossibility of the union that man eternally dreams: the reuniting of the original bisexual self, sundered by the wrath of the gods (as in the myth Plato attributes in the *Symposium* to Aristophanes). This mystery none of the official critics or scholars of Shakespeare has understood as well as the American poet and novelist John Peale Bishop, who wea es the image that embodies it into his own work early and late, culminating in a novel called, aptly enough, *Act of Darkness.*

His first explicit reference to it, however, appears in an earlier novel, *The Huntsmen Are Up in America,* whose protagonist is named "Brakespeare." Describing the city of Venice, Bishop writes, as if by the way, "it was only there, I am sure, that the ceremony could have been found that would have wed Desdemona to her black Moor." And he glosses that seemingly casual metaphor in a poem entitled "Speaking of Poetry."

> The ceremony must be found
> that will wed Desdemona to the huge Moor.
> It is not enough—
> to win the approval of the Senator. . . .
> For then,
> though she may pant again in his black arms
> (his weight as resilient as a Barbary stallion's)
> she will be found
> When the ambassadors of the Venetian state arrive
> again smothered. . . .
> (Tupping is still tupping
> though that particular word is obsolete. . . .)

The allegorical meanings are clear enough: elegance must be married to force, the mind to the body—*married,* not merely yielded up to the kind of unceremonious possession which turns inevitably to destruction. It is ritual, "ceremony," which makes of passionate attraction a true marriage as it makes of passionate perception a true poem; which is to say, the marriage of Desdemona and Othello becomes for Bishop a metaphor for the poetic act itself. Shakespeare, however, seems to have gone further, beyond the aesthetic to the religious; or such at least is the suggestion of "The Phoenix and the Turtle," which can be read as his gloss on the theme:

> So they loved, as love in twain
> Had the essence both in one;
> Two distincts, division none.
> Number there in love was slain. . . .
>
> Property was thus appalled,
> That the self was not the same;
> Single nature's double name
> Neither two nor one was called.

Reason, in itself confounded,
Saw division grow together,
To themselves yet either neither,
Simple were so well compounded. . . .

But what a fantastic notion to turn the Phoenix on her "sole Arabian tree" into a "supersubtle Venetian," and the loyal turtledove into a black and "erring" barbarian. Surely, nothing in Shakespeare's earlier work has prepared us for so extravagant an idealization of a woman, much less of a Moor; and we end by suspecting that, consciously or not, he loaded the deck against himself in *Othello,* wanting to lose the wager whose stakes are, as the Moor himself declares, no less than life and death. Yet the theme is not altogether new in his work, since—unlike Jews and New World savages, each of whom appeared once only in the plays—Moors appear and reappear. And almost always, they are linked by love or lust to white partners.

Before Othello, Shakespeare had already invented four black African characters, two speaking and two, as it were, dumb; and after that play, he is (as we shall see) to invent a fifth, though he will keep him offstage. The first is a kind of Iago in blackface, who, in *Titus Andronicus,* begets on a white-skinned witch the second, a black baby who betrays their secret union. The third is the unsuccessful Moorish suitor of Portia in *The Merchant of Venice,* which also contains the fourth, a Moorish girl whom Launcelot Gobbo has presumably gotten pregnant, and whom Shakespeare disposes of in five lines and one bad pun. The fifth is the King of Tunis, to whom Claribel, daughter of the King of Naples, has been married before the action of *The Tempest* begins.

But it is with Aaron, the Moor of *Titus Andronicus,* that we must begin, if we would understand how long a way Shakespeare had to come before he could portray the black stranger sympathetically and from the inside; for Aaron represents the dark side of his ambivalence, which remained uppermost in his treatment of witches and Jews, but which in the topsy-turvy play of *Othello* is driven underground. Indeed, in the earlier play, any impulse which mitigates horror is resisted; for the genre to which it belongs is precisely a kind of horror-pornography brought to the stage of the time by certain academic bohemians, who found models for it in the surrealist closet drama of the Roman playwright Seneca.

His plays they had first read in the universities, and Senecan tragedy tends to smack therefore of what is called these days "camp," an attitude always congenial to students, involving as it does a kind of condescension to both the subject matter and the audience, combined with a relish in the self-indulgence that condescension makes possible. It is, in fact, precisely the sort of "bloody farce" which Rymer found unpalatable even as adapted and modified by Shakespeare in *Othello*. Yet Elizabethan playgoers apparently loved it—titillated by the tabooed fantasies it released of rape and murder, mayhem and bloody revenge, and troubled not a bit by its tongue-in-cheek tone. And like them, Shakespeare took it all quite seriously; unlike Marlowe or Greene or Kyd, he was not a university dropout, and so writing for the London theater represented to him social climbing rather than cultural slumming.

When he turns, therefore, to the Senecan form in *Titus Andronicus,* he loads the play with allusions to and quotations (some in the original) from Vergil and Horace and Ovid, as if to prove himself the cultural equal of his ex-academic colleagues—and in the process loses all possibility of ironic detachment. In *Titus Andronicus,* then, "camp" is replaced by obsession; which is to say, its author seems less the manipulator of someone else's nightmare than the victim of his own Indeed, once past the show of classical learning, we become aware that in this earliest of his tragedies, Shakespeare has already been possessed by the themes and plot configurations which he will not be able to exorcise until almost the end of his career.

The specifics of that terror, Aaron, who functions as a chorus as well as an actor from start to close, recapitulates in Act V.

> For I must talk of murders, rapes, and massacres,
> Acts of black night, abominable deeds,
> Complots of mischief, treason, villainies,
> Ruthful to hear, yet piteously performed. . . .

Aaron is, however, by no means directly responsible for most of the horrors he recounts, only, somehow, *symbolic* of them all, an embodiment of the psychic blackness they figure forth, as if the play were not merely one more projection upon blacks of intolerable white guilt, but an analysis of the mechanism itself. Certainly he is labeled with almost every opprobrious name invented by terrified whites for black Africans: "incarnate devil," "coal-black Moor," "wall-eyed slave," "black dog," "this barbarous Moor, / This ravenous tiger, this accursèd devil," "inhuman dog," "unhallowed slave," "misbelieving Moor."

"Devil," "dog," and "slave": these are, after "black" itself, the chief epithets on which the revilers of Aaron ring changes. And we realize that, though "black" and "slave" are specifically reserved for "thick-lipped" Moors, "dog" and "devil" are mythic insults also applicable, as in *The Merchant of Venice,* to Jews. Aaron's very name, of course, connects him with Jewish tradition; and like the tribe of Shylock, but unlike Othello and the Prince of Morocco, he is even described as "misbelieving" and "irreligious," an enemy of the True God. Yet here, of course, Shakespeare gets into trouble, having no true believers to set against the pagan, only Titus and his sons, who are also pagans, though Roman, as, indeed, he seems sometimes to forget, permitting, for instance, a clown entering the scene to swear by "Saint Stephen," first Christian martyr to the Jews.

It is, at any rate, the blasphemous black man from the "antres vast and deserts idle" of godless Africa whom Shakespeare intends Aaron to represent—thus suiting the expectations of an audience to whom Moors seemed creatures more diabolical than human—the enemies of Christendom. And it is thus that Aaron, with a candor verging on burlesque, speaks of himself.

> Let fools do good, and fair men call for grace;
> Aaron will have his soul black like his face.

As a matter of fact, Aaron describes himself in such stereotypical terms over and over, until he comes to seem more an allegorical figure in a speaking pageant than the real antagonist of a tragedy. At the point where his villainy is first found out, for example, he seems tempted momentarily to seek refuge in stony silence, like Iago at a similar moment in *Othello;* but he cannot resist proclaiming his vocation for evil.

> Even now I curse the day—and yet, I think,
> Few come within the compass of my curse—
> Wherein I did not some notorious ill:
> As kill a man, or else devise his death;
> Ravish a maid, or plot the way to do it;
> Accuse some innocent, and forswear myself;
> Set deadly enmity between two friends;
> Make poor men's cattle break their necks;
> Set fire on barns and haystacks in the night,
> And bid the owners quench them with their tears.

And lest we forget, he is given one more sacrilegious speech before being buried waist deep in the earth and left to starve.

> Oh, why should wrath be mute, and fury dumb?
> I am no baby, I, that with base prayers

I should repent the evils I have done.
Ten thousand worse than ever yet I did
Would I perform if I might have my will.
If one good deed in all my life I did,
I do repent it from my very soul.

Actually, we see him do few of the fell deeds of which he boasts, though he does stab an old Nurse to death on stage, crying "Weeke, weeke!" in mocking imitation of a stuck pig. And we watch him trick Titus Andronicus into allowing him to chop off his own hand in the vain hope of saving his sons, whose heads are sent back in grim recompense. Aaron, however, commits no crime which equals in horror Titus's own final atrocity of feeding to a mother pasties made of the blood and bones of her two sons, who had earlier raped his daughter. And yet Titus is portrayed finally not as a villain, but as an equivocal figure, essentially noble, though excessive in his rage and more than half mad by the end—one, in any event, more deserving of pity than revulsion. Aaron, however, remains a villain unqualified, since his evil is established more in speech than action, by the role he plays rather than the atrocities he commits.

Most disconcerting to the modern reader in this regard is his peripheral connection with the crime that constitutes the heart of the play's fantasy: the rape and mutilation of Titus Andronicus's chaste daughter, Lavinia, for which Shakespeare had found the model in Ovid's tale of Philomela and Tereus. In our tradition, the black has been the rapist par excellence for a century or more; and to demote him from sexual aggressor to mere sideline plotter and egger-on seems to deprive him of his mythic potency. Moreover, Aaron is neither, like Othello, too old for lust nor, like the Prince of Morocco, too dignified. He is introduced into the play, in fact, as the lover of the captured Queen of the Goths, Tamora; and in his own catalogue of horrors he has helped perpetrate, he lists rape in second place: "murders, rapes, and massacres," which in the specification which follows becomes "ravish a maid."

But the rape around which this play revolves is actually performed by Demetrius and Chiron, the two sons of Tamora, herself the second stranger in the classic world: a witch-mother from across the Alps, who seems another version of Queen Margaret, the "banning hag" of Shakespeare's first tetralogy. Like Margaret, she marries the ruler of the land that has conquered her own, whom she then betrays, bringing into the imperial household the twin horrors of adultery and cuckoldry and into the state treason and dissension. This time, however, to make matters worse, the adulterous queen couples with no compatriot of her royal husband, or even her own; but with a "slave," the color of whose skin makes manifest the blackness of both their hearts and of the lust that links them. It is the only bond, the play suggests, which can possibly join black and white, and one which must bring destruction as a consequence. Yet in her plot to avenge on Titus Andronicus the death of her son at Roman hands, she uses not her Moorish paramour but that dead white boy's two surviving white brothers, who rape Titus's daughter on the decapitated body of her lover, then cut out her tongue and lop off her hands to forestall disclosure.

Aaron, in his desire to seem the world's sole bugaboo, tries hard to claim a share in that rape, boasting:

> Indeed, I was their tutor to instruct them.
> That codding spirit had they from their mother,
> As sure a card as ever won the set.
> That bloody mind, I think, they learned of me,
> As true a dog as ever fought at head.

But it will not work. Shakespeare may even have been aware that something in his audience's imagination, of which we moderns are the troubled heirs, demanded that the rapist be the "coal-black Moor"; but his own deep fantasy insisted that the deed of darkness be done by those spoiled sons of the witch, from whom descend all the later would-be rapists of the pure daughter, like Caliban in *The Tempest* and Cloten in *Cymbeline.* Cloten, in fact, plans, precisely like Demetrius and Chiron, to ravish Imogen on her lover's "trunk," but ends himself a headless corpse, whom she, mistaking for that lover, embraces. Such ironies, however, are beyond Shakespeare's range in *Titus Andronicus,* in which the daughter is first ravished, then revenged, and finally killed in honor's name by her father—but not before she has held in her unhealed stumps a basin to catch the blood of her ravishers.

Aaron's end is quite different, however, from that of those white ravishers, being cued not by the disclosure of his small part in Lavinia's violation, but by the birth to his royal mistress of a "coal-black calf," a baby whose color declares it undeniably his. Despite the orders of its ruthless mother ("christen it with thy dagger's point"), he decides to save the child, thus betraying a humanity he has hitherto concealed and which presumably could only function in relation to one as black as he. But fleeing with the baby, he is captured and persuaded to talk in order to save its life once more, though talking, he knows, will mean his own death. It is a risky venture, at best, in which much is certain to be lost and nothing sure to be won, which may explain the special bitterness of his final words.

Somewhat earlier, however, he had been moved to strike a rather different note in a speech reflecting not the paranoia about blacks which Shakespeare shared with the pit, but that strange sympathy for strangers, which, coming unbidden and unforeseen, had once lent eloquence to Joan and Shylock. "Stay, murderous villains!" Aaron says to Demetrius and Chiron, who stand ready to "broach the tadpole" on their swords. "Will you kill your brother?" Then he launches into a praise of being black. He has already signaled the theme in his reproach to the Nurse who had brought him the child, presumably to be killed, crying, " 'Zounds, ye whore! Is black so base a hue?" But this time he launches into a full-scale defense of his "complexion":

> What, what, ye sanguine, shallow-hearted boys!
> Ye white-limed walls! Ye alehouse painted signs!
> Coal-black is better than another hue
> In that it scorns to bear another hue;
> For all the water in the ocean
> Can never turn the swan's black legs to white,
> Although she lave them hourly in the flood.

With this, we have moved within striking distance of Morocco's plea, "Mislike me not for my complexion," though his tone is modulated by the courtesy appropriate to a black suitor wooing a white bride, rather than inflamed by the proud resentment of a black father whose white mistress has borne a child black like him.

> Bring me the fairest creature northward born,
> Where Phoebus' fire scare thaws the icicles,
> And let us make incision for your love,
> To prove whose blood is reddest, his or mine.
> I tell thee, lady, this aspéct of mine
> Hath feared the valiant. By my love, I swear
> The best-regarded virgins of our clime
> Have loved it too. I would not change this hue,
> Except to steal your thoughts, my gentle Queen.

Before he is through, however, Morocco has begun to sound even more like his black successor than his predecessor, especially toward the conclusion of his second speech, where in a few lines he manages to suggest the whole range of Othello's rhetoric: the immense dignity, verging on stuffiness; the taste for bombast and exotic place names; the underlying pathos, slipping over into self-pity.

By this scimitar
That slew the Sophy and a Persian prince,
That won three fields of Sultan Solyman,
I would outstare the sternest eyes that look,
Outbrave the heart most daring on the earth,
Pluck the young sucking cubs from the she-bear,
Yea, mock the lion when he roars for prey,
To win thee, lady. But, alas the while!
If Hercules and Lichas play at dice
Which is the better man, the greater throw
May turn by fortune from the weaker hand.

Othello, however, makes no full-scale apology for his blackness ever—either in the voice of the courtier or the Machiavel. Though Iago, Roderigo, and Brabantio cry through the streets of Venice and before its highest tribunal insults to his "hue" as vile as any howled at Aaron by his enemies, the Moor ignores them completely, confining himself in rebuttal to denying the charges of witchcraft which have been leveled against him. And of all the self-doubts which plague him later on, when he is convinced that Desdemona has played him false with Michael Cassio, the suspicion that his "complexion" may have foredoomed the match occurs to him only in passing.

Haply, for I am black
And have not those soft parts of conversation
That chamberers have, or for I am declined
Into the vale of years—yet that's not much—
She's gone. . . .

Almost immediately, he passes from considerations of color to the problem of manners, and then to the disparity of age, which apparently troubles him more; for, unlike Aaron or Morocco, he seems most often to consider himself what the Duke has declared him, "far more fair than black." Indeed, he uses the epithet "black" as a pejorative almost as detachedly as if he were himself white, speaking not only generally of "black Vengeance" but even in specific reference to himself, as when he says of his wife, "Her name, that was as fresh / As Dian's visage, is now begrimed and black / As mine own face." Mythologically speaking, Othello is really black only before we see him; after his first appearance, he is archetypally white, though a stranger still, as long as he remains in Venice: a white stranger in blackface.

With the move to Cyprus, however, everything changes once more; for Cyprus is a strange, almost magical island, an anti-Venice, less like the idyllic Belmont of *The Merchant of Venice* than the Ephesus of *The Comedy of Errors*. There black is white and white is black, and the marriage sheets become a shroud, as the act of love is transformed into murder. Cyprus is, however, inhabited by no "dark-working sorcerers that change the mind" or "soul-killing witches that deform the body," only by soldiers and whores, an occupying force and its camp followers. Its sole evil genius arrives with the same fleet that brings its governor and his new bride, but Iago works, as he has boasted, "by wit and not by witchcraft. . . ." Nonetheless, Cyprus remains a place in which all the proverbial antinomies are confused: a "fair island" to which certain Venetians are carried by a "foul and violent tempest," which "hath so banged the Turks / That their designment halts" and threatened war becomes unforeseen peace.

"If after every tempest come such calms," Othello says, taking his "fair warrior" in his arms, "may the winds blow till they have wakened death!" Scarcely has he settled into his bridal bed, however, when "foul rout" shatters the peace of the "fair island," turning night into day, as Venetian fights Venetian senselessly. "Are we turned Turks," Othello cries, disturbed by the "monstrous" transmogrifications around him, "and to ourselves do that / Which Heaven hath forbid the Ottomites?" Quite as on the lonely heath of *Macbeth*, "fair is foul, and foul is fair" in Cyprus, though the symbol of confusion this time is not the witches' cauldron but the soldier's flagon.

In Shakespeare, however, these two symbols are everywhere associated with each other, and both with lust—witchcraft and drunkenness and unbridled passion being to him interchangeable metaphors for the process of downward transformation which makes Turks of Christians and animals of men. "Oh God," cries Cassio, the only drunk in Shakespeare who is not a clown or villain, "that men should put an enemy in their mouths to steal away their brains! That we should, with joy, pleasance, revel, and applause, transform ourselves into beasts!" And the identification of the "invisible spirit of wine" with the figure of the archetypal witch, Circe, is clear. So, too, is the identification of drunkenness and female evil in *Macbeth,* in which, just before the patricidal murder of the King, Lady Macbeth cries to her dilatory husband, "Was the hope drunk? / Wherein you dressed yourself? Hath it slept since? / And wakes it now, to look so green and pale. . . ." And when, a moment later, she has moved on to the actual planning of the deed, it is wine she chooses as her weapon, leaving the knife to be wielded by her husband.

—his two chamberlains
Will I with wine and wassail so convince
That memory, the warder of the brain,
Shall be a fume, and the receipt of reason
A limbec only. When in swinish sleep
Their drenchèd natures lie as in a death,
What cannot you and I perform. . . .

And with the phrase "swinish sleep," we are back on Circe's magical isle.

But this is not the end, for having worked her enchantment on the "sleepy grooms," she moves front stage to boast: "That which hath made them drunk hath made me bold, / What hath quenched them hath given me fire." And though she talks of wine no more thereafter, water instead becoming the theme between her and her shattered husband, the topic is taken up by the Porter in the famous scene of the knocking at the gate, which only in this context can be really understood. For a little while, it seems, in fact, as if Shakespeare has shaken off the hysteria stirred in him by the thought of drink in the period of the tragedies and is returning to the blither mood in which he created such hilarious and sympathetic drunks as Sir Toby Belch and Falstaff. But Falstaff is dead, alas; and though he may lie, as the Hostess asserts, in "Arthur's bosom," the Porter who rises in his place speaks from within the gates of hell; so that his quips, however funny, smack of death and damnation. "And drink, sir, is a great provoker of three things. . . . Marry, sir, nose-painting, sleep, and urine. Lechery, sir, it provokes and unprovokes. It provokes the desire, but it takes away the performance. Therefore much drink may be said to be an equivocator. . . ."

Cassio, on the other hand, is not funny at all, becoming sloppily religious when under the influence and solemnly reciting antialcoholic platitudes when sobering up. "Every inordinate cup is unblest, and the ingredient is a devil." To this, Iago responds, as is his wont, with counter-commonplaces. "Come, come, good wine is a good familiar creature, if it be well used. Exclaim no more against it. . . . You or any man living may be drunk at some time, man." Yet in this play, only Cassio is shown really drunk; and, indeed, his drunkenness marks the beginning of the catastrophe. Being cashiered as a result, he turns to Iago, who suggests he work on Othello through Desdemona, since, he assures him, "Our General's wife is now the General." But this feeds Othello's paranoid fantasies, thus releasing the second "devil" of Cyprus: "the green-eyed monster which doth mock / The meat it feeds on," and turning one "not easily jealous" into a near maniac, who, rising from an epileptic "ecstasy," shouts at his suspected wife, "I am glad to see you mad." What he means, apparently, but cannot otherwise confess, is: I am mad to see you glad; and as if to prove it, he slaps her face in the presence of a visiting Venetian dignitary, her father's kinsman.

The downward transformation of Cassio on Cyprus is not so spectacular, perhaps, but quite as drastic; for he becomes an affected maker of exaggerated compliments, a snatcher of kisses a shade more ardent than courtesy allows, a mocker at fond and foolish women, and of course, a bad drunk, first boastful, then violent, and at last maudlin. What he was before we can only surmise from the fact that Othello had preferred him for a lieutenancy to begin with, and that, at the play's end, the Senators of Venice have appointed him governor in Othello's place. We see almost nothing of him in Act I, in which he serves only as a messenger between the Moor and the Senate; and he seems (or acts?) totally ignorant of the connection between Othello and Desdemona, asking "To who?" when Iago tells him the Moor is married. Later, however, we learn from Desdemona that Cassio had actually come "a-wooing" with his general, even defending him against her playful attacks. Shakespeare seems, as a matter of fact, more than a little uncertain about just who Michael Cassio is, speaking of him on various occasions as if he were a Florentine, a Venetian, and a Veronese; and seeming to change his mind about whether or not he is, like his prototype in Cinthio, married.

The first reference to him is by Iago, who speaks of "Michael Cassio, a Florentine, / a fellow almost damned in a fair wife"; but clearly he is intended to be a bachelor when he reappears on Cyprus. The phrase is, however, fascinating in its own right, since it represents the initial use of the key word "fair" in a play, for which it would, indeed, provide an apt epigraph, if we took it to refer to Othello rather than Cassio. Certainly, it has long troubled the commentators, though perhaps it can be read—wrenching the syntax only a little—as meaning almost damned by a weakness for other men's fair wives. And in that case, Iago's later description of Cassio as one ". . . framed to make women false" could serve as a gloss upon it.

He should, in any event, be played with a touch of irony, for he is a shade too familiar with Emilia, a shade too courtly with Desdemona, and much too cold-blooded in his trifling with Bianca to seem wholly sympathetic, however unfairly he is treated by Othello. And when, totally under the influence, he insists to Iago that in heaven itself he will outrank him still ("Aye, but, by your leave. . . . the Lieutenant is to be saved before the Ancient"), we are tempted momentarily to side with the snubbed villain. Indeed, it even seems possible that though Cassio's line of descent runs back through Bassanio all the way to the young man of the *Sonnets,* this time Shakespeare himself is a little wary of his professional charm. Certainly he bestows on him no happy ending except a better job, but this his sources and the tragic form had predetermined, leaving no suitable woman alive at the action's end.

Even as Cassio is degraded, Desdemona is redeemed on Cyprus, purged of all the equivocal witchlike qualities she still seems in Act I to share with Portia and their common ancestress, Medea. True, we learn on Cyprus of her father's death, for which in some sense she is responsible. But the sting is gone, since by the time his brother, Gratiano, announces, "thy father's dead. / Thy match was mortal to him, and pure grief / Shore his old thread in twain," she herself has been murdered. He speaks in fact to a corpse (which is to say, to one who has made amends for everything), saying:

> I am glad thy father's dead. . . .
> Did he live now,
> This sight would make him do a desperate turn—
> Yea, curse his better angel from his side,
> And fall to reprobation.

Moreover, even on Cyprus, Desdemona is plagued by the minor vice of telling under pressure not lies exactly, but something less than the whole troubling truth. Yet only the whole truth might have saved her and Othello at the moment when, asked about her missing handkerchief, she stutters and equivocates.

> OTH: Is 't lost? Is 't gone? Speak, is it out o' the way?
> DES: Heaven bless us!
> OTH: Say you?
> DES: It is not lost, but what an if it were?
> OTH: How!
> DES: I say it is not lost.
> OTH: Fetch 't, let me see it.
> DES: Why, so I can, sir, but I will not now. . . .

And she continues to lie still to the very end of her life, though at that point she lies only in order to exculpate her husband, for his sake.

She seems, finally, the very embodiment of the female lie or, rather, of the lie men lie to themselves about the female. And her transformation from witch to forgiving victim is motivated by no probabilities of the waking world, only by the exigencies of Shakespeare's dream, in which the women whom men destroy, on the verge of their deaths, declare the men guiltless, white not black. Emilia falls out of that dream, to be sure, exposing, even before the thrust that kills her, both her husband and Desdemona's, calling Othello a "blacker devil." But not so Desdemona, who, rising from the dead, as it were, declares first that "Nobody," then that she herself has "done this deed." And only on that lovely lie will Shakespeare let her die a second, final death, with the words: "Commend me to my kind lord. Oh, farewell!"

If we find such deathbed humility insufferable rather than moving, it is not only because the notion of the all-forgiving woman has come to seem an offense to the dignity of that sex but also because we sense that it implies as well a diminution, a symbolic castration of the male. Certainly, this seems the case with Othello, who has been deprived, at the play's conclusion, of all the masculinity his mythic Moorishness implied: not only the nightmare terror of blackness exploited by Iago and the exotic glamor for which Desdemona first loved him but even the repressed savagery released by his jealousy. All, all has been exorcised and bleached away by Iago's active malice and Desdemona's passive love. What remains—the impotent dignity and desperate pride, along with a certain obdurate simplicity—make him seem a Morocco who has, in fact, changed his hue to steal the thoughts of his white "gentle Queen," rather than an unrepented "coal-black" Aaron. He has become, in short, *colorless:* a provincial gentleman-warrior, a downright English soldier fallen among foreigners; which means that he no longer functions archetypally even as a stranger, much less a black.

It is those around him who have become, in a complementary reversal of roles, such strangers as Italians seemed to Elizabethan Englishmen. Shakespeare, however, does not here use that ethnic label pejoratively, as he will later in *Cymbeline* to distinguish Iachimo, "slight thing of Italy," from the virtuous Romans around him. Iago may, indeed, be the prototype of that later villain; but Shakespeare seems to have felt the need in his case for an implicit comparison with strangers even more remote and menacing. "Spartan dog," he calls him at one point; but, more typically, "dog" unqualified, along with "devil" and "damnèd villain," quite as if he were another Shylock. Moreover, he has Iago twice refer to his "tribe": identified the first time as "all the tribe of Hell," but left unspecified the second, when he says, "Good Heaven, the souls of all my tribe defend. . . ." And in the phrase, we hear the very accents of the archetypal Jew, as is appropriate, after all, to one whose name is the Italian equivalent of Jacob, later called "Israel," the "supplanter" who became the "contender with God."

Moreover, Iago is also called repeatedly, as the play moves toward its end, a slave: "damnèd slave," "oh, cursèd slave," "damnèd slave," "this slave." But "slave" is, we remember, the epithet especially associated with Aaron the Moor, who is addressed contemptuously as a "wall-eyed slave," and himself refers to his child, in affectionate deprecation, as a "thick-lipped slave." It is an insult attached in Shakespeare's mind specifically to blacks. "Bondslaves and pagans shall our statesmen be," Brabantio howls in rage. The reference, of course, is to Othello before he is officially declared "fair" by the head of state. And, indeed, he *had* actually been a slave, as he reminds us rehearsing the tales with which he first won Desdemona's love. "Wherein I spake of most disastrous chances . . . Of being taken by the insolent foe / And sold to slavery. . . ."

Iago, has, in short, become, before *Othello* is over, anything signified for Shakespeare at the beginning of his career by the word "Moor." Rejected, the fool first turns "foul," making explicit the implicit pun, then becomes the other antonym of "fair," which is to say, black. Meanwhile, the black prince has turned first "fair," then, in an unforeseen reversal, has become the fool. "Oh, murderous coxcomb!" Emilia cries at the moment of their mutual transformation, "What should such a fool / Do with so good a wife?" And though there is some ambiguity, surely it is Othello she addresses, not Iago; for Othello bestows that epithet on himself thrice over before he is done, "O fool! Fool! Fool!"

It should be possible, then, to mount a production of the play in which Othello would be acted by a white man in a black mask and Iago by a black in a white one so that in the final scene they can unmask (perhaps at the moment that Iago turns to silence) and reveal the reversal of their mythic roles by showing their "true colors." Best of all, however, might be for them to exchange masks at this juncture, showing the audience, in the brief interval when both faces are bare, that they are the same man—black or white, as contemporary fashion demands, it scarcely matters. To do this properly would probably require a shift from stage to screen; in which case, indeed, masks might be dispensed with entirely, the two characters, played by the same actor, appearing instead in circus make-up, the grotesque blackface and whiteface appropriate to a pair of clowns. And those faces would bleach and darken respectively scene by scene, almost frame by frame, so that somewhere toward the end of the third act, perhaps, they would for an instant be the same "hue."

At any rate, Iago must be, for the play to have its full impact, quite black—masked black, painted black, or merely acted black—at the point when Othello, trying twice to kill him, is twice disarmed. Thus it would be made clear that though his first vain attempt leaves Othello feeling impotent, it also brings him the beginnings of self-recognition. "I am not valiant neither," he says to the dying Emilia, with whom, for some dream reason, he is left alone on stage, "but every puny whipster gets my sword. / But why should honor outlive honesty? / Let it go all."

Not, however, until he has tried the second time—Iago and the whole group of Venetians returning quite as mysteriously as they have left—does Othello fully understand the reasons for his failure. "I look down toward his feet," he says of Iago, "but that's a fable. / If that thou be'st a devil, I cannot kill thee." And though Iago has no cloven hoof, as in the "fable," he proves in some sense a genuine devil, since he will not fall to Othello's sword. "I bleed, sir," he cries, "but not killed." And now, at last, Othello must be aware that to kill Iago he has to kill himself; for he cannot destroy the blackness at the center of his own soul by striking at its shadow projection.

Yet for a little while he dissimulates, talking not about

suicide but precisely about that "honor" which he is presumably now willing to let go: "An honorable murderer, if you will, / For naught did I hate, but all in honor." The reversion is, perhaps, inevitable after the death of Emilia, because with her, the last representation of the female principle has vanished from the stage. Othello, therefore, must make his final gesture in a world of men without women, among soldiers and politicians to whom "honor," "good name," and "reputation" are the highest values. It is an impressive group, indeed, which has gathered for the final unmasking, the living embodiment of the patriarchal principle: three governors of Cyprus (Othello being flanked by Montano, his predecessor, and Cassio, who is to succeed him) plus those two surrogates for Desdemona's father, Gratiano and Lodovico. And behind them stands the power of the state, represented by a band of nameless "Officers"; while in their midst, their shadow and scapegoat dumbly awaits his sentencing.

It is a world whose central symbol is the sword, the phallic significance of which Shakespeare takes pains to make clear. "Behold, I have a weapon," Othello says just before his second disarming. "A better never did itself sustain / Upon a soldier's thigh." It is presumably his last weapon, so that when it in turn is taken, his guards relax their vigilance. But with a third, concealed until that moment God knows where, Othello kills himself. "This did I fear," Cassio comments after the fact, "but thought he had no weapon." And this, indeed, Othello himself must have believed, until knowing himself his own dearest enemy, his potency was magically restored, though only long enough for him to die and, dying, kiss the cold lips of a corpse. "To die upon a kiss," he says, oddly reechoing the last words of Romeo ("Thus with a kiss I die") and evoking the pun, which Shakespeare so much loved, on "die" meaning "come" as well as "go."

What stays in our minds, however, is not Othello's closing

erotic couplet, but the longer speech framed between it and the despairing cry of "O fool! Fool! Fool!"—a speech whose central images come from politics and war. "I have done the state some service, and they know 't," the Moor begins, as if, after all, he has learned nothing, understood nothing. And when he goes on to speak of himself as "one that loved not wisely but too well. . . ." his obtuseness seems too much to bear. But the opening platitudes are overwhelmed by deeper mythic material, as he seeks in a final burst of grandiloquence to project everything he wants to kill in himself upon the ultimate enemy, the total stranger. Predictably enough, he does not allude at all to his own actual "complexion," having forgotten (along with us) that he was ever a Moor, and identifying himself instead with the common foe, whom, cheated by the fair-foul tempest, he had not encountered: the Turk.

And say besides that in Aleppo once,
Where a malignant and turbaned Turk
Beat a Venetian and traduced the state,
I took by the throat the circumcisèd dog
And smote him, thus.

In these final lines, however, the figure of the Turk, whom he impales upon his sword in stabbing himself, begins almost imperceptibly to fade into that other alien archetype, the Jew. "Circumcisèd dog," though obviously applicable enough to a Moslem, is ambiguous at least, reminding us also of Shylock, who in Abraham's name sought to impose his "merry bond." Moreover, the shadow of the Jew has already fallen across Othello's final speech at an earlier point, when, speaking of his own failure to appreciate Desdemona's true worth, he refers to himself as "one whose hand, / Like the base Judean, threw a pearl away / Richer than all his tribe. . . ." And here the Jewish stranger with whom he identifies himself is not Father

Abraham but Judas, thus seeming to equate the "pearl" if not with Christ himself, whom that Jew betrayed, at least with salvation in the abstract.

Since that "pearl" is also Desdemona, however, we are left finally with a mythological equation unprecedented in Shakespeare. The metamorphosis of golden girl to pearl-pale maiden was difficult enough to accept in terms of his usual practice, but the further transformation of that pearl-pale maiden into the Pearl of Great Price seems unresolvably alien. It implies, in fact, the belief that love for a good woman saves, but that her rejection damns; and such romantic theology seems more appropriate to the mid-eighteenth or the early thirteenth centuries than to the seventeenth, to Dante's time or Samuel Richardson's, not Shakespeare's.

Perhaps we should, therefore, abandon the misleading text of the First Folio and read "Indian" for "Judean," following the First Quarto instead: "Like the base Indian, threw a pearl away / Richer than all his tribe. . . ." By the time *Othello* was written, the first English explorations of the New World had already occurred, and the audiences had learned to associate the word "tribe" not only with Jews but with those red men whose contempt for gold and precious stones had already become proverbial. Such a reading will, at any rate, deliver us from the necessity of interpreting Desdemona as a kind of belated Beatrice or pre-Pamela, in contempt of Shakespeare's deepest mythological bias, and will leave us looking forward to his concern with the New World savage ("a born devil, on whose nature / Nurture can never stick. . . ."), perceptible here and there in *Pericles* and *Henry VIII* and at the very center of *The Tempest*.

SONNET 146

Poor soul, the center of my sinful earth,
Feed not these rebel powers that thee array,
Why dost thou pine within and suffer dearth,
Painting thy outward walls so costly gay?
Why so large cost, having so short a lease,
Dost thou upon thy fading mansion spend?
Shall worms, inheritors of this excess,
Eat up thy charge? Is this thy body's end?
Then, soul, live thou upon thy servant's loss,
And let that pine to aggravate thy store.
Buy terms divine in selling hours of dross,
Within be fed, without be rich no more.
  So shalt thou feed on Death, that feeds on men,
  And Death once dead, there's no more dying then.

IV

The New World Savage as Stranger: or “ ’Tis new to thee.”

If *Othello* disconcerts by suggesting at its very end a mythological equivalence of Indian and Jew, *The Tempest* even more disconcertingly begins proposing a similar equivalence of Indian and African. Throughout that play, in fact, Shakespeare exploits the archetypal ambiguity of the New World and ancient Carthage as alternative versions of a polar strangeness, which Europe has kept redefining for nearly two millennia in order to know itself. Twice over we are told that the voyage whose second and unintended landfall was a "brave new world" had made its first, quite intentionally, in the city where Aeneas had, at a god's behest, abandoned the "Widow Dido." And the spokesman both times is the garrulous old councilor, Gonzalo, who, summing up the play's action in its last act, says, quite succinctly for a change:

> In one voyage
> Did Claribel her husband find at Tunis
> And Ferdinand, her brother, found a wife
> Where he himself was lost, Prospero his dukedom
> In a poor isle, and all of us ourselves
> When no man was his own.

Earlier, however, he had been less terse and more specific, suggesting (in an interchange with those scornful Neapolitan courtiers: Sebastian, Alonso, and Antonio) certain parallels between their story and that of the original traveler to the West, Aeneas.

> GON: Methinks our garments are now as fresh as when we put them on first in Afric, at the marriage of the King's fair daughter, Claribel, to the King of Tunis.
> SEB: 'Twas a sweet marriage, and we prosper well in our return.
> ADR: Tunis was never graced before with such a paragon to their Queen.
> GON: Not since Widow Dido's time. . . .
> ADR: "Widow Dido," said you? You make me study of that. She was of Carthage, not of Tunis.
> GON: This Tunis, sir, was Carthage.

But "Carthage" is a corruption of *Quarthadasht,* meaning "new town," an appropriate name for what was once the westernmost Phoenician colony; and its Greek equivalent is "Neapolis," which becomes "Napoli" and "Naples," memorializing a second westward voyage to a second New World. It is doubtful that Shakespeare was aware of both these etymologies; yet they so suit the pattern of a play inspired by the opening of a third and final West, that we cannot dismiss the possibility out of hand.

His concern with Dido's Carthage is as old as his obsession with the black stranger, evoked first in the seductive words spoken by Tamora, faithless wife of the Roman Emperor, to Aaron the Moor.

> And—after conflict such as was supposed
> The wandering Prince and Dido once enjoyed,
> When with a happy storm they were surprised,
> And curtained with a counsel-keeping cave—
> We may, each wreathèd in the other's arms,
> Our pastimes done, possess a golden slumber. . . .

How much is already present in *Titus Andronicus* of the pattern that reappears in part in *The Merchant of Venice* and *Othello* and recurs fully in *The Tempest:* "a happy storm," a cave, the sexual union of white and black, played out against a Vergilian music. In Vergil, to be sure, there are basic differences, since not only is his African a female and at home, his European a male and "wandering," but both are imagined as Asians by birth, who solely by disparate adoption come to stand for Carthage and Rome, the opponents in a long-drawn, bitter war of worlds. Only once (except for the brief quip about Launcelot Gobbo's pregnant Moorish girl) did Shakespeare represent Africa by a woman: in *Antony and Cleopatra,* that anti-*Aeneid* in which the hero chooses the "tawny" Queen over patriarchal Rome, thus insuring the destruction of them both and his replacement by the almost-sexless Octavius.

More typically, Shakespeare imagines the reconciliation of the worlds that fell apart with Aeneas's flight and Dido's suicide in terms of marriage between a black prince and a fair princess. That union, however, he could not before *The Tempest* quite manage to make work. As we have already noticed, it is portrayed in *Titus Andronicus* as an obscenity eventuating in total disaster, in *Othello* as a failed happy ending turned by distrust to murder. And in *Pericles,* it recurs, like the fading ghost of itself, as a device on the shield of an unsuccessful suitor of Thaisa: "a black Ethiope reaching at the sun." How astonishing, then, to discover that impossible-desirable union achieved at last in *The Tempest,* or rather before *The Tempest* properly begins, as if none of the other reconciliations in the play could occur until it had been accomplished.

In *The Tempest,* however, the black-fair encounter, from initiation to consummation, is summed up in a handful of lines in a single scene of Act II, then resumed in less than half as many in Act V, so that in many productions it tends to be lost. Yet Shakespeare manages to tell a good deal about it finally, though he shows nothing on stage, since the companions of the King of Naples repeat in bitterness after the shipwreck their original objections to the match: "That would not bless our Europe with your daughter, / But rather lose her to an African. . . . You were kneeled to, and importuned otherwise, / By all of us. . . ." And they go on to remind him that Claribel herself had only reluctantly agreed to the marriage: ". . . the fair soul herself / Weighed between loathness and obedience. . . ."

Moreover, we actually witness the growing regret of the King, to whom his casting away and the presumed death of his son, Ferdinand, seem a punishment for having compelled, against the will of all those closest to him, so ill-assorted a match in so distant a land.

> Would I had never
> Married my daughter there! For, coming thence,
> My son is lost and, in my rate, she too,
> Who is so far from Italy removed
> I ne'er again shall see her.

And we are allowed to overhear, as well, the growing hope of his villainous brother Sebastian as he realizes that thanks to the ill-fated African venture, only the King himself now stands between him and the throne, Ferdinand being surely doomed and Claribel as good as dead.

> She that is Queen of Tunis, she that dwells
> Ten leagues beyond man's life, she that from Naples
> Can have no note, unless the sun were post—
> The man i' the moon's too slow—till newborn chins
> Be rough and razorable.

This insistence on the remoteness of North Africa from southern Europe may seem a little absurd, not only in the light of actual geography but of Shakespeare's own conventions elsewhere, particularly in *Antony and Cleopatra,* in which the characters shuttle back and forth between Alexandria and Rome as if they were no more distant from each other than, say, Belmont and Venice. But such exaggeration is important to all the meanings of the play, including its suggestion that to succeed, the black-white marriage must be removed as far as possible from the world in which Shakespeare had previously demonstrated its inevitable failure. This time around, the fair princess is transported quite out of Europe into the territory of her black prince, where she, along with her kith and kind, become strangers, disoriented to the point where "no man was his own," until each finds a new center and a new self.

Her new self, Claribel presumably discovers in Tunis; but the royal entourage which does stay with her in that alien world, discovers that having made the voyage, it cannot return to its own until it has been cast up by a fair-foul tempest in one alien to both Africa and Europe, quite off the archetypal North-South axis of Mediterranean civilization with which Shakespeare has been hitherto obsessed. It is an East-West (which is to say, a transatlantic) axis along which *The Tempest* moves, though Shakespeare could not quite confess it, so alien did he find the reorientation of all Europe which the discovery of America was, like some new magnetic pole, just then compelling. Three hundred years later, D. H. Lawrence, in describing the impulses to which Shakespeare was responding, described also the mythic drift of *The Tempest:*

> About the time of the Renaissance, however, this circuit exhausted itself, as the Italian-African circuit had been exhausted a thousand years before. Italy suddenly scintillated, and was finished in her polar potentiality. The old stability of Europe was gone, the old circle of vital flow was broken. It was then that

> Europe fell directly into polar unison with America. Europe and America became the great poles of negative and positive vitalism. . . .
>
> When the great magnetic sway of the medieval polarity broke, those units which were liberated fell under the sway of new vital currents in the air, and they were borne helplessly as birds migrate, without knowing or willing, down the great magnetic wind towards America, towards the centrality of the New World. . . .

For Shakespeare, however, it was not quite so simple, since he thought of the "great magnetic wind towards America" as blowing not from Europe itself, but from Africa or, at least, via Africa.

Moreover, even his first Europeans ashore in the New World, Prospero and Miranda, discover, quite like the first English explorers of Virginia and the first Spanish expedition to San Salvador, that the world new to them is already inhabited by men more different from them than any Africans. These strange beings the first actual discoverers of America had called "Indians," assuming they had reached—for so Columbus's maps seemed to indicate—the "Indies," which is to say, certain outlying islands of Asia. But when Columbus's cartography had been revealed as more wrong than right (the world, though round, proving much vaster than he was prepared to believe), endless ethnographic speculations began. Were they, the ethnomythographers of Europe asked, these red-skinned inhabitants of a world really new, stray scions of Shem or Japheth or Ham, displaced Hebrews or Moors, Welshmen or Mongolians? Or were they, bold speculators suggested, plunging the councils of the church into embittered debate, not humans at all, though two-legged animals uncomfortably like men in appearance, but monsters or freaks, lower creatures intended to slave for a higher humanity like asses or horses or oxen.

If Shakespeare seems inclined, on the one hand, to deny all human status to the single aborigine of his isle, Caliban, making him the by-blow of a demon mother, on the other hand, he insists that, on his mother's side, he was an African. Certainly, this makes a kind of mythological sense, particularly since Shakespeare had in *Othello* associated the cannibals, of whose name Caliban is an anagram, with the native land of the Moor. In any case, his mother, "the foul witch Sycorax," had been—in a kind of caricature of the exile of Prospero and his infant daughter—deported from Algiers, where she was born.

> This damned witch Sycorax,
> For mischiefs manifold, and sorceries terrible
> To enter human hearing, from Argier,
> Thou know'st, was banished. . . .
> This blue-eyed hag was hither brought with child,
> And here was left by the sailors.

Morocco, Mauritania, Egypt, Tunis, and now Algiers to complete the series. It is as if Shakespeare had wanted, before finishing his work, to specify region by region the whole Mediterranean shore of Africa, which was for him, of course, all the Africa there was, its sub-Saharan interior as unknown as Northwest America. It is from that shore, at any rate, that the "blue-eyed hag" (her eyes not really "blue," the commentators hasten to assure us, like those of some fair girl, but only ringed and bagged in blue) is purported to have brought not just an heir but the magic to wrest the New World island from the spirits who inhabited it in perfect freedom before her coming. Those spirits, and in particular Ariel, represent, surely, the powers of the imagination which before any foot had touched its soil, already possessed the New World of the West in myth and dream.

And to those spirits, Shakespeare seems willing at the play's end (or so at least he assures us through the white magician, Prospero) to give back that newfound land, whose subjugation to her clottish son the witch-mother had vainly planned. Sycorax, along with Claribel, however, remains offstage throughout, the one already dead, the other lost to an Africa as far removed as Arcturus. They exist as memories only, as if to make clear that the Africa-Europe axis exists only in the remembered past; for after Prospero's arrival, the island becomes a point on a new line joining not only East and West but also a past behind the past of Africa to a present beyond any which present Europe could conceive.

Yet the enormous span of time implicit in this mythology is concealed at first by the very compression and brevity of *The Tempest,* which is, notoriously, the tightest of all Shakespeare's plays, observing with uncharacteristic punctiliousness the classical unities of space and time. Its fictional span is very nearly identical with its playing time, and all its action (barring a brief shipboard introduction) occurs on one small island, which we imagine as not much larger than the theater in which it is played. We dare not forget, however, the immense body of discordant, almost irreconcilable, archetypal material which *The Tempest* contains, myths associated with two ultimate poles of Shakespeare's world: its margins of strangeness and wonder on the East as well as the West.

The world of *The Tempest* is still, nominally, the same Mediterranean world through which Shakespeare's imagination had ranged from the beginning of his career; but that imagination is here straining against its traditional boundaries. On the one hand, his mythological materials take him to its oriental limits in Antioch and Tyre, Mytilene and Pentapolis, Tarsus and Ephesus; and on the other, to the occidental edge of the ancient world, to a place which we sense must surely be beyond the Pillars of Hercules, even across the vast Atlantic. But Shakespeare insists, rather equivocally (there being in *The*

Tempest double space, as there is in *Othello* double time), on putting Prospero's island back into the Mediterranean, somewhere toward the setting sun, on past Tunis. He has, however, to expand the size of that inland sea immensely, as we have already begun to observe, in order to contain a world at once so remote and so new. Deep in the European imagination, all journeys westward are identified with a motion in time from past to future; and that archetypal identification Shakespeare exploits in *The Tempest,* a work of art which is itself a journey from Anatolia to America, from "once upon a time" to right now, from legend to chronicle.

One body of mythological material on which he drew belongs to the oldest strata of inherited story available to him: the kind of "mouldy" tale he had associated with "ancient Gower" in *Pericles,* but which originated in fact in the Hellenistic culture which had first flourished on the eastern rim of the Mediterranean and came so oddly to possess the imagination of Elizabethan and Jacobean England. The other is emerging, even as he writes, from chronicles and journals and letters, some not even in print when *The Tempest* was first produced, as well as from the gossip of friends and friends of friends about the Jamestown Colony and the "stormy Bermoothes": a New World which seemed to the English of Renaissance times as fabulous and remote as the neverlands of the Greek romances. We must take quite seriously the cry of wonder which Shakespeare placed on Miranda's lips, "O brave new world," though, ironically, it is the sight of some aging old-world villains which prompts it; and the response of her father must represent, in some sense, the poet's own reservations: " 'Tis new to thee."

Whatever Shakespeare's own antiutopian bias, however, his play is about notions of the new just then in the air—of a New World, first of all, but also of new men, inhabitants of that world who were at first as new to old Europeans as the latter were to Miranda.

'Ban, 'Ban, Cacaliban
Has a new master.—Get a new man.

In short, the myth of the new and the West, which constitutes one-half of the main archetypal content of *The Tempest,* is quite simply the myth of America and of the Indian, who is the last stranger in Shakespeare—the last stranger, in fact, whom this globe can know, until we meet, on his own territory or in ours, the first extraterrestial, whom until now we have only fantasized and dreamed.

With the discovery and settlement of America, certain possibilities of wonder were temporarily foreclosed, since once East and West were revealed as a continuum, the bipolarity upon which myths had so long been nurtured could no longer be sustained even in the deep imagination. Ever since Aristotle, and probably before, men had surmised that the earth was round; but in proving it, Columbus robbed even that hypothesis of its magical allure: "the hemispheres rounded and tied, the unknown to the known." Walt Whitman, with his taste for profaning mysteries, might have found that cause for celebration; but it has proved an almost fatal blow to the marvelous, which only the invention of space travel promises to revive.

Worst of all, however, was to have discovered in the hemisphere of water which the Christian Aristotelians had postulated as uninhabited, *il mondo senza gente,* men who, whatever their superficial divergences from Europeans, Asians, and Africans, had finally to be accepted as children of Adam, too. For Shakespeare, however, at the moment of writing *The Tempest,* the new man emerging from the watery West, like some strange fish with legs, still seemed an ultimate stranger. And to him and his world we shall in due course return; though of all aspects of *The Tempest,* its Western mythos is these days the most explored. Indeed, thanks to such political commentators as Franz Fanon, as well as certain more adventurous literary critics like Frank Kermode, no respectable production of the play these days can afford to ignore the sense in which it is a parable of transatlantic imperialism, the colonization of the West.

Considerably less well explored and understood is the complementary myth of the East, which constitutes the pole of memory as opposed to the pole of prophecy in *The Tempest*. Its seed is to be found in the tale of *Apollonius of Tyre*, which Ben Jonson may have found insufferably antiquated (he called it "mouldy"), but which possessed Shakespeare throughout his writing life and came to so extraordinary a flowering in the last plays. The *Apollonius of Tyre* legend is not so much a single story as a little anthology, a kind of grab bag of folk motifs linked together in that loose, episodic form which Hellenism invented and the later Middle Ages and the Renaissance so loved. That antiform is the romance, and though, as in most really popular literature, its middle tends to consume both beginning and end, it has finally a characteristic movement or pattern, which can itself be interpreted archetypally, a movement in two stages from absolute horror to total redemption.

The first stage represents what anthropologists might call the triumph of exogamy over endogamy, which means, in fairy-tale terms, the defeat of father-daughter incest, real or threatened, by the impulse which leads to marrying someone else, that is, one dreamed or wished-for before known. In the complex web of Apollonian story, the incestuous father is sometimes shown as resisting until death his daughter's suitors, finding them such total strangers to the flesh of his flesh, that a union with any of them is tantamount to miscegenation. But sometimes he is portrayed as himself conquering a reluctance he recognizes as unworthy and giving up his daughter to her alien lover after providing the merest sham of opposition in order, he assures himself, to sweeten their love with the savor of rebellion. Most typically, however, he appears one or more times in both roles, malign and kindly, since in the dream sequence of romance, the most multilayered ambivalences can be serially indulged.

In any case, Stage I of the Apollonius pattern, ending as it does in a wedding and a father's defeat, is not unlike the mythos of New Comedy. But Stage II reveals its essential difference, as the happy ending of marriage yields to the happier ending of restoration, and presumably dead children and wives —castaways, preserved rather than destroyed by tempests—are revealed to a final, miraculous music as alive and/or nubile: in some sense, *as good as new.* Such restorations, it must be understood, are natural rather than supernatural, symbols of "the triumph of time" rather than of the special intervention of Providence. They are, therefore, not instantaneous, but require customarily the span of a generation for their working out, some fourteen or fifteen or sixteen years. Whatever this does to the unity of time, it provides a period long enough for the deflowered maiden to reappear, which is to say, long enough for a rejected wife to attain a second, spiritual puberty as a nun or for a castaway girl baby to have become capable of producing girl babies of her own. The "miracle" which Apollonian comedy celebrates is not that of the unity of the sexes in marriage, but that of natural immortality, the eternal return of which marriage is the first stage, begetting the second. But that process can only begin after the witch-mother has been destroyed, the witch-daughter has become Ariel, and the ogre-father has turned himself into a good magician.

Some sense of all this seems to have moved Shakespeare from the very first, from the moment when, quite gratuitously, he introduced certain elements of the myth of restoration into what was surely his first comic play and perhaps even his first venture of any kind in drama, *The Comedy of Errors.* Like *Titus Andronicus,* it is a self-consciously classicizing effort, almost academic in many respects, and not least in its fable, which seems more researched than invented, combining as it does a main plot lifted from Plautus's *Menaechmi* with a complicating situation derived from that other surviving Roman play about doubles, the *Amphitruo*. Both plots, in any case—that of the identical twins whose resemblance is their comic fate and that of the god who puts on a resemblance to seduce an honest wife—are atypically remote from the Menandrian pattern of boy-outwits-father-gets-girl favored by Plautus and Terence.

But if this avoidance of standard New Comedy on Shakespeare's part seems revealing enough, even more revealing is the frame in which he chose to enclose his tale of confusion twice confounded. Quite inappropriate in theme and tone, since it has nothing to do with twins and its bittersweetness ill suits the farcical tone of the rest, that frame somehow occurred to Shakespeare as he sought to explain the separation of the twin brothers from each other and their sundered parents. And it came from the mythological storehouse of *Apollonius of Tyre:* the story of the casting away of a mother at the moment of giving birth and of her restoration to sons and husband after an immural of more than thirty years as "abbess" in the convent of Diana of Ephesus. That the goddess is, in fact, the Black Diana of the witches, Shakespeare never quite admits, though he does make the city a place of sorcery.

In any case, he is not yet ready to do full justice to the myth of children lost at sea and found on land, carried off in a tempest and recovered through "the triumph of time." Even the great natural symbols so essential to the archetype seem to baffle him. The storm-tormented ocean rolls distantly offstage, and the verse in which he tries to evoke it falls oddly flat, as if he had no sense of what all that weltering water might signify.

> A league from Epidamnum had we sailed
> Before the always-wind-obeying deep

Gave any tragic instance of our harm.
But longer did we not retain much hope,
For what obscurèd light the heavens did grant
Did but convey unto our fearful minds
A doubtful warrant of immediate death. . . .

Nor does he seem to understand any better the import of time itself; doubling the generational gap between shipwreck and restoration ("Thirty-three years have I but gone in travail . . . and till this present hour / My heavy burden ne'er deliverèd"), as if more interested in getting the mother safely on the other side of the menopause than in allowing years enough for a girl child to reach nubility. There are, of course, no girl children at all in *The Comedy of Errors,* only the two Antipholuses with their two Dromios, twinned sons and their matching male servants. The shadow of father-daughter incest cannot, therefore, fall upon the happy ending, in which the father, in fact, oddly fades to silence as brother embraces brother, servant jests with servant; and the last serious word is the mother's: "After so long grief, such nativity!" Yet as we know, having read *Henry VI, Part I,* the conflict of father and daughter had already begun to haunt Shakespeare; though it would be long, long before he could see how the girl child's "gross revolt" represented not a tainted will, but the force of "great creating Nature" itself, against which no tyranny could prevail, especially one grounded in life-denying incest.

For nearly twenty years, in fact, the Apollonian theme went underground in Shakespeare's work, until—as if he himself were living the myth—a generation had elapsed, and it was ready for a second birth. During the first decade it was replaced, despite his real reluctance on this score, by the Menandrian pattern itself; and where he resisted still, by variants of the Pyramus and Thisbe legend, which, as we have already noticed, operates on various levels in *A Midsummer Night's*

Dream, Romeo and Juliet, and rather peripherally in *The Merchant of Venice.* In the casket scene of that play, indeed, the Apollonius mythos comes close to resurrection, though in so expurgated a form that it has to be reconstructed rather than simply felt. To be sure, the puzzle central to the Apollonius archetype is present for the first time; and if we have been reading Claude Lévi-Strauss, we know this signals the presence of incest as well. "Between the puzzle solution and incest," that most literary of all anthropologists says, "there exists a relationship, not external and of fact, but internal and of reason. . . . Like the solved puzzle, incest brings together elements doomed to remain separate. . . ."

But *The Merchant of Venice* is not so much a play about an enigma as a second enigma concealing the first. The incestuous father is postulated as dead to begin with, and the penalty for failing his impossible test is made lifelong celibacy rather than immediate execution. Most confusing of all, however, is the inversion of the true incest riddle (what does the desired and forbidden girl conceal—a heart of gold or silver or lead?) into the pseudoenigma (which casket—gold, silver, or lead—contains the desired and forbidden girl?). Only in *Pericles, Prince of Tyre,* does Shakespeare confess the aboriginal enigma whose answer is the leaden secret of incest.

> I am no viper, yet I feed
> On mother's flesh which did me breed.
> I sought a husband, in which labor
> I found that kindness in a father.
> He's father, son, and husband mild;
> I mother, wife, and yet his child.
> How that may be, and yet in two,
> As you will live, resolve it you.

The appeal in the last three words seems to parody Portia's appeal to Bassanio, "Reply, reply." And when Pericles has resolved the riddle (which only a profound reluctance to face so unpalatable a truth could have made mysterious to anyone), he finds in his answer an image for Antiochus's daughter which sends us back to Belmont once more.

> Fair glass of light, I loved you, and could still,
> Were not this glorious casket stored with ill.

But the deviousness of *The Merchant of Venice* simply baffles us again, unless we remember, returning to it, the clue provided by *Pericles,* in which the "ancient Gower" explains whatever the dramatic action and the interspersed dumb show leave unclear. Yet, though a final revelation of the meaning of the caskets, it by no means represents Shakespeare's next word on the subject after *The Merchant,* since, over the intervening decade, he writes *Othello, Hamlet,* and *Lear,* in each of which a lovely daughter brings death to an overfond father. But such tragedies reflect Shakespeare's furthest remove from what is most reassuring in the mythology of *Apollonius of Tyre*—except, perhaps, for *Lear,* in which the three caskets are, as it were, made flesh in Goneril, Regan, and Cordelia. In its final scene, there is, certainly, a recognition of Cordelia's worth, plus the hint of her restoration. However, not her lover but her repentant father takes in his arms at the close the golden girl who had, in the beginning, returned such leaden echoes to his appeals for love, responding, "Nothing. . . . Nothing," as if his words bounced from the walls of an empty tomb.

It is an odd and equivocal scene, this "Protestant Pietà," closer in its iconography to the Victorian world of Little Nell and Little Eva than to the more orthodox Middle Ages. Moreover, unlike Dickens or Harriet Beecher Stowe, Shakespeare promises for one moment to end with a resurrection in this world, rather than the next, as the dead Cordelia seems to draw breath. "This feather stirs, she lives," the hopeful father cries. "If it be so, / It is a chance which does redeem all sorrows / That ever I have felt." Yet in an instant, he is convinced that he has been self-deceived; and though before his heart cracks finally he returns to the dream of restoration, all ends in the ambiguity of despair. "Do you see this?" he implores those around him. "Look on her, look, her lips, / Look there, look there!" What he sees, dying, however, no one living shares, so that whatever is restored belongs to a world inhabited neither by his fellow actors nor by the audience, for whom the Duke of Albany speaks, saying, "Bear them from hence. Our present business / Is general woe." And what leaves the stage are two corpses.

It is with *Pericles* that Shakespeare embarks on his final series of plays, which include also *Cymbeline, The Winter's Tale,* and *The Tempest,* and which (whatever other elements they may contain) are all of them reworkings, with shifting emphases and varying experiments in structure, of the Apollonius myth. Not only are the necessary gaps of time provided in each, but the sea, too, so essential to the full archetype, is at work in all, even in the teeth of probability, since without the sea, there can be no tempests, and without tempests, no shipwrecks to begin the plot. But seacoasts are required as well: symbolic representations of the border between eternity and time, upon which waif after waif can be safely beached. Even Bohemia—to the scandal of all good geographers ever since—is provided a shore line, lest *The Winter's Tale* lack an ocean and Perdita a beach to receive her. And in *Cymbeline,* at a certain point, as Quiller-Couch was once moved to remark testily: "Heaven knows why—every character in the play has set sail for Milford Haven."

Moreover, in all, restoration is made of what had seemed—what would have been by the nightmare logic of tragedy—forever lost: in *Cymbeline,* a pair of sons, plus a girl who functions simultaneously as wife, sister, and daughter; and in *The Winter's Tale,* both such a girl, cast away as an infant, and a wife long held in secret for a somewhat stagey "resurrection" scene. Indeed, *The Winter's Tale* is an adaptation of the Apollonius archetype almost as complex as *Pericles* itself, for Shakespeare's immediate source, Greene's *Pandosto: The Triumph of Time,* embodies in only slightly bowdlerized form almost the whole original legend. The riddle, for instance, so intimately linked to the incest secret, survives in Greene's prose romance, benignly recast as a puzzle oracle: "the King shall live without an heir if that which is lost be not found." Greene will not, however, permit achieved incest in his tale, presenting it instead as a narrowly averted catastrophe, in which Pandosto, who is his Leontes, really loses his wife and ends wooing his unrecognized grown daughter. Indeed, as Greene tells the story, denied that daughter, Pandosto chooses suicide, a catastrophe Shakespeare avoids by keeping Hermione alive long enough to insure a happy ending for her repentant husband.

Only once, then, did Shakespeare permit himself—or perhaps rather felt himself compelled—to deal overtly with father-daughter incest, not as dreamed and repressed, but performed, punished, and publicly exposed, as it is by the end of Act II, scene iv, of *Pericles.*

> Antiochus from incest lived not free;
> For which, the most high gods not minding longer
> To withhold the vengeance that they had in store,
> Due to this heinous capital offense,
> Even in the height and pride of all his glory,
> When he was seated in a chariot
> Of an inestimable value, and his daughter with him,
> A fire from Heaven came and shrivelled up
> Their bodies, even to loathing; . . .

This announcement is made by Helicanus, a lord of Tyre, at a point when Pericles has, as it were, been born again and has fallen in love for a second time, with Thaisa, daughter of Simonides, King of Pentapolis. His first love for the daughter of Antiochus had turned to loathing when he guessed her secret;

and fleeing the wrath of her evil father, he had been swallowed down and cast up again by the sea. But this time, too, there is a test to be passed before marriage, though Thaisa returns his love, a tourney set up by her father to winnow the suitors she has drawn to Pentapolis.

Thaisa and her father constitute, in short, an alternative, benign version of the incestuous couple from whose vengeance Pericles had so narrowly escaped; but in this version, the king-father turns out to be only *playing* at forbidding the match. We overhear him musing on his daughter's declaration that come what may, she will be Pericles's bride.

> 'Tis well, mistress. Your choice agrees with mine.
> I like that well. Nay, how absolute she's in't,
> Not minding whether I dislike or no!
> Well, I do commend her choice,
> And will no longer have it be delayed.
> Soft! Here he comes. I must dissemble it.

We are, therefore, not deceived, as she is, when, a moment later, he screams at her suitor, quite like old Brabantio before him, "Thou hast bewitched my daughter, and thou art / A villain." Nor are we misled when Thaisa answers as Desdemona did, absolving her lover of the guilt of seduction, and her father responds:

> I'll tame you. I'll bring you in subjection.
> Will you, not having my consent,
> Bestow your love and your affections
> Upon a stranger?

"Stranger" is the key word—the familiar epithet evoking images of the black ram tupping the white ewe, which is to say, projections of a father's forbidden and unconfessed lust ("This accident is not unlike my dream").

In *Pericles,* however, neither the father dies, as in *Othello,* nor the daughter, as in the variations on the theme of Pyramus and Thisbe; for the threat is turned in an instant, as if by the omnipotent magic of wish, into a blessing.

> Therefore hear you, mistress. Either frame
> Your will to mine—and you, sir, hear you,
> Either be ruled by me, or I will make you—
> Man and wife.

The two lovers, thus blessed, are hurried off to bed by the old man himself, who having entered in the guise of "loathéd" Antiochus, exits as the "good" Simonides, thus ending Stage I of the Apollonius archetype.

> It pleaseth me so well that I will see you wed,
> And then, with what haste you can, get you to bed.

Act III begins, like *The Tempest,* in the middle of a monstrous storm, which, before blowing itself out, has presided over the birth of a girl child to Pericles and Thaisa and the apparent death of the mother, who is sealed into a coffin and cast into the sea. Actually still alive, Thaisa is tossed ashore at Ephesus, where she is revived from her trance and inducted into a nunnery in which she awaits the intended happy ending under the protection of Diana. Her daughter has meanwhile been christened Marina, presumably in honor of the sea which was her childbed, though actually, it would seem, after the Indian mistress of Cortez. That Spanish-American Pocahontas had before her baptism been called Malintzin; but her romantic adventures as Marina had stirred the imagination of all Catholic Europe, to which she represented, perhaps, the hope of an alliance in love between Old World and New. It is, in any event, Shakespeare's Marina who constitutes the center of Stage II of *Pericles,* which reaches its first climax when a jealous stepmother, to whom she has been entrusted by her bereaved father, orders her murder.

Her would-be killer, however, makes the mistake of tempting her to the rim of the always-salvational sea, so that with the sudden intervention of a band of pirates, what he had intended to be her tomb becomes instead an avenue of escape and eventual restoration. "I'll swear she's dead, / And thrown into the sea," the frustrated assassin says, assuming no other fate possible for the ravished girl, who, in fact, is taken to Mytilene and sold to the keeper of a brothel. Here the logic of the myth demands really that she be confronted by her father, without—after fourteen years of separation—recognition on either side. Only in this way can the pattern be fulfilled: the deliberate incest avoided in one generation accomplished unwittingly in the next. Shakespeare, however, characteristically shies away from this, splitting the second-generation father into Pericles and Lysimachus, as he had the first-generation father into Antiochus and Simonides.

It is not Pericles, at any rate, but Lysimachus, Governor of Mytilene, who enters the whorehouse in which Marina has until then successfully defended her virginity against all comers by the chilling sageness and chastity of her speech. "Fie, fie, upon her!" the baffled bawd has cried out earlier. "She's able to freeze the god Priapus, and undo a whole generation." Indeed, before she has finished with Lysimachus, he, too, is undone, claiming that he "came with no ill intent" to begin with, though, as a matter of fact, he had bandied lewd jokes in obvious impatience with Boult, the brothel keeper.

> LYS: Well, call forth, call forth.
> BOULT: For flesh and blood, sir, white and red, you shall see a rose; and she were a rose indeed, if she had but—
> LYS: What, prithee?
> BOULT: O, sir, I can be modest.

This is Shakespeare's last pun on "prick," unspoken in a place where the "god Priapus" has been frozen; yet Lysimachus seems even at this point unblunted enough. "Faith," he says on first seeing Marina—and in this sea-drenched play, the metaphor seems inevitable—"she would serve after a long voyage at sea."

Nonetheless, he is finally no more her ravisher than her father, and, therefore, they can be married to each other (the matter dispatched, in fact, with a few rather perfunctory lines) after the true father has claimed that daughter so long lost to him, as well as his miraculously preserved wife. Gower sums it all up in the induction to his final chorus, Stages I and II rendered in a half-dozen lines.

> In Antiochus and his daughter you have heard
> Of monstrous lust the due and just reward.
> In Pericles, his Queen and daughter, seen,
> Although assailed with fortune fierce and keen,
> Virtue preserved from fell destruction's blast,
> Led on by Heaven and crowned with joy at last.

And to this, it seems necessary only to add that the restorations occurred, of course, in Ephesus, on the very lintel of that temple, where two decades before, Shakespeare had imagined his first restored mother, the daughterless Aemilia of *The Comedy of Errors.*

Gower may remind us thus at the play's end of the overt incest with which it began, but it is only in the first two acts, so oddly disjoined from all which follows, that Shakespeare confronts directly the crime of Antiochus. These first two acts, however, many eminent scholars and critics have denied were Shakespeare's at all. And, indeed, the problem of the authorship of *Pericles* as a whole seems a vexed, even an insoluble one, though beginning with Act III, certain lines occur which are so extraordinary that any refusal to attribute them to Shakespeare means postulating another major poet in the early seventeenth century. But the verse of Acts I and II is flat and undistinguished throughout, as if the poet who wrote them, and whom we might as well call Shakespeare, had somehow been scared *stiff,* perhaps by the myth's revelation of certain material hitherto buried deep in his own psyche. Not even the thought of a tempest at sea can evoke anything more moving than:

> For now the wind begins to blow.
> Thunder above and deeps below
> Make such unquiet that the ship
> Should house him safe is wrecked and split,
> And he, good Prince, having all lost,
> By waves from coast to coast is tossed.

Even poor Gower, trapped in his rhymed tetrameters, comes closer to actual poetry after Act III.

> Their vessel shakes
> On Neptune's billow. Half the flood
> Hath their keel cut; but Fortune's mood
> Varies again. The grisled North
> Disgorges such a tempest forth
> That, as a duck for life that dives,
> So up and down the poor ship drives.

But when Pericles is released to unrhymed pentameter, we begin to hear—not everywhere or constantly, but at intervals—a singular music, altered a little from anything Shakespeare had made earlier, yet undeniably his for all the unaccustomed counterpoint of the sea, which sounds beneath it like another voice.

> A terrible childbed hast thou had, my dear.
> No light, no fire, the unfriendly elements
> Forgot thee utterly. Nor have I time
> To give thee hallowed to thy grave, but straight
> Must cast thee, scarcely coffined, in the ooze,
> Where, for a monument upon thy bones,

And aye-remaining lamps, the belching whale
And humming water must o'erwhelm thy corpse,
Lying with simple shells.

. . . .

Give me a gash, put me to present pain,
Lest this great sea of joys rushing upon me
O'erbear the shores of my mortality,
And drown me with their sweetness.—Oh, come hither,
Thou that beget'st him that did thee beget;
Thou that wast born at sea, buried at Tarsus,
And found at sea again!

At the next stage, this is distilled to the magical ten words which Thaisa speaks—"Did you not name a tempest, / A birth, and death?"—and we are ready for *The Tempest.* It is all there, no matter how Shakespeare first encountered *Pericles:* whether, in fact, he was asked to complete someone else's clumsy beginning; or at the end of his career, took up an abandoned early effort of his own; or even merely patched and emended a work entirely by another author, scarcely knowing he had transformed it utterly. No matter how he began, he ended by finding what he, quite like his own misguided kings, thought he had buried forever years before: not only certain mythic themes but their intended music.

Pericles was, contemporary witnesses tell us, an immense popular success. But Shakespeare seems to have felt uneasy about its structure, which had so directly transposed the form of the prose romance to the stage, suspecting, perhaps, that its sprawling, episodic antishape somehow belied the vision toward which the play tended: "a tempest, / A birth, and death" experienced simultaneously, instantaneously, and in joy. He had returned via the Apollonius legend to two of the oldest, deepest metaphors for essential religious experience: the vision and the voyage, the tedious voyage toward eternity through time and the unmeditated ecstasy of the timeless vision. And he sought, therefore, not out of some last-minute conversion to neoclassicism, but rather from an awareness of the specific obligations of his task, to unify in a way possible only to drama (as opposed to epic or romance) the sense of the voyage and the structure of the vision.

To accomplish this end, he condenses and simplifies in all possible ways the myth he had so loosely handled in *Pericles,* squeezing the dozen or so years that have made Miranda a woman into a single improbable retrospective speech, reducing a half-dozen fabled cities into one tight little island, and fusing three father-daughter pairs, with their attendant foils and split-offs, to one daughter of the father and one father of the daughter. Corresponding to each, there is an other-worldly double, an elemental: the gross shadow of the father, compounded of earth and water in Caliban; the ethereal anima of the daughter, compounded of fire and air in Ariel. Caliban and Ariel, however, seem finally projections rather than real characters, who, within the action of the play, can be made to vanish at the wave of Prospero's hand.

Indeed, no character appears on scene, except for Miranda, until called up by spells or with the tempest's aid. How unreal, therefore, even the quarreling group of Neapolitans seem, unable to accomplish good or ill, except within the limits of Prospero's scheme, an oddly futureless, unfertile lot, being entirely without women. Only what Prospero remembers can attain his island, and what his memory holds are men alone: fathers and sons, kings and councilors, and, especially, fratricidal brothers, Cain and Abel twice over, but transported to a world in which their hatred is impotent. Moreover, they seem to grow less real as the play progresses, this cast of supernumeraries left over from old tragedies—except for Ferdinand, the single representative of his generation, needed to replace the father of the daughter as the father declines into age, or perhaps rather to deliver the father from his last temptation as the daughter reaches puberty.

Prospero is, in short, not merely all the male characters in an almost all-male play, but its omnipotent author as well, able to trap both actors and audience—for they are one—in the theater of his mind. Other characters in Shakespeare's earlier plays seem similarly to control in whole or part the action of the drama around them, but after the more festive comedies, such manipulators of their own plays (one thinks of Iago or Claudius or Edmund or Macbeth), which is to say, of their own destinies, tend to work evil, being usurpers in fact or in intent, and operating on a level of "wit" compatible with politics. Shakespeare, however, finds it as hard to believe in good politics as he does in good witchcraft, imagining only Henry V as an exemplar of the first and Prospero of the second. Unlike the redeemed Prince Hal, Prospero combats evil politics not with good politics but with good witchcraft—or as he, the master of arts, prefers to call it, "art." It is a word which meant to Shakespeare first of all "magic," but something new as well, since it was just then assuming (the *Oxford English Dictionary* lists a clear usage of this sort by 1620) its modern sense: the sense which makes it possible to call *The Tempest* "a work of art."

Prospero is in any case no usurper, but a genuine duke ("*Non sans Droict*" being the slogan of the coat of arms Shakespeare composed for himself, his final boast) and, by the same token a true artist, capable of providing an idyllic dream, a bright vision, and a good trip for everyone. Of all the other plot manipulators in the Shakespearean corpus, he seems closest to Vincentio, the Duke in *Measure for Measure,* who, like him, loved study more than his official duties. But that "Duke of dark corners" proved in the end a creature more cunning than artful, despite his unchallenged legitimacy. Even his apparent abdication proved a way of getting certain dirty work done without soiling his own hands, and he ends, not like Prospero with an act of renunciation, but by demanding the kind of happy ending more appropriate to a young man than a mature ruler of the city. It is an ending made doubtly equivocal, moreover, since the girl he claims as his reward—and whom he has all but delivered into the power of unmitigated evil—is a "sister"-daughter, espoused to One greater than a mere politician playing Providence. And in no case does she seem intended for Duke Vincentio, whose age puts him, even as his clerical disguise declares, in the position of being her "good Father."

Shakespeare could not imagine a protagonist suitable for his supreme Apollonian tragedy until time had taught him to conceive a duke eternally on guard against incest, actual and symbolic, and, by the same token, immune to the temptation to believe he is doing anything more than *pretending* to be God when he imposes his fantasies on others. It is Prospero's greatest virtue to know that he merely *plays* at power, that is, composes fictions based on his own dreams, which can influence the lives of others only when the heavens are favorable. "I find my zenith doth depend upon / A most auspicious star," he tells Miranda early in the action, "whose influence / If now I court not, but omit, my fortunes / Will ever after droop." And to keep his limitations ever in our minds, Shakespeare portrays him as continually making and unmaking smaller plays within the larger play, whose actors shift from role to role at his command, though one, his boy star Ariel, in every interval returns to demand his "freedom," which is to say, the power to write his own plots.

Usually the interior dramas which we watch him plan and execute involve not just actor-spirits, who play now harpies, now sea nymphs, now a pack of pursuing hounds, but human actors as well, who never shift their parts within the larger plot. And once, he presides invisible, as Ferdinand and

Miranda, both fixed forever in their lovers' roles, perform with no help from the spirit world the sham Pyramus and Thisbe story he has persuaded them it is their fate to re-enact. And when they seal their bond of love—in secret, as they think—he comments with all the pride appropriate to one who is the author of, as well as the third actor in, the piece.

> So glad of this as they I cannot be,
> Who are surprised withal, but my rejoicing
> At nothing can be more.

The last such inner play, however—the masque of Juno, Ceres, and Iris—is presented not, like its predecessors, intertwined with the surrounding action, but properly introduced and distanced, as in the theater: "No tongue! All eyes! Be silent." While it lasts, therefore, all actors on the stage except for the performing spirits are converted into an audience, at one with the beholders in the house—both those long dead and us the living. But this means that the larger play, in which they have been acting until that moment, along with the smaller play, which now as they act they watch, has become a metaphor for the illusory lives all men enact in the still greater theater of the world. "All the world's a stage, / And all the men and women merely players," the familiar line has it, turning myth into platitude. Sonnet 15 manages to say it better, however, honoring the commonplace without profaning the mystery: ". . . this huge stage presenteth naught but shows / Whereon the stars in secret influence comment. . . ."

Most inner plays in Shakespeare are interrupted—like *The Mousetrap* in *Hamlet,* which is stopped midway, or Bottom's production in *A Midsummer Night's Dream,* which is shorn of its epilogue. And, indeed, their incompletion seems essential rather than accidental, a part of their significance. Only in *The Taming of the Shrew* is a play within a play allowed to run full course; but in that instance, it swallows up the enclosing action, leaving it an unfinished frame. More typically,

The Tempest's masque is stopped before its end by Prospero, its author, who interrupts its course, remembering urgent matters which belong to the enclosing plot. Before its start, he had already explained to his would-be son-in-law that the actors in his play within a play were really projections of a world within his head: "Spirits which by mine art / I have from their confines called to enact / My present fancies." And moved by the magic of it all, that boy, naïve almost as Miranda herself, has cried, "So rare a wondered father and a wise / Makes this place Paradise." Indeed, enchanted by the show, he seems willing never to return to the land where he will someday be king, saying, "Let me live here ever."

But no one, not even a "wise" and "wondered" father, can live forever in the world of his fancy, which far from being "Paradise," is only a desert island from which finally all must move back into their respective real worlds. Remembering quite un-Paradisal matters, Prospero stops his masque mid-course; dismisses his spirits with a brusque, "Well done! Avoid, no more!"; and tells Ferdinand:

> Our revels now are ended. These our actors,
> As I foretold you, were all spirits, and
> Are melted into air, into thin air.
> And, like the baseless fabric of this vision,
> The cloud-capped towers, the gorgeous palaces,
> The solemn temples, the great globe itself—
> Yea, all which it inherit—shall dissolve
> And, like this insubstantial pageant faded,
> Leave not a rack behind.

The lines have become justly, though unfortunately, famous to the point where they are almost as unavailable to us as the *Mona Lisa*. But one set of their meanings at least must be redeemed in any contemporary production, the actor of Prospero lingering over the theatrical metaphors "globe," "pageant," and "rack," rather than the too-familiar "dreams" and "sleep" which follow. Only thus can he make clear to the audience the reference to their own immediate situation, on which so much of the speech's significance depends.

The pun on "globe" which Shakespeare makes through Prospero is perhaps irrecoverable, except for those aware that the Globe was a theater in which Shakespeare's own company had acted. But somehow an analogous way must be found to break the illusion for contemporary beholders of the action, leaving them aware that insofar as they have forgotten they are watching a play, they have been had. Only when the first level of illusion has been thus broken, can it be reconstituted on a second convolution, where we believe *again* in our own reality as well as in that of the actors on stage who do not vanish at Prospero's behest, like those New World spirits so oddly disguised as Hellenistic nymphs and reapers and goddesses. To be sure, Prospero's own words insist on the evanescence of *all* life; but they are spoken at the close of what is twice described (first by Ferdinand and then by Prospero himself) as a "vision." "A most majestic vision," the young man calls it; but the older one refers to it as a "baseless fabric."

We must, therefore, distinguish temporarily its level of reality from that of all which follows, including even the last play within a play, in which Miranda and Ferdinand are *"playing at chess."* "If this prove / A vision of the island," says the King of Naples, "one dear son / Shall I twice lose." But Prospero has assured him in advance that what he beholds is something truer: a "wonder" rather than a "vision." By the time we have reached the Epilogue, all *The Tempest* will have been revealed as a "vision" of restoration and liberation, actual only at the Day of Judgment, our own lives will presumably appear no more real and no less.

But in Acts IV and V, despite Prospero's prophetic Epilogue to the masque, we must still make discriminations in the world of maya, lest we fall out of the play too soon. In Act IV, it is the point of Shakespeare's duplicitous game to make seem superreal the crew of drunken louts whose coming Prospero confides, in an aside, to us alone:

> I had forgot that foul conspiracy
> Of the beast Caliban and his confederates
> Against my life. The minute of their plot
> Is almost come.

The audiences at the early performances of *The Tempest* must have been especially predisposed to believe thus in Caliban and Stephano and Trinculo, since their "plot" is derived not from a lapsed Greek mythology, but from current travel books. Like Shakespeare, some of them were familiar, at first or second hand, with accounts of the famous Somers's shipwreck and rescue in the Bermudas, or compendia of explorers' narratives such as Richard Eden's *History of Travaille in the West and East Indies,* or even with Montaigne's reflections on the alternative life-style of the savages in French Antarctica. And almost any of them might have seen living Indians at court receptions or country fairs, as Shakespeare reminds us in *Henry VIII:* "Or have we some strange Indian with the great tool come to Court, the women so besiege us?" Moreover, at the moment when *The Tempest* was being shown for the first time, bazaars were in progress to raise money for the imperiled Jamestown Colony. Within the play itself, Shakespeare refers early on to "the still-vexed Bermoothes," then later twice over to the Indian on exhibition: "When they will not give a doit to relieve a lame beggar, they will lay out ten to see a dead Indian." "Do you put tricks upon 's with salvages and men of Ind . . . ?" How appropriate, then, that the most distinguished of such visitors-on-show, Pocahontas, though she arrived in England a bit too late to meet Shakespeare (she had to content herself with a drunken Ben Jonson), did attend a performance of *The Tempest.*

In any event, once Shakespeare had moved in his search for

archetypal material from East to West, from then to now, from a symbolic language so old that no one could fail to recognize it as myth to one so new that scarcely anyone could distinguish it from actuality, he changed the level of credence demanded from his audiences, thus endangering the essential meanings as well as the crystalline form of his voyage-vision. And that danger was further aggravated by his growing concern with the political implications of the Caliban world, to which he had initially turned for reasons quite unpolitical. The very tag by which Caliban is described in the dramatis personae, "a savage and deformed slave," suggests the focus of that concern.

To be sure, the word "slave" is ambiguous in Shakespeare, meaning sometimes (as in the case of Iago) one so vile that only total subjugation to another seems an appropriate fate, and sometimes one actually thus subjugated (like Othello), whether he deserves it or not. Read either way, however, Caliban's label raises themes of colonialism and race; and taken all together, such themes evoke the place in which, for two hundred years, white Europeans had been confronting them in fact as well as theory, the land already called by Shakespeare's time "America," though he uses the word only once in a joke and never in *The Tempest.*

There seems little doubt, however, that America was on Shakespeare's mind, particularly at the point in Act II when he puts into the mouth of that kindly but ineffectual old windbag, Gonzalo, the speech beginning, "Had I the plantation of this isle, my lord—" and ending, "I would with such perfection govern, sir, / To excel the Golden Age." There is something especially pathetic about the constantly interrupted speech of one who, having been unable to save Prospero and Miranda (he contented himself with smuggling the Duke's favorite books aboard their rotting ship), can now scarcely hold his listeners' attention long enough to make his points. But they are important points, all the same.

I' the commonwealth I would by contraries
Execute all things, for no kind of traffic
Would I admit, no name of magistrate.
Letters should not be known; riches, poverty,
And use of service none; . . .
all men idle, all;
And women too, but innocent and pure; . . .
All things in common nature should produce
Without sweat or endeavor.

And when Shakespeare allows this vision to be mocked through the foul mouths of the bad brothers, Sebastian and Antonio, it is Montaigne's dream of a communist utopia in the New World he is allowing them to vilify. For the very words he attributes to Gonzalo he has lifted from Florio's translation of the French skeptic, whose skepticism seems to have failed him for once in his essay "Of the Cannibals."

Montaigne had begun by reading the accounts of returned travelers from Brazil about the life lived by man-eating savages on the banks of the Amazon and, comparing their way of life with that lived by his European neighbors, had moved toward a kind of cultural relativism. "Chacun appelle barbarie," he commented, "ce qui n'est pas de son usage" ("Each calls 'savagery' customs different from his own"). It is the observation of a protoanthropologist, a contributor to the *Encyclopédie* born before his time. And beginning thus, he inevitably ends up with a sentimental paradox worthy of Rousseau: that the New World barbarians are, in some sense, less barbarous than the European ones, providing at least, for all their cannibalism, models for a perfect commonwealth, the Golden Age restored. If there is the merest hint of irony in all this, it is quite gone from Gonzalo's version, which leaves all the ironical qualification to his interlocutors, who observe aside, "The latter end of his commonwealth forgets the beginning." And this can be read as meaning not only that the old councilor, carried away by his own rhetoric, forgets how he has begun his speech before concluding it but also that he has forgotten the Fall in the garden with which the whole history of human society began.

Certainly Shakespeare is on their side in the debate, utter, even hopeless villains though they may be, for the events of the play prove them, not Gonzalo, right. Indeed, that old man himself, who has begun by observing of the New World, "Here everything is advantageous to life," ends by confessing, "All torment, trouble, wonder, and amazement / Inhabits here. Some heavenly power guide us / Out of this fearful country!" The pun on "maze" is clearly intended, the image it suggests being picked up later by Alonso who says, "This is as strange a maze as e'er men trod." Indeed, the maze seems as central to the mythology of the West in *The Tempest* as the riddle is to the mythology of the East. And with its emergence, the two archetypal equations which underlie the play's action are made completely manifest: the East = the past = incest = the riddle; the West = the future = rape and miscegenation = the maze. "And there is in this business more than nature / Was ever conduct of," Alonso continues. "Some oracle / Must rectify our knowledge." But Prospero proves "oracle" enough, unriddling the enigma, unwinding the maze in his actions as well as his words.

To seek the past, the fable of his life signifies, is to leave action for books and to end up enisled with a nubile daughter in an ultimate travesty of the endogamous family, an incestuous *ménage à deux*. But in place of the East he dreams, the common source of Rome and Carthage and the "mouldy tale" of *Apollonius of Tyre,* he wakes to find the West, a beach more strange and fearful than the "still-vexed Bermoothes." Here rape and miscegenation threaten the daughter too dearly loved in an ultimate travesty of the exogamous family. And instead of himself—that is, the past—repeated in the child that daughter bears, he can look forward only to total strangers, monsters as grandchildren—that is, a future utterly alien to anything he knows.

The identification of incest with the riddle is traditional enough to seem convincing, even without the testimony of Claude Lévi-Strauss; but that of miscegenation-rape with the maze may seem at first arbitrary and implausible. Yet a moment's reflection on the myth of Crete reminds us that the latter identification, too, is rooted in ancient mythology; for at the center of the first of all mazes, the labyrinth, there lay in wait the Minotaur, bestial product of woman's lust to be possessed, without due rite or ceremony, by the horned beast, monstrously hung but bereft of human speech. And Caliban is, in effect, a New World Minotaur, inheritor by *Mutterrecht* of a little world which proves, therefore, a maze to all European castaways, even those who dream it Paradise regained. But Caliban exists in history as well as myth, or more properly, perhaps, represents myth in the process of becoming history: the Minotaur rediscovered in the Indian.

His very name is meant to indicate as much, since it is "cannibal" anagrammatized and "cannibal" is derived from "Carib," first tribal Indian name made known to Europe. Caliban seems to have been created, on his historical side, by a fusion in Shakespeare's imagination of Columbus's first New World savages with Montaigne's Brazilians, Somers's native Bermudans, and those Patagonian "giants" encountered by Pigafetta during his trip around the world with Magellan, strange creatures whose chief god was called, like Caliban's mother's, "Setebos." But to say that Caliban was for Shakespeare an Indian means that he was a problem, since the age had not been able to decide what in fact Indians were. And, in a certain sense, *The Tempest* must be understood as an attempt to answer that troubling question on the basis of both ancient preconceptions and new information about the inhabitants of the Americas.

That Caliban seems to be part fish has always troubled

some readers of Shakespeare, though the characterization is apt enough for a native of the hemisphere which medieval scholars had believed to be all water. He is portrayed finally as a creature of the mud flats who has managed to climb onto land at long last, but has not yet acclimatized himself to the higher elements of air and fire. Humanoid without being quite human, though a step above what he himself describes as "apes / With foreheads villainous low," he is as the play draws to its close called more and more exclusively "monster": "servant-monster," "brave monster," "man-monster," or simply "monster" unqualified. And the point is to identify him with a kind of subhuman freak imagined in Europe even before the discovery of red men in America: the *homme sauvage* or "savage man," who, in the nightmares of Mediterranean humanists, had been endowed with sexual powers vastly in excess of their own. Such monstrous virility Shakespeare attributes to Caliban, associating him not with cannibalism, after all, but with unbridled lust, as Prospero reminds us when he answers Caliban's charges of exploitation and appropriation with the countercharge:

I have used thee,
Filth as thou art, with human care, and lodged thee
In mine own cell till thou didst seek to violate
The honor of my child.

And Caliban, glorying in the accusation, answers:

Oh ho, oh ho! Would 't had been done!
Thou didst prevent me. I had peopled else
The isle with Calibans.

He becomes thus the first nonwhite rapist in white man's literature, ancestor of innumerable Indian warriors and skulking niggers who have threatened ever since in print, as well as on stage and screen, the fragile honor of their oppressors' daughters. And it is his unredeemable carnality which, as both

Prospero and Miranda insist, condemns him to eternal slavery, since, incapable of being educated to virtue, he must be controlled by force. "A devil, a born devil, on whose nature / Nurture never can stick," the master of arts describes him. And his daughter, more explicitly racist, concurs: "But thy vile race, / Though thou didst learn, had that in't which good natures / Could not abide to be with."

This charge Caliban never directly answers, though with his usual generosity, Shakespeare permits him an eloquent plea on his own behalf, less relevant, perhaps, but quite as moving as Shylock's.

This island's mine, by Sycorax my mother,
Which thou takest from me. When thou camest first,
Thou strokedst me, and madest much of me, wouldst give me
Water with berries in 't. And teach me how
To name the bigger light, and how the less,
That burn by day and night. And then I loved thee,
And showed thee all the qualities o' th' isle. . . .
Cursèd be I that did so! . . .
For I am all the subjects that you have,
Which first was mine own king. And here you sty me
In this hard rock whiles you do keep from me
The rest o' th' island.

There is, moreover, a kind of music in Caliban's speech, one is tempted to say a "natural rhythm," quite remote from Shylock's tone; for the Jew is postulated as an enemy of all sweet sound, whereas the New World savage is a singer of songs and a maker of poems, especially when he remembers the virginal world he inhabited before the coming of patriarchal power.

Prospero thinks of his island kingdom as a place to be subdued, hewed, trimmed, and ordered, so that, indeed, the chief use of his slave is to chop down trees and pile logs for the fire. But Caliban remembers a world of unprofaned magic, a living nature, in which reality had not yet quite been separated from dream, nor waking from sleeping:

Be not afeared. The isle is full of noises,
Sounds and sweet airs that give delight and hurt not.
Sometimes a thousand twangling instruments
Will hum about my ears, and sometimes voices,
That, if I then had waked after long sleep,
Will make me sleep again. And then, in dreaming,
The clouds methought would open and show riches
Ready to drop upon me, that when I waked,
I cried to dream again.

Once awakened from the long dream of primitive life, fallen out of the mother into the world of the father, there is no falling back into that intra-uterine sleep, only the hope for another kind of happiness, a new freedom on the farther side of slavery. Even drunk, Caliban remains a poet and visionary, singing that new freedom in a new kind of song.

No more dams I'll make for fish.
Nor fetch in firing
At requiring,
Nor scrape trencher, nor wash dish.
'Ban, 'Ban, Cacaliban
Has a new master.—Get a new man.
Freedom, heyday! Heyday, freedom! Freedom,
heyday, freedom.

Particularly in its Whitmanian long last lines—howled, we are told by the two mocking European clowns who listen—he has created something new under the sun: the first American poem.

And what has this in common with the Old World pastoral elegance of the marriage masque, in which Prospero compels certain more "temperate" spirits to speak for the top of his mind, even as the rebellious Caliban does for the depths of his soul.

You nymphs, called Naiads, of the windring brooks,
With your sedged crowns and ever-harmless looks,
Leave your crisp channels, and on this green land
Answer your summons. Juno does command.
Come, temperate nymphs. . . .

They simply cannot see eye to eye, the bookman and the logman, for while one is planning marriage, the other is plotting rape, since the savage (as even Gonzalo seems to know, providing that "Letters should not be known. . . ." in his commonwealth) prefers freedom to culture and would rather breed new Americans in passion than himself become a new European in cold blood. But against Prospero's "art" he is powerless and must abide, therefore, enslaved and desexed until some outside deliverer comes to his rescue.

That outside deliverer turns out to be, alas, the team of Stephano and Trinculo, the scum of the Old World promising themselves unaccustomed glory in the New and attempting to use against their old masters the New World savage, converted by whisky to their cause. But a drunken revolution is a comic one, and joining the clowns who would be kings, Caliban turns drunken, too, which is to say, becomes a clown himself. Indeed, the subject of drunkenness haunts *The Tempest* early and late quite as compulsively as it does *Macbeth* or *Othello*. But it has lost its tragic implications, providing only occasions for jokes, from the first scene, with its sodden sailors, to the last, from which Stephano and Trinculo exit "reeling ripe" and prophesying that they will remain "pickled forever." "What a thrice-double ass / Was I," Caliban comments toward the play's close, "to take this drunkard for a god." And we remember how only a little while before, he had cried, "That's a brave god, and bears celestial liquor," thus preparing to become the first drunken Indian in Western literature.

Together with Stephano and Trinculo, in any case, he had plotted a slave's revolt against what Shakespeare believed to be proper authority. Caliban, in fact, was the tactician of this fool's rebellion, suggesting, out of his fantasies of revenge, means to destroy their common enemy: "with a log / Batter his skull, or paunch him with a stake, / Or cut his weasand with thy knife." But especially he insists that they must first take from the master of arts the instruments which give him a fatal advantage over them all: his books, which is to say, those symbols of a literate technology with which the ruling classes of Europe controlled the subliterates of two worlds. The theme recurs almost obsessively in his speeches: "Having first seized his books. . . . Remember / First to possess his books, for without them / He's but a sot. . . . Burn but his books." Yet the revolt is foredoomed because Stephano and Trinculo prove interested only in the trashy insignia of power, while Caliban is dreaming not just the substitution of one master for another but the annihilation of all authority and all culture, a world eternally without slaves and clowns.

Moreover, Prospero has been aware of what they plotted from the very start, only awaiting the proper moment to quash it. By the time he has hunted them down, however, with dogs called "Fury" and "Tyrant," the whole history of imperialist America has been prophetically revealed to us in brief parable: * from the initial act of expropriation through the Indian wars to the setting up of reservations, and from the beginnings of black slavery to the first revolts and evasions. With even more astonishing prescience, *The Tempest* foreshadows as well the emergence of that democracy of fugitive white slaves, deprived and cultureless refugees from a Europe they never owned, which D. H. Lawrence was so bitterly to describe. And it prophesies, finally, like some inspired piece of science fiction before its time, the revolt against the printed

* Appropriately enough, one of the hounds pursuing two runaway slave girls in Harriet Beecher Stowe's *Uncle Tom's Cabin* is also called "Fury," whether in tribute to the prescience of Shakespeare (whom Mrs. Stowe knew well) or by apt coincidence it is hard to be sure.

page, the anti-Gutenberg rebellion for which Marshall McLuhan is currently a chief spokesman.

Thus fallen into history, however, has Shakespeare not also fallen out of his own myth, for what, after all, has America to do with *Apollonius of Tyre,* the guilt of expropriating ex-Europeans with that of incestuous fathers? It is easy enough to perceive on the literal level of his fable common images which betrayed Shakespeare from legend to chronicle: the sea voyage itself, for instance, along with the attendant circumstances of storm and shipwreck and miraculous salvation. In the most general sense, moreover, both the Old World of Apollonius and the New World of Caliban are worlds inhabited by terrifying and hostile strangers or, conversely, ones in which the castaway European feels himself a stranger in a strange land. Indeed, the word "strange" appears everywhere in *The Tempest,* not only in the speeches of the shipwrecked Neapolitans but in the stage directions as well: "strange drowsiness," "strange beast," *"strange music," "strange Shapes,"* "strange stare," "strange story"—all climaxing in Alonso's description of Caliban: "This is a strange thing as e'er I looked on."

These last words are only spoken, however, after Prospero's unknotting of the web he has woven; before, it is themselves and their plight which the displaced Europeans find superlatively "strange." And this sense of total alienation stirs in them not only "wonder, and amazement" but "trouble" and "torment," too, which is to say, the pangs of guilt. It is not merely that all of them are in fact guilty of treachery and usurpation in respect to each other but that having entered so alien a realm, however inadvertently, they become also guilty, on the metaphorical level, of rape and miscegenation. They are all, in short, Calibans, for America was at once virgin and someone else's before they came—and this they dimly surmise.

The figure of Caliban, at any rate, casts its shadow upon two utopian visions at once: that of Montaigne-Gonzalo, on the one hand, and that of Shakespeare-Prospero, on the other, the dream of a political utopia and the vision of sexuality redeemed. Inside the skin of every free man, Mark Twain was to observe three centuries later, there is a slave; and Shakespeare has concurred in advance, adding, And a monster as well! But all this Prospero has somehow temporarily forgotten, as the play which Shakespeare let him write moves—inexorably, it seems—toward its intended happy endings.

He has acted the stern father just long and hard enough to confirm the love which propinquity has bred. And, the marriage he has hoped for now assured, he delivers to the not-quite bridegroom two frenetic sermons against premarital sex, sexual consummation a moment too soon. Having first ritually intoned the admonition:

> If thou dost break her virgin knot before
> All sanctimonious ceremonies may
> With full and holy rite be ministered,
> No sweet aspersion shall the Heavens let fall
> To make this contract grow; but barren hate,
> Sour-eyed disdain, and discord shall bestrew
> The union of your bed with weeds so loathly
> That you shall hate it both.

he bustles off to make some arrangements for the prothalamion masque, then returns with a brusquer, more colloquial warning:

> Look thou be true. Do not give dalliance
> Too much the rein. The strongest oaths are straw
> To the fire i' the blood. Be more abstemious,
> Or else, good night your vow!

And reflecting on that double injunction, a reader is likely to remember not only the ill-fated marriages of, say, Othello and Desdemona or Romeo and Juliet—legal enough, yet without "all sanctimonious ceremonies" or paternal blessings—but also the odd couplet in *Pericles* in which Shakespeare seems to identify incest and premarital sex.

> But being played upon before your time,
> Hell only danceth at so harsh a chime.

In this case, Prospero seems determined to insure the "full and holy rite" he himself has demanded, becoming a kind of playwright-priest as he frames the marriage masque. Not only does he choose for the occasion the most ritual of all dramatic forms, but he insists also that its actors portray a carefully screened selection of classical divinities. Unlike Gonzalo's utopian vision, which imagined a new society based on free sexuality (for Gonzalo speaks of all things being held in common and mentions no marriage), Shakespeare's utopia begins and ends with the family. It is a kind of puritan Eden he projects, not gray, but full of sober grace, a Paradise regained worthy of John Milton, in which not unredeemed nature but married chastity insures fertility without destructive passion. "Honor, riches, marriage blessing," Juno sings to the young couple, "long continuance, and increasing. . . ." And Ceres adds (ritually transforming Gonzalo's earlier formulation, "But Nature should bring forth, / Of it own kind, all foison, all abundance. . . ."), "Earth's increase, foison plenty, / Barns and garners never empty. . . ."

And what a really New World that would be, in which Juno presides along with her sister Ceres, but from which one-third of the Triple Goddess—all in her that is equivocal and dangerous and which Venus figures forth, along with her blind son—has been excluded. Iris, who acts as chorus in the masque, has earlier reassured a troubled Ceres:

> Of her society
> Be not afraid. I met Her Deity
> Cutting the clouds towards Paphos, and her son
> Dove-drawn with her. Here thought they to have done

Some wanton charm upon this man and maid,
Whose vows are, that no bedright shall be paid
Till Hymen's torch be lighted. But in vain,
Mars's hot minion is returned again.
Her waspish-headed son has broke his arrows,
Swears he will shoot no more, but play with sparrows. . . .

Yet precisely at this point of the ceremony Prospero is forced to interrupt his own fantasy of love purified: "PROSPERO *starts suddenly, and speaks. After which . . . they heavily vanish*." It is of the politics of Caliban that he speaks in fact, the "foul conspiracy" entered into with Stephano and Trinculo against his legitimate authority and his life. But in order to deal with such matters, he is compelled to dismiss his sexual vision along with the spirits who enact it to the world of "dreams." In the waking world, illusory though it may be, what is demanded of the enemies of Aphrodite is constant vigilance, an authoritarian control of both body and state, microcosm and macrocosm, which are mirror images of each other. And remembering this dismal truth, Prospero also remembers his age and his mortality, concluding the epilogue to the masque:

Sir, I am vexed.
Bear with my weakness, my old brain is troubled.
Be not disturbed with my infirmity. . . .
A turn or two I'll walk,
To still my beating mind.

Once alone, however, he shakes off his weariness in anger, and thinking still of Caliban, cries:

A devil, a born devil . . .
on whom my pains,
Humanely taken, all, all lost, quite lost.

And as with age his body uglier grows,
So his mind cankers. I will plague them all,
Even to roaring.

It is himself, however, who is to blame for having forgotten that only in the world of art and make-believe does the "waspish-headed son" of Aphrodite turn "boy right out." In the world of nature, he turns Caliban, that is, he grows old and ugly quite like all men. But this Prospero is not yet prepared to admit, for admitting it, he would have to confess his kinship with Caliban; and to this confession he comes, like Shakespeare himself, slowly and reluctantly.

Yet from the start of his career, Shakespeare had been obsessed by the dark image of those lustful mother's sons from whom Caliban descends on one side, just as he descends from Montaigne's cannibals on the other. From the time of Demetrius and Chiron's successful rape of Lavinia in *Titus Andronicus* to that of Cloten's failed attempt on Imogen in *Cymbeline,* such enemies of the father's daughter had haunted him. Comic and villainous at once, stupid to the point almost of inarticulateness, they seem more like walking phalluses than complete men, or, in Shakespeare's own image, eyeless, noseless, mouthless "trunks." In *Cymbeline,* indeed, he seems on the verge of suggesting that in terms of their sexuality, *all* men are Clotens —even that purest of heroes, the man not born of woman, finally indistinguishable from the basest of rapist-buffoons.

How sure Imogen is, dismissing the grotesque suit of Cloten, that he is of less worth than the least garment of her beloved; but how incapable she proves of telling him from that lover once he has put on those garments and lost his own head. It is not just that she recognizes Posthumus's clothes but also that she thinks she knows his godlike body, the flesh she had embraced in love.

A headless man! The garments of Posthumus!
I know the shape of 's leg. This is his hand,
His foot Mercurial, his Martial thigh,
The brawns of Hercules. . . .

And as she throws herself on the abhorred "trunk" in unwitting travesty of all those *Liebestod* scenes created by Shakespeare on the model of Pyramus and Thisbe, we suspect momentarily that perhaps Cloten was right, that he would have "fit" her sexually quite as well as Posthumus's clothes had fit his frame.

But it remains a passing thought even in *Cymbeline,* dissipated by the felicitous recognitions and reversals which follow. And in *The Tempest,* Shakespeare seems at first to be playing quite another game, making the ithyphallic Caliban utterly different in "race" from the Prince, who, knowing what slavery is for, deserves finally to be free. It is not just by forswearing premarital sex that Ferdinand passes the magician-father's test, though this, too, is required of him; and twice over he makes formal protestation of his innocence. "The most opportune place, the strong'st suggestion / Our worser genius can, shall never melt / Mine honor into lust," he vows first, then adds, "The white cold virgin snow upon my heart / Abates the ardor of my liver." But words are not enough, being in themselves a kind of vicarious sensual indulgence.

It is a prior *ascesis* that is required. And this Ferdinand has performed by enduring, king's son that he is, the slavery which Caliban, a hag's by-blow, had sought to subvert. Yet it is only for her sake, he assures Miranda, that he would bear the yoke.

I am, in my condition,
A prince, Miranda . . .
and would no more endure
This wooden slavery than to suffer
The flesh fly blow my mouth. Hear my soul speak.

The very instant I saw you, did
My heart fly to your service, there resides,
To make me slave to it, and for your sake
Am I this patient logman.

How different the voice of the bridegroom from that of the rapist: the one murmuring submissively, "I must remove / Some thousands of these logs, and pile them up. . . ."; the other crying in revolt, ". . . or with a log / Batter his skull. . . ."

Even such service, however, with the vows that follow, does not quite suffice for Prospero, who insists that before the marriage can be consummated Ferdinand must learn the meaning of "play" as well as work. And for this end (as well as for others he does not yet himself suspect), he mounts his two final plays within the play: first the elaborate vision-masque, to which Ferdinand is a spectator, and next the game of chess, in which he becomes an actor. The latter constitutes perhaps the oddest moment in this strangest of plays—an epitome, in scarcely more than thirty words, of all the rest—as Prospero draws the curtain of the inner stage to reveal what Gonzalo calls "a most high miracle," though in fact it is only the two lovers *"playing at chess."*

"What is this maid with whom thou wast at play?" Ferdinand's royal father asks when they have spoken their four or five lines and turned to watch their audience in wonder. In his mouth, the final word assumes for a moment erotic as well as theatrical overtones; but their encounter is formal and distant, a board between them and the men they move not flesh but carved and painted wood. To be sure, Miranda's first speech to her lover has been, "Sweet lord, you play me false" —another pun on the key verb of the tiny scene. And the shadow of betrayal falls across their happy ending, as we have seen it fall across such resolutions from *Love's Labor's Lost* to *The Merchant of Venice.* This time, however, it seems only a flirtatious joke, a charm against distaster that will not come.

And the last words we hear before they merge with the beholders on the outer stage are "fair play," a phrase which reminds us by contrast, how, at the beginning of it all in Act I, Miranda and Prospero had echoed back and forth, "foul play. . . . foul play": "By foul play, as thou say'st, were we heaved thence. . . ."

Yet the wordless game they have played at playing all the while—the play within the play within the play—is a game of war not love, in which the players "wrangle" for "kingdoms." Moreover, on its mock battlefield, the strongest piece is the queen; and the combat ends always with the cry, "Checkmate!", meaning "The king is dead!", the old man left without a move. Small wonder, then, that Prospero remains so uncharacteristically taciturn throughout the exchange which follows, responding not at all, for instance, when Ferdinand hails him as a "second father." It is small comfort for one who knows he has lost his only daughter, as the rules of the larger game require.

He seems, in fact, to be more interested in Ariel than anything else, whispering asides into that servile ear, as he prepares for a final valediction: "My Ariel, chick. . . . to the elements / Be free, and fare thou well!" Earlier he has called him "industrious servant" "my tricksy spirit," "my diligence," "my bird," "my delicate Ariel"; at one point he even declared that he loves "dearly" the elemental whom he must now abandon along with his art and his island. He bids Ariel adieu much as if he were giving up for a second time his Miranda, or rather what in Miranda is dearest to him: the epicene charm of early puberty, in which boy and girl, daughter and wife, slave and free, body and soul, flicker and merge like light and shadow in a flame.

Moreover, Ariel seems also the boy actor, implicit in all the women's parts which Shakespeare ever wrote, made explicit at last. "Bravely the figure of this harpy has thou / Performed, my Ariel," Prospero congratulates him after one of his female impersonations, "a grace it had, devouring." But the truly faithful actor ("Of my instructions has thou nothing bated. . . .") exists only as the embodiment of an author's fancy; and that fancy once abjured must disappear forever from his stage. Precisely such an abjuration, however, Prospero has made.

> But this rough magic
> I here abjure, and when I have required
> Some heavenly music—which even now I do . . .
> I'll break my staff,
> Bury it certain fathoms in the earth,
> And deeper than did ever plummet sound
> I'll drown my book.

Thus bidding the anima-actor farewell should mean, too, leaving the shadow-clown behind, the dark underside of the imagination which had also to be enlisted before a new world of culture could be constructed in the midst of waters most men fear to sail. So Prospero has explained in fact to his daughter when she has complained of Caliban, " 'Tis a villain, sir, / I do not love to look on."

> But, as 'tis,
> We cannot miss him. He does make our fire,
> Fetch in our wood, and serves in offices
> That profit us. What ho! Slave! Caliban!
> Thou earth, thou! Speak.

Yet having dismissed Ariel to his "elements" (which is to say, to air and fire), how can Caliban not similarly be released to his, to the "earth" after which he is called and the water which laves it, to the island of the mother, in short, which he has all along desired to repossess.

And there is a sense in which Caliban has, since Prospero's abdication, taken over the island and the play. Being, that is (like Joan and Shylock), a truly mythic character, less invented than discovered, he has continued to live on in the public domain, becoming, in spite of Shakespeare, the hero, not the villain of the piece. Especially as black writers have learned in the last decades to invert the racist mythology of their former masters, he has been remade in fiction and drama into a central symbol both for their old indignities and the possibility of revolt against them. The exponents of *négritude* tend to read *The Tempest* as a kind of prefiguration of Melville's *Benito Cereno:* a parable of slave trade and slave rebellion and the fatal link which joins Europe, Africa, and America in guilt and terror.

Aimé Césaire, for instance—in a play less well known in the West than in Eastern Europe, Africa itself, and Asia—has rewritten Shakespeare's fable so that what disrupts Prospero's classicizing masque is not just the drunken plot of a slave and two clowns but the epiphany of a Congolese god, a dark divinity which the master of arts had failed to take into account. Such rewritings of *The Tempest* are true enough to a part of what moved Shakespeare at his most prophetic unconscious depths. But they leave out, on the one hand, what is specifically Indian rather than African in Caliban; and on the other, they ignore the sense in which he represents not merely the oppressed nonwhite minorities in America but *all* America insofar as that country remains Europe's bad nigger.

This D. H. Lawrence knew, and writers for the popular European press dare not forget even now, the mythological identification coming to the surface without reflection whenever they are most moved to rage against a culture they know to be an extension of their own, but long to believe to be totally alien. So, for example, an English journalist commenting in retrospect on the assassination of John F. Kennedy was moved to write that "the murder of the President" held up "a mirror to America which reflects such a Caliban image of brutishness and corruption that her enemies can only view it with glee. . . ."

In Shakespeare's conclusion to *The Tempest,* however, the total complexity is preserved. At first, it appears as if he is willing to grant the "savage and deformed slave" no future at all, as Prospero, in what seems more an exorcism than a proper farewell, first cries impatiently, "Go, sirrah, to my cell," then, ignoring Caliban's promise to reform, "Go to, away!" And Caliban, exiting on the line, seems rather to disappear than leave the stage. Yet we have the sense somehow that he will dog Prospero's footsteps until his death, the distorted shadow, which lay before him in the morning, following after in the evening of his life. Prospero has, in fact, implied as much, declaring, just after Ariel enters for a last time, *"driving in* CALIBAN, STEPHANO, *and* TRINCULO, *in their stolen apparel":*

> Two of these fellows you
> Must know and own, this thing of darkness I
> Acknowledge mine.

The "I" and "you" suspended in brief hiatus at the endings of the run-on lines define two kinds of man: the one remade in the New World, whatever its origin, and resolved now to return; the other unchanged, though chastened by its voyage into the unknown. There is special ambiguity, however, in the phrase "this thing of darkness I," which seems for a moment completely to identify the occultist Duke with the "savage and deformed slave"; but it is qualified by the sentence's end, "acknowledge mine." Yet there is a ritual ring to the formula, all the same: *"This thing of darkness I / Acknowledge mine,"* as if, through Prospero, all Europe were accepting responsibility for what was to remain forever malign in the America just then being created by conquest and enslavement.

But he speaks on a psychological level, too, as indeed he must, since, in general, the oppression of minorities always implies the repression of certain elements in the psyche of the oppressors with which those minorities are identified. And more particularly, the Anglo-Saxon "plantation" of the New World was somehow early linked, by analogy at least, with the puritan rejection of "cakes and ale" and unbridled sexuality—clearing the woods and subduing the savage, being metaphors for ascetic control. Such early English ventures into the New World as Roanoke and the Bermudas and even Jamestown were, to be sure, cavalier in spirit and motivation and sometimes carried with them actual magicians and poets. But as those settlements moved northward, eschewing slavery for a few in favor of work for all, it was the Malvolios who began to set the tone, not the Duke Orsinos, in love with love, or the masters of arts, like Prospero.

Yet Prospero could have warned such *émigrés* that even the noblest of puritan dreams, the making of marriage into a myth as potent as courtly adultery, was doomed unless the Caliban principle was given its due. But this means that the patriarchal consciousness must acknowledge the dark motivations, the maternal residue, which, even when they do not write the plots we live, mar those which our best magic strives to make come true. It is Prospero's own residual lust which has broken the spell of the marriage masque; and confessing this, he knows himself checkmate once more.

There is, in any case, a note of melancholy in Prospero's last speeches which undercuts the euphoria of a conclusion that he himself has worked for from the start. Not only have the two young lovers found each other, but the whole Neapolitan party has found forgiveness and self-knowledge and, for the moment, a modicum of peace. And Prospero himself has found again his lost dukedom. Why, then, does he talk chiefly of death as all presumably prepare to depart for home?

> And in the morn
> I'll bring you to your ship, and so to Naples,

Where I have hope to see the nuptial
Of these our dear-belovèd solemnized,
And thence retire me to my Milan, where
Every third thought shall be my grave.

Especially odd is his insistence on the number three: one thought out of three, rather than two or ten or a hundred. Is it only a conventional turn of phrase, or an offhand acceptance of a number as magic almost as seven?

The clue lies surely in the earlier lines in which, formally giving his daughter away to Ferdinand, Prospero explains, "I have given you a third of mine own life, / Or that for which I live. . . ." But this, too, is a little cryptic, suggesting several explanations, none wholly satisfactory in itself. Perhaps, hearing it, we are supposed to think of Prospero as having lived for his own sake, then for his long dead wife's, and finally for Miranda's. Or perhaps we are, rather, meant to remember that a man's life is divided into past, present, and future, the last of which Miranda represents. Or maybe, after all, we are being reminded that that for which Prospero lives is symbolized by the trinity of Ariel, Caliban, Miranda: two offspring of his fancy and one living human child. Or most simply of all, the reference may merely be to Miranda's age, which, since she is fourteen or fifteen, comes to one-third of forty-five, which is to say, the age of Prospero-Shakespeare at the moment of writing the play.

In any case, we must think of Prospero as turning toward death at the play's conclusion, which means away from Milan, insofar as Milan represents the kind of real life which he has assured us earlier is also "such stuff / As dreams are made on." We can be certain that everyone else will make it back to a world in which they believe, since he himself guarantees them "calm seas, auspicious gales, / And sail so expeditious" and he has always proved as good as his word. But they are already leaving the stage as he makes his promise—his beloved Miranda and Ariel along with the courtiers and clowns—so that, ironically, his last words, "Please you, draw near," are spoken to their departing backs.

We must imagine him, therefore—as we, too, prepare to leave the theater—absolutely alone: enisled, isolated in the abandoned playing space. For a long time his back is to us, as the other actors' are to him; and we remain, as it were, invisible. Then turning on his heel, slowly, slowly, he discovers us: beings he has neither invented nor evoked by charms and who survive the ebbing of his fantasy. And knowing at last that he, too, is an actor, a "walking shadow" like the rest, he steps forward to speak the Epilogue, which begins as a conventional-enough plaudite.

> Now my charms are all o'erthrown,
> And what strength I have's mine own,
> Which is most faint. Now, 'tis true,
> I must be here confined by you,
> Or sent to Naples. Let me not,
> Since I have my dukedom got,
> And pardoned the deceiver, dwell
> In this bare island by your spell,
> But release me from my bands
> With the help of your good hands.

But the word "hands" suggests a pair of puns which take us as far from the theater as from the magic isle. A verbal pun is sufficient to make the helping hand of a rescuer into the applause of a gratified audience. Then, by a visual pun, the hands struck together to clap become a pair of touching palms lifted in prayer; and we are ready for the final couplet of the Epilogue, which is a paraphrase of the last verses of the Pater Noster.

> As you from crimes would pardoned be,
> Let your indulgence set me free.

It is an oddly orthodox ending to a play otherwise more pagan than Christian, more occultist than pious—a last minute reversion from the certain knowledge of death to the eternal hope of life. Yet it is truly faithful not only to the meanings of the Apollonius myth but also to the nature of art on its ultimate borders, where it becomes scarcely distinguishable from sorcery. Prospero, the artist-magician, has never—he realizes at this point, and we with him—been inside the play at all; but the play, being one of his dreams, has been inside him. Not necessity, therefore, but wish has controlled the action; and unlike a tragic hero, he does not have to die with the plot he set in motion. Yet he must be abandoned at its close, since in the land of wish nothing fails like success.

Only the failure, the castaway, the irredeemable stranger succeeds in dreams—dream-magic being granted in exile and loneliness—a means to drive out the usurper or to create a "brave new world" in which love is ceremonial innocence. But the perfection of the dream is the dream's ending, and the dreamer must finally let fall his cloak and wand, bid the powers of air depart, stand outside the last illusion. Only then, knowing himself naked as all men are naked, estranged as all men are estranged, a slave as all men are slaves, can he learn to ask the prayers of others as he had once sought their applause.

> or else my project fails,
> Which was to please. Now I want
> Spirits to enforce, art to enchant,
> And my ending is despair
> Unless I be relieved by prayer. . . .

EPILOGUE

No epilogue, I pray you, for your play needs no excuse. Never excuse, for when the players are all dead, there need none to be blamed.

Duke Theseus to Bottom in
A Midsummer Night's Dream

INDEX